Llewellyn's

Sabbats

ALMANAC

Samhain 2009
to
Mabon 2010

Llewellyn's Sabbats Almanac:
Samhain 2009 to Mabon 2010

Cover art © Carolyn Vibbert/Susan and Co.
Cover design by Ellen Dahl
Editing by Ed Day
Interior Art: © Carolyn Vibbert/Susan and Co., excluding illustrations on pages 147, 225, and 296, which are © Carol Coogan

You can order annuals and books from *New Worlds*, Llewellyn's catalog. To request a free copy call toll free: 1-877-NEW WRLD, or order online by visiting our Web site at http://subscriptions.llewellyn.com

ISBN: 978-0-7387-1496-7

Llewellyn Worldwide
2143 Wooddale Drive
Woodbury, MN 55125-2989
www.llewellyn.com

Printed in the United States of America

2009

JANUARY
S	M	T	W	T	F	S
				1	2	3
4	5	6	7	8	9	10
11	12	13	14	15	16	17
18	19	20	21	22	23	24
25	26	27	28	29	30	31

FEBRUARY
S	M	T	W	T	F	S
1	2	3	4	5	6	7
8	9	10	11	12	13	14
15	16	17	18	19	20	21
22	23	24	25	26	27	28

MARCH
S	M	T	W	T	F	S
1	2	3	4	5	6	7
8	9	10	11	12	13	14
15	16	17	18	19	20	21
22	23	24	25	26	27	28
29	30	31				

APRIL
S	M	T	W	T	F	S
			1	2	3	4
5	6	7	8	9	10	11
12	13	14	15	16	17	18
19	20	21	22	23	24	25
26	27	28	29	30		

MAY
S	M	T	W	T	F	S
					1	2
3	4	5	6	7	8	9
10	11	12	13	14	15	16
17	18	19	20	21	22	23
24	25	26	27	28	29	30
31						

JUNE
S	M	T	W	T	F	S
	1	2	3	4	5	6
7	8	9	10	11	12	13
14	15	16	17	18	19	20
21	22	23	24	25	26	27
28	29	30				

JULY
S	M	T	W	T	F	S
			1	2	3	4
5	6	7	8	9	10	11
12	13	14	15	16	17	18
19	20	21	22	23	24	25
26	27	28	29	30	31	

AUGUST
S	M	T	W	T	F	S
						1
2	3	4	5	6	7	8
9	10	11	12	13	14	15
16	17	18	19	20	21	22
23	24	25	26	27	28	29
30	31					

SEPTEMBER
S	M	T	W	T	F	S
		1	2	3	4	5
6	7	8	9	10	11	12
13	14	15	16	17	18	19
20	21	22	23	24	25	26
27	28	29	30			

OCTOBER
S	M	T	W	T	F	S
				1	2	3
4	5	6	7	8	9	10
11	12	13	14	15	16	17
18	19	20	21	22	23	24
25	26	27	28	29	30	31

NOVEMBER
S	M	T	W	T	F	S
1	2	3	4	5	6	7
8	9	10	11	12	13	14
15	16	17	18	19	20	21
22	23	24	25	26	27	28
29	30					

DECEMBER
S	M	T	W	T	F	S
		1	2	3	4	5
6	7	8	9	10	11	12
13	14	15	16	17	18	19
20	21	22	23	24	25	26
27	28	29	30	31		

2010

JANUARY
S	M	T	W	T	F	S
					1	2
3	4	5	6	7	8	9
10	11	12	13	14	15	16
17	18	19	20	21	22	23
24	25	26	27	28	29	30
31						

FEBRUARY
S	M	T	W	T	F	S
	1	2	3	4	5	6
7	8	9	10	11	12	13
14	15	16	17	18	19	20
21	22	23	24	25	26	27
28						

MARCH
S	M	T	W	T	F	S
	1	2	3	4	5	6
7	8	9	10	11	12	13
14	15	16	17	18	19	20
21	22	23	24	25	26	27
28	29	30	31			

APRIL
S	M	T	W	T	F	S
				1	2	3
4	5	6	7	8	9	10
11	12	13	14	15	16	17
18	19	20	21	22	23	24
25	26	27	28	29	30	

MAY
S	M	T	W	T	F	S
						1
2	3	4	5	6	7	8
9	10	11	12	13	14	15
16	17	18	19	20	21	22
23	24	25	26	27	28	29
30	31					

JUNE
S	M	T	W	T	F	S
		1	2	3	4	5
6	7	8	9	10	11	12
13	14	15	16	17	18	19
20	21	22	23	24	25	26
27	28	29	30			

JULY
S	M	T	W	T	F	S
				1	2	3
4	5	6	7	8	9	10
11	12	13	14	15	16	17
18	19	20	21	22	23	24
25	26	27	28	29	30	31

AUGUST
S	M	T	W	T	F	S
1	2	3	4	5	6	7
8	9	10	11	12	13	14
15	16	17	18	19	20	21
22	23	24	25	26	27	28
29	30	31				

SEPTEMBER
S	M	T	W	T	F	S
			1	2	3	4
5	6	7	8	9	10	11
12	13	14	15	16	17	18
19	20	21	22	23	24	25
26	27	28	29	30		

OCTOBER
S	M	T	W	T	F	S
					1	2
3	4	5	6	7	8	9
10	11	12	13	14	15	16
17	18	19	20	21	22	23
24	25	26	27	28	29	30
31						

NOVEMBER
S	M	T	W	T	F	S
	1	2	3	4	5	6
7	8	9	10	11	12	13
14	15	16	17	18	19	20
21	22	23	24	25	26	27
28	29	30				

DECEMBER
S	M	T	W	T	F	S
			1	2	3	4
5	6	7	8	9	10	11
12	13	14	15	16	17	18
19	20	21	22	23	24	25
26	27	28	29	30	31	

Contents

Ostara

Beltane

Litha

Lammas

Contents

Mabon

Introduction

NEARLY EVERYONE HAS A favorite sabbat. There are always ways to enhance any holiday. This annual edition of the Sabbats Almanac provides a wealth of lore, celebrations, creative projects, and recipes to enhance your holiday.

For this inaugural edition, a mix of up-and-coming writers—Thuri Calafia, Gede Parma, and Michelle Skye—join more established writers—Deborah Blake, Ellen Dugan, Ann Moura, Raven Grimassi, and Oberon Zell-Ravenheart—in sharing their ideas and wisdom. These include that of a Green Witch, Garden Witch, a view from Down Under, and in the case of Zell-Ravenheart, a unique way to incorporate Mabon into an eighteen-month ritual cycle. Each of these writers also closes the chapter with an extended ritual, most of which are suitable for both solitaries and covens (except Mabon).

In addition to these personal insights and rituals, specialists in astrology, history, cooking, crafts, and family impart their expertise throughout.

Fern Feto Spring gives an overview of planetary influences most relevant for each sabbat season and provides details and a short ritual for selected actions. A Full Moon is discussed each sabbat.

Dan Furst explores the realm of old-world Pagans—the customs, parallels between different religions, and their connection to celebrations today.

Kristin Madden conjures up a feast for each festival that includes an appetizer, entrée, dessert, and beverage.

Silver RavenWolf offers instructions on craft projects that can also be incorporated into your practice.

Lydia M. Crabtree focuses on activities the entire family can share to commemorate each sabbat.

About the Authors

Deborah Blake is a Wiccan high priestess who has been leading her current group, Blue Moon Circle, for four years. She is the author of two Llewellyn books: *Circle, Coven and Grove: A Year of Magickal Practice* and *Everyday Witch A to Z: An Amusing, Inspiring & Informative Guide to the Wonderful World of Witchcraft*. Her third book, *Goddess in the Details*, came out in 2009. Her award-winning short story, "Dead and (Mostly) Gone" is included in the *Pagan Anthology of Short Fiction: 13 Prize Winning Tales* (Llewellyn, October 2008). When not writing, Deborah runs the Artisans' Guild, a cooperative shop she founded with a friend, and works as a jewelry-maker, tarot reader, ordained minister, and an intuitive energy healer. She lives in a 100-year-old farmhouse in rural upstate New York with five cats who supervise all her activities, both magickal and mundane.

Thuri Calafia is the author of *Dedicant: A Witch's Circle of Fire* and the upcoming *Initiate: A Witch's Circle of Water*. She is an ordained minister and Wiccan high priestess, teacher, and creator of the Circles system and Circles School. She is actively involved in the Pagan community in the Pacific Northwest, teaching Circles classes, presenting open Full Moon rituals, and Witches' afternoon teas (fund-raisers for local Pagan organizations and charities). She lives with her beloved Labrador, Miss Alyssa Ramone.

Lydia M. Crabtree is the cofounder and high priestess of Family Wiccan Traditions International (www.familywiccantradition.org). Lydia is dedicated to promoting family as the first and most important coven in a Witch's life. Featured in the *CIRCLE Magazine*, *Modern Witch Magazine*, and *The Witches' Voice*, Lydia has been dedicated to researching families as they relate to spiritual practice during her training in occult practices. Her bachelor's of science degree in psychology, with minors in theater and journalism, has positioned Lydia to present entertaining, informative seminars. Besides multiple visits to Starbridge Sanctuary festivals and StarFest in Georgia, she has presented at PantheaCon in San Jose, California; ConVocation 2008 in Troy, Michigan; Turning Wheel Festival 2007 in Georgia; and Pagan Unity Festival 2008 in Brentwood, Tennessee. Lydia's first book on family spirituality will be published by Llewellyn in 2010. You may contact Lydia at Lydia@lydiacrabtree.com or visit her website www.lydiacrabtree.com.

Ellen Dugan, the "Garden Witch," is an award-winning author and psychic-clairvoyant. A practicing Witch for more than twenty-five years, she is the author of ten Llewellyn books: *Garden Witchery, Elements of Witchcraft, Cottage Witchery, Autumn Equinox, The Enchanted Cat, Herb Magic for Beginners, Natural Witchery, How to Enchant a Man* and her latest book, *A Garden Witch's Herbal*. Ellen wholeheartedly encourages folks to personalize their spellcraft—to go outside and to get their hands dirty to discover the wonder and magick of the natural world. Ellen and her family live in Missouri. For further information, visit her website at www.ellendugan.com.

Fern Feto Spring has been practicing astrology since 1990, studying with a variety of teachers, including Steven Forrest, Rio Olesky, and Asata Gabriel. She is also a graduate of Steven Forrest's apprenticeship program, and has a master's degree from Sonoma State University. Fern is the co-author (with Jen Zurick) of *Simply Sacred: Everyday Relationship Magic*, a forthcoming book from Clean Sisters Press, and writes for *The Mountain Astrologer*, Llewellyn, Starlines Calendars, and Astrocenter. She also has an astro blog: www.wisestars.wordpress.com. Fern teaches astrology at Diana's Grove Mystery School and sees private clients in the San Francisco Bay Area and nationally.

Dan Furst has been an actor, singer, writer, astrologer, and ceremonial artist in the United States, Europe, Japan, and India. He has lived in Egypt since 2004 to research and write *Double Harmonies*, a book about the ancient Egyptian sound science and sacred music. His first book, *Dance of the Moon*, was published by Llewellyn Worldwide in July 2009. His *Universal Festival Calendar*, published since 1998, is on his website at www.hermes3.net/ufc .htm. He's a medicine theater priest, clown, and sound shaman, having played the Green Man, the Holly King, Jupiter, Saturn, Neptune, Pan, the Sun Banana, and others at many sabbats.

Raven Grimassi is the author of seven books on Wicca and Witchcraft, including the award-winning *Wiccan Mysteries*, *Wiccan Magick, Italian Witchcraft, Hereditary Witchcraft, The Encyclopedia of Wicca & Witchcraft* (awarded Best Non-Fiction Book 2001 by the Coalition of Visionary Resources), *Beltane*, and *The Witches' Craft*. A teacher and practitioner of the Craft for nearly thirty years, he is trained in the family tradition of Italian Witchcraft (also known as Stregheria), and is also an initiate of several Wiccan traditions, including Brittic Wicca and the Pictish-Gaelic tradition. He is currently the directing elder of the Arician Ways. Grimassi has also worked as both a writer and editor for several magazines over the past decade, including *The Shadow's Edge* (a publication focusing on Italian Witchcraft) and *Raven's Call* (a journal of modern Wicca, witchcraft, and magick).

Kristin Madden is the author of ten books to date, including *The Book of Shamanic Healing, Mabon*, and *Festival Feasts*. Raised in a shamanic home, Kristin has had ongoing experience with both Eastern and Western mystic paths since 1972. She is the dean of Ardantane's School of Shamanic Studies and has appeared on radio and television throughout North America. In her other life, she runs a wildlife rehabilitation clinic and works as a field biologist.

Ann Moura was born in 1947 and raised in a family of oral tradition from her mother and maternal grandmother. Ann felt a need to write about her Green Witch heritage to preserve it. She holds both bachelor's of arts and master's of arts degrees in history and writes from family training and personal experience. Her books with Llewellyn Publications include: *Green Witchcraft: Folk Magic, Fairy Lore, & Herb Craft*; *Green Witchcraft II: Balancing Light & Shadow*; *Green Witchcraft III: The Manual*; *Green Magic: The Sacred Connection to Nature*; *Grimoire for the Green Witch: A Complete Book of Shadows*; and *Tarot for the Green Witch*. She can be contacted through her website at www.annmourasgarden.com.

Gede Parma of Australia is the author of *Spirited: Taking Paganism Beyond the Circle*, a book that goes beyond the basics for young Pagans who are yearning for insight into the philosophy and spirituality of Paganism. Parma, co-founder and an initiated priest of Coven of the WildWood, has been an active member of his local Pagan community for years. A staff writer for *Copper Moon E-zine,* he has contributed articles to other books and e-zines geared toward Pagan young adults. For further information, visit www.gedeparma.com.

Silver RavenWolf is a widely published author, including bestsellers like *Solitary Witch* and *Teen Witch*. An artist, photographer, and Internet entrepreneur, she also heads the Black Forest Clan, a Wiccan organization that consists of sixty covens in twenty-nine states and three international groups. A wife of twenty-nine years, mother of four grown children, and grandmother, Silver has been interviewed by the *New York Times*, the *Wall Street Journal*, *US News & World Report*, and *A&E Biography*. Visit her at www.silverravenwolf.com.

Michelle Skye, a practicing Witch for more than ten years and author of *Goddess Alive!* and *Goddess Afoot!* (both from Llewellyn), has been working with the Fey since she was a child. Although solitary, Michelle presents workshops and classes in southeastern Massachussetts and at Womongathering, a Goddess festival in Pennsylvania. An ordained minister with the Universal Life Church, she performs legal handfastings, weddings, and other spiritual rites. Michelle shares her home with elfy husband Michael and the little Witch-in-training Neisa.

Oberon Zell-Ravenheart, a renowned wizard and elder in the worldwide magickal community, was instrumental in the coalescence of modern Neopaganism. In 1962, he co-founded the Church of All Worlds and through his publication of *Green Egg* magazine (started in 1968), he was the first to apply the terms *Pagan* and *Neopagan* to the newly emerging nature religions. He is also founder and headmaster of the online Grey School of Wizardry. Oberon now lives in Sonoma County, California, with his beloved lifemate Morning Glory. He is the primary artist of The Mythic Images Collection, producing beautiful jewelry and altar figurines of gods, goddesses, and mythological creatures. Oberon has written *Grimoire for the Apprentice Wizard* (2004), *Companion for the Apprentice Wizard* (2006), *Creating Circles & Ceremonies* (with Morning Glory, 2006), *A Wizard's Bestiary* (with Ash DeKirk, 2007), and *Green Egg Omelette* (2008).

Samhain

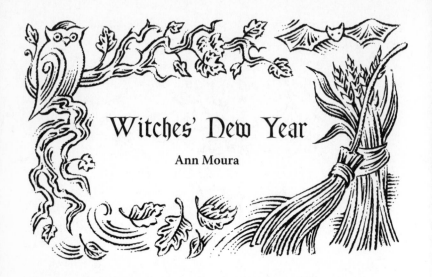

Witches' Dew Year

Ann Moura

SAMHAIN IS THE FINAL harvest of the season. Root vegetables, squashes, pumpkins, beans, winter wheat, and colorful Indian corn are gathered for the winter. Fields lie fallow, home gardens are bedded down and covered with mulch or hay, while seeds begin their slumber. Herds are culled, meats are smoked and cured, and the hunting season begins. Samhain marks the start of the New Year for some Pagans, but for all, it is the time of remembering the dead and communicating with spirits.

Seasonal colors are black for spirit contact and the Goddess as Crone, and orange for harvest and the God as Hunter. Nocturnal and carrion animals, such as cats, bats, owls, crows, ravens, and vultures symbolize the fleeting proximity of the world of shadows and specters. Such stones as labradorite, obsidian, and black onyx are used in meditation as gateways to underworld, while herbs are used throughout the month, during the holiday, and in ritual to flavor beverages (cinnamon, clove, or anise), to cleanse and purify an area with their fragrance (sage, patchouli, purple heather, or myrrh), and to imbue divination tools with psychic energy (mugwort or cypress). Appropriate offerings for visiting spirits are violets, lilacs, apples (symbolizing immortality with their inner pentagrams), and pomegranates (whose juicy seeds are the legendary food of the underworld).

At Autumn Equinox, the fading light of the Sun indicates that the God has entered the underworld to rule. The Goddess, alone as Crone, withdraws her fertility from the Earth in preparation for winter and enters the underworld at Samhain. Now is when the God passes into her to be reborn at Yule. His transition makes thin the veil between the worlds, making spirit communication easier, for in that timeless moment all is hallows (holy) and the tomb of the Goddess as Crone becomes the womb of the Goddess as Mother. The mystery of Samhain is that the god of fertility and self-sacrifice is also the hunter who gathers the dead and rules underworld, and that the fertile Mother Goddess is also the barren Crone through whom all must pass for rebirth. Death is a passage, not a state of being.

Various deities from different cultures and regions are associated with guiding spirits to underworld. Among these are the Horned Hunter leading the Wild Hunt, Hermes, and Anubis, or Hecate, Black Annis, Nicneven, and the Cailleach Bheara. Other deities are considered underworld rulers, including the Lord of Shadows, Arawn, Dis, Osiris, or Hades, and the Crone, Rhiannon, Hel, or Persephone. Deities of choice may be incorporated into the Samhain sabbat through an introductory dramatization of their myths or by naming them as the god and the goddess in the ritual.

While the archetypal mythologies vary depending upon the pantheon and the Craft tradition, the underworld is generally seen as having two realms. Some see the dim, tranquil Shadowland as a place where spirits rest, releasing the stress and pains of the past life and becoming refreshed and reenergized. A spirit might leave this realm and seek rebirth almost at once, or enter into the bright and active Summerland to experience a period of blissful harmony and joy, perhaps even reuniting with loved ones who passed before. This is a place to consider what is best for personal growth and decide what further experience is needed for spiritual development. A spirit may consider traveling to other worlds, becoming a spirit guide to someone, or reincarnating in physical form in a location suited to the life lesson to be learned. Some spirits are confused upon passing, becoming earthbound or wanderers until guided to the light. Others choose to remain near loved ones, a familiar place, or their gravesite until they become aware that they can move on. At Samhain we greet the spirits kindly, instinctively aware of our connection for we are all of the same essence, making the same passage through life, death, rest, and rebirth.

Samhain affords us a time to honor the ancestors both known and unknown, commune more easily with our departed loved ones and spirit guides, and assist spirits who seek to move on. We divine the future year and investigate our own past lives through meditative mirror gazing. Because we can more easily contact spirits, this is an opportunity to bless them, to learn from them, to receive a message, and to offer our aid to those spirits in need. In some traditions, this is a time to tend gravesites, cleaning and decorating them with flowers and leaving offerings and mementos. In the home, a shrine may be created on a shelf or table by arranging photos and keepsakes of departed loved ones, along with flowers and an offering of salt and bread. Here a white candle may be lit in remembrance, for this is the essence of Samhain.

⚜

Although I was raised in a family tradition of Green Witchcraft, which I have passed along to my now-adult children, over the years I have adopted into my Craft those Wiccan and secular elements that appeal to me, so some of my holiday customs will be quite familiar to most Pagans. Samhain is my favorite time of year, for this is one of those great turning points on the wheel of the year. Some years this holiday becomes as hectic as Yule and I do not have time for all my usual observances, especially because I usually attend several public sabbat rituals and still perform my private ritual at home. There are so many activities and events to choose from that selecting among the customs makes each year's celebration familiar, yet unique.

Early October is the time to start decorating the house inside and out with the fall leaves, pumpkins, gourds, Indian corn, and knickknacks of the season. By blending the holy eve of Halloween with the summer's end of Samhain, the house abounds with plenty of depictions of haunted houses and figures of Witches, goblins, bats, cats, and ravens, along with autumnal wreaths on the doors and floral arrangements on the indoor shrines and altar. Scented candles are lit most of the month, filling the home with a fall fragrance of spiced pumpkin, mulled cider, and patchouli. Pomegranates show up at the grocery store this time of year and I always buy one to keep until Samhain, when it will be buried in the backyard as food for the passing spirits.

The Full Moon of October is an ideal time for taking outside a large bowl of spring water and charging it in the moonlight for psychic power and spirit communication. This water may then be bottled and labeled for use during the following year as needed to enhance meditations, divinations, spirit work, and journeying. By mid-October, the altar is decorated for the season and a shrine is set up indoors to honor the dead. With a black, shrouded figurine representing the Goddess as the Crone, two small bowls are placed before it, one with salt and the other with bread. A white votive candle is lit between the bowls, and small, framed photos of departed family members are set up around the figurine. Sitting before the shrine, I can meditate and remember things from the past, speak to the spirits, and let the ancestors know they are not forgotten.

On Samhain morning, I change the cinnamon-scented besom by the front door, placing the old one in the garden to return to the earth. A homemade charm dedicated to the elementals with a circle of vine and two sticks crossed at the center—decorated at the quarters with a holed stone for earth, a feather for air, a piece of lava for fire, and a shell for water—is removed from the old besom and hung on the new to keep negative energies from entering the house.

Besides changing the besom at the front door, the day of Samhain is a good time for wiping down a crystal ball with a mugwort wash to enhance psychic energies, divinations, and other activities. I like to do a wheel-of-the-year tarot reading, showing me how the energies are aligned for the coming year. I shuffle the deck and cut it into two stacks. The left stack represents the major influence of a month, and the right stack represents the major event of a month. A card is pulled from the top of each stack and placed side by side for each month of the year starting with November to form a circle of months. By interpreting the paired cards in relation to each other, and also with those of the following months, a sequence of possible events and influences can be seen. With this knowledge, you can work with, or around those energies. Keeping a list of the pulled cards with the interpretations noted allows you to keep track as the year progresses.

By early evening on Samhain, an apple or a pomegranate is buried in the backyard as food for the passing spirits. Supper may include a place setting for departed relatives with a portion of the meal served to them along with a favorite beverage, cider, or beer. For the more traditional Dumb Supper, set bread, salt, and cider or beer at the extra place to honor the ancestors during the family meal, which is eaten in silence. Another version of this custom involves doing everything by candlelight in silence and backwards. You walk backwards around the table as you set it, the meal begins with the dessert, and the spirits are invoked and bid farewell in silence. In my home, however, the deceased loved ones are invited to attend the dinner, and we serve them the same as ourselves. During the meal we are free to talk about their lives, share family stories, and reminisce. This is how family heritage is passed on to the next generation and a connection is forged with the ancestors. Often we are rewarded with signs of the honored guest being present, leaving us with a warm and comfortable sensation. I always make a hearty soup this time of year that includes items from the last harvest—carrots, potatoes, and beans—along with smoked ham. Sometimes the soup is made earlier in the month and Samhain is celebrated with a roasted meat and stuffed acorn squash or mini-pumpkins, but always there is apple cider warmed with cinnamon and cloves. Banana-nut bread and pumpkin pie are standard desserts, and of course, there is always plenty of candy to hand out to children who come trick-or-treating.

A carved jack-o'-lantern, without a candle, is placed outside by the front door a couple of weeks before Samhain. After the early evening sabbat ritual, a consecrated white votive candle, anointed with a blend of pomegranate and violet oils to invite good and protective spirits to visit, is placed inside the pumpkin and lit. This candle shows the way to passing spirits, so that with the candle at the front door and the pomegranate in the backyard, a spirit is greeted when entering and nourished upon leaving. With an early ritual, there is time to greet the trick-or-treaters throughout the night.

Dressing up and perhaps wearing a mask is part of the fun; it lets your inner child come out to play. This is important, for it is through play that we are relaxed and most receptive to the spirits. By opening the door to strangers dressed in costumes and handing out candy, you are giving a vicarious offering to the spirits. This is a unique way of bringing the living closer to the departed in an atmosphere that is both casual and exciting, and yet it generates energy for spirit manifestations. It also allows people to brush gently with the reality of the death passage so that, in a subtle way, they may recognize that we are all spirits, only some are in a physical form while others are not.

Late at night when the doorbell is no longer ringing is a good time for a black-mirror meditation. If you don't have a black mirror, a regular mirror will work. Place the mirror upright on a table in a darkened room and set a black candle in front of it. Light the candle and gaze into the mirror and ask to see your ancestors. Your face will soon morph into other forms and you will see a variety of people going far back in time. If you like, you can also use this mirror to see your own past lives. Some of the faces you see may be male or female or even nonhuman or extraterrestrial, for the spirit is immortal and eternal, but humans are a recent form on this planet.

Because the veil between the worlds is thin, spirit communication may be accomplished through mediumship; the use of a spirit board; divination with tools such as tarot cards, runes, ogham fews, or a pendulum; or with automatic writing by holding a pen to a blank paper and letting it move of its own accord for a message or in response to queries.

During Samhain the cycle of life, death, and rebirth becomes clearer, and departed loved ones are nearer. This is the beginning of the New Year, when cleansings and renewals are performed. By smudging the home with sage and by burning at the Samhain sabbat ritual a paper on which you have written that which you wish to release, you clear out any negativity that may have lingered from the previous year. By celebrating the cycle of nature, you regain balance. By lighting a candle at a shrine to the ancestors, you remember from whence you came.

Celestial Sway

Fern Feto Spring

THE SAMHAIN SEASON BEGINS with a waxing Moon in fiery Aries on October 31. The Sun and Mercury in Scorpio square Mars in Leo add to a growing theme of intensity, activity, and challenge. Mercury, the planet of communication, is amplified by its placement next to the Sun, and both are in a dynamic relationship with Mars. With the Sun and Mercury in Scorpio, intense and meaningful communications are now emphasized. It may be wise to choose words carefully, as the square with Mars could result in tense and combative interactions with others if diplomacy and tact are neglected. Venus in Libra, and in trine to Jupiter, can help smooth rough edges, with the planet of love and social interactions in its ruling sign of Libra, and in sync with Jupiter, the planet of generosity and expansion.

On October 30, Saturn transited out of its 2½-year journey through Mercury-ruled Virgo, and progressed into Libra, ruled by the planet Venus. This emphasizes the need to pay more attention to Libran traits such as diplomacy, tact, balance, and attunement to others. It's important to modify the more challenging Libran qualities such as superficiality, conflict avoidance, and indecisiveness.

As Saturn moves into Libra, it squares Pluto, which is now firmly settled in early Capricorn. This planetary relationship is poised to initiate a time of major change and transformation in our personal and collective consciousness. Be ready to let go of old structures and relationship patterns, and patiently prepare for a new reality to emerge.

Samhain Mercury in Scorpio Ritual

As you reach through the veil to commune with your beloved dead this Samhain, try to think of anything you might need to communicate to move forward in your life. Are there things that you may have avoided saying aloud because you were afraid of conflict? Apologies that have been left unsaid out of pride or fear? Now is a great time to relieve any burden you might be carrying in regard to those who have crossed over, or even those who are still embodied.

Samhain Mercury Magic

You can ritualize this process on Samhain Eve by writing the words you need to speak in a letter, poem, or other form and placing it in front of a picture of the person(s) with whom you want to communicate. Light a yellow candle and let it burn down, imagining that the person intended received your message. You may even want to say the words aloud, speaking directly to the picture. Over the course of the coming days, look for a response in your dreams or your waking life. You may be surprised at the manner in which you receive your reply!

Full Moon in Taurus

The Full Moon in Taurus comes on November 3. This Moon emphasizes the balance and tension between spirit/Scorpio and body/Taurus. Themes arising in your life now concern your relationship to the unseen and the core mysteries of life and also your connection to building solid foundations and structures in the physical world. Conflicts between resources (money, skills, time, etc.) you share with others and those saved for yourself may also be a concern now.

The Sun and Moon continue to square Mars in Leo, so this Full Moon may have an explosive and attention-getting energy that is hard to ignore. Neptune also moves direct on November 4, bringing our spiritual awareness, dreams, and fantasies back out into the light of consciousness.

Look to where the Full Moon falls in the houses of your chart for a more specific interpretation of how this lunar event will affect your life. Look to which house cusp Taurus rules, and which Scorpio rules for an understanding of the house pairs to be activated.

Full Moon in Taurus through the Houses

1st and 7th: Self-identity/the Other, partnerships

2nd and 8th: Personal skills and resources/Shared energies and resources

3rd and 9th: Communication and the immediate environment/Meaning and expansion of consciousness

4th and 10th: Home, family, and deep self/Public persona, career, and destiny

5th and 11th: Self-expression, creativity, and spontaneity/Community, humanity, and the future

6th and 12th: Service to others and in the world/Service to spirit, and retreat

Venus in Scorpio

Venus transitions into Scorpio on November 9, joining the Sun and Mercury. This planetary focus on Scorpio emphasizes the need to engage in personal relationships with a focus on depth and intensity. If there is an issue that has been avoided in intimate partnerships, now is the time to get to the bottom of it and bring attention to the hidden dynamics that might have created it. Since Mercury is involved, this means making the time and space to sit down and talk about anything that has been put on the back burner. Putting off these conversations now could result in these pots boiling over in unpleasant ways in the future.

Venus is the planet of love and relationships and her placement in our charts shows how we give and receive love. As Venus transits through Scorpio, we are all asked to learn how to express our love in ways that embody the more positive Scorpio qualities while avoiding its challenging traits. Scorpio can bring a deeply healing and transformative energy to relationships, but can also try to avoid the pain of rejection and betrayal by making preemptive strikes: "I'll hurt you before you have the chance to hurt me."

By making a commitment to bravely facing our vulnerability and fears in relationships at this time, and being willing to go deeper, we can navigate this intense period with, if not grace, at least a sense of empowerment and transformation.

New Moon in Scorpio

The New Moon in Scorpio on November 16 is trine Uranus and square Neptune, offering the opportunity to open up to new and unexpected ways of connecting and relating to others. It will be important though, with the square to Neptune, to keep one foot in the world of reality and not move too quickly into something that may be hard to get out of later.

Opening up to spiritual guidance with a grain of salt will help you make the most of this New Moon energy. Though the messages that you get now may seem enchanting and magical, only time will tell if they can deliver what you really need, as opposed to what you may want in the moment.

New Moon Magic

Invoke Persephone, the hostess to the underworld, and burn a purple candle for her. Ask Persephone for guidance in helping you to divine what you really need to move through the darkness of winter. Cut open a pomegranate and eat the seeds. As you eat, set the intention that every seed that you swallow is a seed that will grow into fruition, guiding you along your path, and providing you with the spiritual sustenance you need on your journey. Continue to eat as many seeds as you want, assigning different areas of life to each (romance, work, etc.), and asking that they grow and be fruitful.

The Old Ways

Dan Furst

FOR MOST PEOPLE, THE customs of Samhain day on November 1 are a dim memory. The old folk symbols that have survived and are still happily revived every year are all from Samhain Eve, on October 31. It's been better known since the Christian Middle Ages as Hallowe'en, that is, the night before All Hallows, the feast of All Saints, followed on November 2 by All Souls Day. In both its ancient Celtic/Druidic/Norse rites and its newer Christian meaning, the Samhain season has always been a time when the living remember and honor the dead, affirm their links with beloved ancestors, and gather the strength to brave the dark forces of Earth and the Underworld as the leaves fall, the winds get chilly, and the long, dark nights come near.

This is why the most important of the Samhain rites has always been the fire of purification. Rites of dissolving and dispelling all of the old grief, pain, rage, and hate of the old season, so that they will not burden the Earth or the community of people in the months to come, are crucial to all four of the midseason sabbats, though the purification is done in different ways in each: chase-the-devil comedies abound at Imbolc, and erotic love blesses both land and lovers on May Night. The ones at Lughnasadh in August are enlivened by beer, wine, and all other kinds of cleansing water. But the Samhain purification fire is the most spectacular of all—it is not only big, it's the only ritual fire that in some communities is called a bonfire. Why is this, and why must the community do the great cleansing fire of Samhain really well? We'll find out soon, after we start the feast at its beginning, on Hallowe'en.

Everyone knows what the symbols of this night are: ghosts and devils, skeletons and jack-o'-lanterns, black cats, and spiders. What is less known is that some of these symbols are truly universal, used in cultures throughout the world. Everywhere in the world the Triple Goddess—who has just made her transition from Mother to Wise Woman in this Libra month—is busy at her web and her loom just before Samhain Eve ends at dawn on November 1. The Hopi of North America, like other peoples on every continent, call their creator goddess Spider Woman, the one who mends the torn web of the old year so that it will be supple and firm again as the new year begins. Long before Samhain Eve was called Hallowe'en, European peoples held weaver goddess festivals on October 31, honoring the art of weaving and the virtues of patience, diligence, service, and care for beauty that it requires. This is why the black spider has always been one of the most common Hallowe'en symbols.

At sunset on October 31, the Sun was said to enter the gates of the underworld, creating an opening for malicious spirits to fly out and work mayhem on the Earth for the next forty-eight hours. The spirits of departed ancestors were also welcomed to their family homes on Samhain Eve, so the children's custom of dressing as ghosts and ghouls, and going door to door for treats echoes the ancient practice of placing food offerings near the door to placate the malicious spirits that are apt to be about on this night, and to stop them from coming inside along with the good ghosts.

It's easy enough to see why central and western Europeans would associate the Scorpio month with death and regeneration. The end of October and early November are an obvious weather marker and transition time when birds migrate, animals begin to hibernate, and the leaves flame out in sunny colors before they start to fall. Amid all this season's other reminders of mortality, Samhain has always offered an open door of communication between Earth and the spirit world, to be traveled by shamans and Witches, and feared by the less skilled. October 31 is the Norse Festival of the Thin Veil, so-called because the Veiled Woman rules this night when the opaque barrier between the worlds of the living and the dead became transparent, so the two realms could see each other.

The soulscape travelers make a point of getting back by November 3, when the solemn rites of consecration and purification begin. The three months from Samhain's fires through the Great Cold that ends in February are the Wise Woman phase of the Triple Goddess cycle, when the women of the community are protected and empowerment by Cailleach, the Veiled Woman. Her name resembles the Hindu Kali because the severe, terrifying side of the Wise Woman is honored now.

The universal premise of this season, wherever peoples in the Northern Hemisphere celebrate it, is that the time of purification is at hand. Families and fields alike are to be cleansed of all grudges and fears. Homecoming festivals are held now not just because the family needs every pair of hands to get the crops in at the end of harvest time, but because light hearts, freed of old bitterness and sorrow through the forgiveness of loved ones, are the likeliest to navigate Ice Moon and the dark time before spring comes again.

It is time to burn away all the old poison in the fires of Samhain. It's called a bonfire because along with wheat chaff and cornhusks, papers with prayers written on them, rags and wood scraps, this fire must have the bones of animals our hunters have killed. It is time to honor the Horned One, whose mighty abundance blesses us this month at Hunter's Moon, to ask and receive the blessing of all the horned elk and deer our men have harvested. The hunters are the first to be purified, as they will be again after the kill.

One of the year's happiest Sahmain bonfires is held in England every November 5 on Guy Fawkes Day, commemorating the day when Fawkes and other conspirators attempted to blow up the British Parliament in 1605. The English have been burning Guy Fawkes in effigy ever since, making it one of England's great spectacles for tourists. How many of them know, as they watch the fireworks and festivities today, that for centuries before Britannia started to become England, their forebears would light the last of the great Samhain bonfires on November 5? And that they would burn an effigy called "the Old Guy" because he represented all the grief and trouble of the Old Year? It is only a happy coincidence that Mr. Fawkes had the same first name. The Old Guy has been around much longer, doing his annual duty of sending trouble up in smoke at Samhain time.

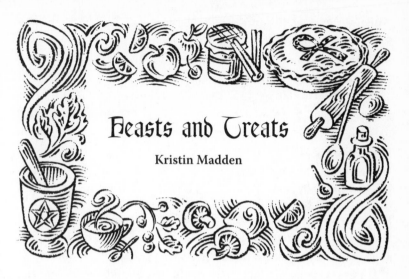

Feasts and Treats

Kristin Madden

PUMPKINS, APPLES, AND THE silliness of Halloween are what often come to mind when most people think of this time of year. Others focus on divination, introspection, and loved ones who have passed into the next world. The foods of Samhain reflect all that is mysterious yet joyful, reminding us of the light to come after the dark times and the never-ending love we share with each other and our ancestors.

Pumpkin Dinner

Why limit pumpkins to jack-o'-lanterns and pie at Samhain? Try them in mysterious new ways to surprise your guests. This baked-pumpkin dinner uses the meaty sweetness of this beautiful fruit to create a surprisingly scrumptious meal. It's even more fun if you gently carve a simple jack-o'-lantern face or other design just into the skin of each pumpkin. Use a little soy sauce to darken your design before baking.

Prep Time: 25 minutes
Cook Time: 2 hours
Serves: 4–8

1 pound stew beef in chunks
3 tablespoons olive oil
4 small baking pumpkins
2 cups brown rice, cooked
1 onion, chopped
3 cloves garlic, chopped
½ cup celery, chopped
2 teaspoons sage
¼ cup grated Gruyère cheese
1 cup chicken stock

Preheat oven to 325 degrees F. In a large frying pan, brown the beef in oil over medium-high heat. Cut the top off the pumpkin and scrape out any seeds or strings, just as you would do for a jack-o'-lantern. In a large bowl, mix together all ingredients except the pumpkin. Stuff the pumpkin loosely with the mixture and put the lid on top. Bake on a greased cookie tin for 90 minutes until a fork inserts easily into the side but the pumpkin is still standing firmly. Serve stuffing with some pumpkin meat added to it.

Black Bean Canapés

Canapés are a marvelous offering at potlucks or feasts. These charming finger foods are fairly simple to make and can be as diverse as your imagination. Black beans bring in the energy of the dark half of the year in a healthy and tasty way. The basil and garlic sauce remind us of all that can be found in the dark, if we are open to the possibilities. And the goat cheese brings in the light that helps us move through the darkness that is inevitably a part of life.

Prep Time: 20 minutes
Cook Time: 5 minutes
Serves: 10–12

2 cups fresh basil
3 cloves garlic, minced
½ cup olive oil

1 can black beans, drained
1 teaspoon lemon juice
1 baguette
6 ounces goat cheese, crumbled

In a blender, purée the basil, garlic, and oil. In a small saucepan, simmer this mixture over medium heat for 5 minutes. Strain liquid into a measuring cup. In a medium bowl, combine the basil and garlic that was strained with the beans and lemon juice. Mash with a fork.

Cut the baguette into ¼-inch rounds. Spread bean mixture on rounds, top with cheese and drizzle with the strained oil.

Double Chocolate Caramel Apples

Is there anyone that didn't love candy and caramel apples as a kid? They were at every party and some people would even give them out for trick-or-treating. Those store-bought kits are okay, but to truly honor the ancestors and your guests, serve these gourmet apples at your Samhain feast or put them out for a potluck offering. Everyone is guaranteed to be pleasantly surprised.

Prep Time: 25 minutes
Chill Time: 1 hour, 45 minutes
Serves: 4

4 apples
4 popsicle sticks or dowels
16 ounces of caramel candies
2 tablespoons water
10 ounces dark chocolate
2 tablespoons butter
4 ounces white chocolate

Remove the stems from the apples and insert the sticks into the stem ends. Cover a baking tin with nonstick spray and/or waxed paper. In a medium bowl, microwave the caramels and water for about 2 minutes, stirring halfway through, until the caramels are completely melted. Dip the apples in the caramel and twirl or spoon over the top until coated. Refrigerate on baking tin for 30 minutes.

In a medium bowl, microwave the dark chocolate and butter for about 2 minutes, stirring every 40 seconds until the chocolate is completely melted. Dip the apples in the chocolate and twirl or spoon over the top until coated.

Refrigerate on baking tin while melting the white chocolate. In a medium bowl, microwave the white chocolate for about 2 minutes, stirring every 40 seconds until the chocolate is completely melted. Drizzle over top of apples and refrigerate for at least an hour.

Pomegranate Sangria

Sangria is a splendid drink combining wine and fruit juice with chunks of fresh fruit. With or without alcohol, this is a perfect Samhain offering of the fruits of this final harvest. The addition of pomegranate reminds us of some of the myths of the season and the promise of light returning once we pass through the shadows. For a non-alcoholic version, replace the wine with red grape and cranberry juices and delete the brandy.

Prep Time: 1 hour, 15 minutes
Chill Time: overnight
Serves: 10–12

1 pear, peeled and cored, cut into large chunks
1 blood orange, sliced
1 cup red grapes, cut in half
2 bottles of red wine
½ cup blackberry brandy
1 cup pomegranate juice
⅓ cup honey

In a large pitcher or bowl, combine all ingredients. Allow to sit at room temperature for an hour. Then refrigerate overnight.

Crafty Crafts

Silver RavenWolf

AS THE NAME IMPLIES, the Crafty Crafts here not only give you a hands-on project that you can share for each of the eight sabbats, they demonstrate how you can incorporate relatively simple activities into your practice.

Each project contains helpful, inspirational techniques to use throughout the holiday season. The Deva of the Season is your connection to an aspect of Mother Nature. The visualizations given are different practice variations on learning how to focus the mind on intended goals. The affirmations match the Deva of the Season and the primary energy of the month, and can be used in meditation, ritual, and spellcasting—or whenever you need a mental boost. The deva, visualization, affirmation, and energy type are designed to flow together to help you created the intended project(s) given. In this way, you aren't just making something . . . you are living the magick.

Deva of the Season: Communication
Scents/Aromas: Pumpkin, Patchouli
Energy: Reward
Visualization: Place a small pumpkin as a centerpiece on the table. On little strips of orange paper, write down items and energies

you desire to draw toward you. Wrap each paper around a decorative, holiday toothpick and secure with tape, ribbon, or glue. As you stick each toothpick into the pumpkin skin, imagine each thing you desire floating up from the pumpkin and into your hands (or close enough to touch). Practice this visualization every day for twenty-one days, beginning October 1. Envision yourself happily sending out your thoughts and receiving the things you desire. Always end your visualization with a smile. Not only does this project provide a great visualization exercise, it can make a very cool holiday centerpiece!

Affirmation: As I connect with Mother Nature, my intuition is heightened. I will always take the right path. I welcome the rewards for which I have worked so hard.

🌿

Samhain's a time when so many energies are melded into one! Honor: a time to honor the dead. Reward: a time to open your arms and accept the rewards you've worked so hard for. Closure: the Wiccan New Year. Communication: it is said that on true Samhain (when the Sun reaches exactly 15 degrees Scorpio) the veil between the worlds (all worlds) is thinnest. What a perfect time to have a heart-to-heart talk with Mother Nature!

Deva Intuition Scrying Glass

This project is designed to combine your inherent intuition with the powerful communication lines of Mother Nature. As you work on the project, use the affirmation given as a mantra during the creative process to heighten the power of your scrying glass. A spirit elixir formula (see next page) can also be dabbed on candles, divination tools, conjuring bags, etc. If refrigerated, it will last about three weeks. The glass itself is a tool to connect you with the communication lines of Mother Nature and heighten your intuition so that you always take the right path. You don't have to stare into the glass; simply state the information that you need while holding the glass, and let Mother Nature do the rest. Cleanse your glass with clear spring water and place under a Full Moon when you feel this is needed.

Supplies

Glass bowl

Large, sterling-silver serving spoon (used is okay)

½ cup spring water

3 tablespoons each: dried eyebright herb, dried spearmint herb, dried patchouli leaves, dried mistletoe bark (totaling 12 teaspoons of herbs, leaves, and bark)

Hammer/mallet

Paintbrush

3-inch, round piece of clear glass

Black acrylic spray paint

Bottle for spirit elixir storage

E600 Glue

Embellishments such as ribbon, rhinestones, and gems

Spirit elixir formula–Pre-preparation instructions: In the glass bowl, mix warmed (not boiling) spring water, eyebright herb, mint herb, patchouli leaves, and mistletoe bark. Allow herbs and bark to steep for twenty-four hours. This is best done on a Full Moon before the Samhain holiday. Strain. Throw out herbs. Bottle the liquid, label, and refrigerate until you are ready to use this mixture.

Basic instructions: Two days before Samhain, pound the spoon head flat with hammer or rubber mallet. You must use a sterling silver spoon because, unlike regular dinnerware, it is soft enough to be flattened. Set aside. With paintbrush, apply your spirit elixir on one side of the glass. Allow to dry completely. Spray this side of the glass with one coat of black paint. Allow to completely dry. Brush the spirit elixir on the dried black surface. Allow to dry completely. Spray this same side with black paint again (not too much—keep your coats thin). Again, allow to dry and follow with one last coat of spirit elixir and one last coat of black spray paint. When the glass is completely dry, glue the flattened spoon head to the painted side of the glass with E600 Glue. This is the best glue I have found for this type of glass/metal bond project. Let it set for twenty-four hours.

Refrigerate any extra spirit elixir. Be sure your bottle is labeled so it will not be consumed by a family member!

The following day, when your Deva Intuition Scrying Glass is completely dry, begin embellishing as you desire with ribbons, rhinestones, flat-backed gemstones, small tile pieces, artificial flowers, etc., around the edges of the glass, on the handle, and on the back—or don't embellish at all. The choice is yours. On Samhain Eve, set the Deva Intuition Scrying Glass outdoors, under the light of the Moon (whatever phase it may be in) beside a burning lantern (candles may not do well at night outdoors in the wind, depending upon the weather). In your mind, surround yourself with white light. Say, "Peace with the gods, peace with nature, peace within," three times, then hold your hands over the face of the mirror and repeat the affirmation given nine times. Finish by saying, "Always a blessing. It always works. Thank you." Sit back and visualize Mother Nature's face in the mirror. Go ahead and talk to her. Tell her what you desire. She will listen. Just remember to keep your communication clear, concise, and your visualizations (mind pictures) with your words as detailed as you can. Rule of magickal thumb: Few spoken words—vibrant pictures that include aroma and sound in your mind.

Cost of this project: Approximately $14.00

Time to complete: This one takes a little longer because you are making the glass over a two-day period and waiting for paint and elixir coats to dry. Total, it took me two hours to complete.

Samhain Pocket Shrine To Honor the Dead

One of Samhain's most important themes in the Wiccan religion revolves around honoring our beloved dead, whether the individual was a friend, relative, co-worker, or even a pet that has passed beyond the veil. The Samhain pocket shrine is extremely easy to make. All you need is a square (or round) metal mint tin, paint or paper, and a collection of items to put into the tin to honor someone you loved. These items can be loose or you can glue them to the inside of the tin with E600 glue. You can cover the outside of the tin with decorative paper, pictures, stamp art, or simply paint it with paint that adheres well to metal (you'll find this at your local hardware store). The theme can be anything that you like—you can include a picture of the person you loved or a picture of something they loved. You can add ribbons or other embellishments outside the tin to achieve a highly decorative project, or a simple, elegant piece. Write a note to the deceased and place it in the shrine if you so desire.

When your pocket shrine is finished, you can put it in a place of honor over the Samhain season, at the dinner table during your Silent Supper, on your altar during Samhain ritual, or carry the shrine to the graveside and leave it there as a gift of love. They will always hear you.

Cost of this project: $2.00 to $11.00 (depending on items used)
Time to complete: 1 hour

Fostering Family

Lydia M. Crabtree

FOR FAMILY COVENS, SAMHAIN reminds us of the endings in our lives: death, divorce, parting with friends, losing jobs, moving from one covenstead into another, and so forth. These endings epitomize what Samhain is for family covens. For partners, Samhain is felt in their lives as they face the empty nest, retirement, and deaths of one another. Although these events can happen at any time of year, Samhain is the place on the wheel of the year at which we learn to best deal with these endings.

For children, Samhain represents the time in their lives from age fifteen until they leave the covenstead. Filled with anticipation and fear, it is much like walking through a haunted house. You know you are going to be scared. You aren't sure when, yet you can't wait for it happen. This is how children feel during the Samhain of their lives. They know they are going to move out, they aren't sure when, yet they can't wait for it to happen.

Luckily, as the final harvest, Samhain teaches us how to deal with these endings. It divulges for us the secrets we need to walk through the darkness and carry on to Yule. The secrets are hidden in the treats we eat, the symbols we create, and the ghosts that haunt us.

Activities

Talk about the Wheel of Life: Death and Rebirth

The most important thing family covens can do is to talk about the wheel that is life, death, and rebirth with their children. Don't wait to answer questions like, "Where does the hamster go when it dies?" Begin the discussion now. Take out pictures of relatives far removed from your children and ask if they think the relatives are gone or not. Then point out the similarities in the faces in the pictures and the faces around your covenstead. If your children are adopted, talk about the mannerisms that are passed on, like a preference for peanut butter and jelly sandwiches or opening one present on Yule night and the rest on Yule morning. Remind children that these things came from the lives of the ancestors in their adoptive line.

Talk also about the fact that as we die, we are sucked back into the light of the source of all things. The place from where all gods and goddesses emanate, and for a time, we are one with them until we are reborn to cycle through the world again. By discussing this type of recycling, your children are learning lessons they can rely upon when death or tragedy strikes their world.

Carve Pumpkins

Talk about the spiritual reasons pumpkins are important. Pumpkin carving is the spiritual light needed for our ancestors to find their way back home to us, bringing messages that we may need to hear. Pumpkins also deflect unwanted spirits from entering a home. Each family coven's spiritual light is unique, and by setting out pumpkins, especially on Samhain Eve, we are helping the spirits to not get confused and visit the wrong families. Pumpkins also represent the light of family coven. Now is the time to tell your children that if it is dark in their life after they have left home, they can remember the pumpkin and return to the covenstead for any help, nourishment, or love they may need.

Tell Scary Stories

The telling of scary stories has a spiritual purpose. They teach us important spiritual lessons: 1. Scary only lasts for a little while. 2. The Spirit of all that is, was, and shall be is present even in the scariest of stories or places. 3. The scariest thing we will ever face is the darkness within ourselves.

A favorite scary story involves creating a spooky house out of cardboard, a flashlight, and a dark room. The spooky house is made so there are three stories and an attic. The story is about four identical children who on Samhain night pass by the haunted house and dare each other to take their flashlights, climb to the attic, and return. The first child goes in, and his or her light is seen on the first floor before it suddenly goes out. The second child goes in, and his or her light is seen on the first floor, then the second floor before the light suddenly goes out. The third child, after much debate, enters the house and his or her light is seen on the first floor, second floor, and third floor, before the light suddenly goes out. The fourth child, feeling responsible for the other three, enters the house where his or her light can be seen moving through the first floor, the second floor and the third floor, searching for the other three children. When the fourth child reaches the attic his or her light mysteriously goes out, and the storyteller builds the suspense as one screaming child comes rushing out of the haunted house. It helps if you jump into the middle of the children, who are now clinging to each other in suspense.

The question, after all the screaming has stopped, is what happened to the other three children. The answer—there was only one child to begin with. The first child was our physical body who enters the spiritual house and can only go to the first floor. The second child is our superficial desires and with the will of those desires can spiritually go farther but not far enough. The third child is our dreams and hopes, which can enter the spiritual house and go farther than the other two, but not far enough. The fourth child is our spiritual self, the part of us that is directly connected with the

Divine. This child can go all the way to the top of the spiritual house and along the way, encounters the other children, recognizing them for who they really are—our physical body, limited and shackled; our superficial desires, egotistic and selfish; our hopes and dreams, drifting without direction; and finally, Divinity, where the child understands that only in unifying the four parts of the spiritual self will he or she be able to conquer the world outside. This revelation is scary, and the underlying lesson of Samhain is that the thing we should fear most is our own unchecked, selfish desires, unchased dreams, and the limits of our physical body unchallenged.

Trick-or-Treat the Old-Fashioned Way

Trick-or-treating started as a ritual where children dressed in disguises would go from house to house asking for treats and threatening the house with tricks. Treats were given in exchange for the children guaranteeing a blessing upon the house. Instead of saying, "Trick or treat!" create a generic blessing for your children (and you) to say at the door:

> *For some candy, we implore you*
> *We'll ask that blessings are poured upon you.*
> *Give us not what we ask, and*
> *We will reveal what is beneath our masks!*
> *Trick or treat!*

For some added fun, use makeup to create a gruesome face beneath the mask you wear, so if someone decides to take you up on your offer, they will get a scare.

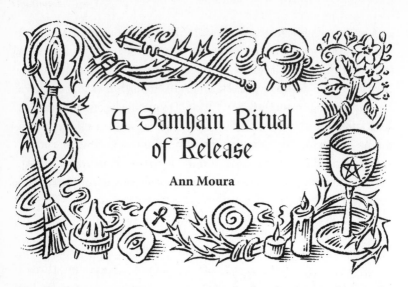

A Samhain Ritual of Release

Ann Moura

THE SAMHAIN SABBAT CELEBRATES the last harvest, releases the old year, initiates the new, and opens the way for winter. On a slip of paper prior to this ritual, write any bad habits or negativity from the past year you desire to banish. With a group, have slips of paper and pens available for people to do this before ritual. Collect the papers and place these on the altar. During the sabbat, a spirit candle will be consecrated for later placement in a jack-o'-lantern to welcome the spirits. An apple or pomegranate will be blessed as well, and then buried in the backyard to nourish the departing spirits. Follow the ritual with a meal or potluck utilizing seasonal foods and beverages such as stuffed roasted game birds or chicken, baked ham, roast beef, corn on the cob, squashes, beans, potatoes, roasted carrots, pumpkin pie, taffy apples, cider, apple juice, dark wine, and beer or ale.

The altar may be a 4 × 2-foot table (or larger) covered with a black cloth (or an autumn color), and set at the north inside the circle area. This ritual may be performed indoors or out—anywhere with enough open space to fit everyone inside the circle. Set three candles (tapers or jar candles) across the back of the altar to represent the Goddess as Crone (black) on the left, the God as Lord of Shadows (black) on the right, and the Harvest of Both (orange) in the middle, or use all black, orange, or deep purple colors. Deity statues or representations (e.g., a shell for the Goddess and an antler for the God) and a cornucopia for the harvest may be placed at the left, right, and center of the altar, respectively, or in front of the altar candles as room permits. Decorate the altar and circle area as desired with autumn leaves, gourds, pumpkins, Indian corn, cornstalks, and acorns.

This ritual is written to accommodate either a solitary or group, with group words and directions in parentheses. Group attendees remain outside the ritual area until after the circle is cast. For group rituals, the words and activities may be divided among those presenting it, but whoever casts the circle also opens it. Attendees may spontaneously repeat certain phrases like "Hail and welcome!" "So mote it be!" and "Merry meet, merry part, and merry meet again!"

On the Goddess side of the altar, place a cup or chalice with a beverage (wine, fruit juice, cider, or apple juice), and for a group include a bottle or pitcher of a non-alcoholic beverage and disposable cups. Also on this side, set the anointing oil (such as clove or patchouli), a bowl of spring water, a bell, a cauldron with a lid, an apple or pomegranate, the slip(s) of paper, and a wand. The besom (ritual broom) goes to the left of the altar.

On the God side, set a plate with a snack such as cornbread or pumpkin bread, and for a group, add individual mini-cupcakes or muffins, cookies, or bread cubes to share. Also on this side, set a bowl of salt, a ritual incense (such as sage, patchouli, or myrrh) and holder, a feather to fan the smoke, matches and a thin taper for lighting candles, a bowl of purple heather, a black votive candle, a white votive candle, and an athame. For a group ritual only, a sword or long knife (not the athame—the ritual knife) goes to the right of the altar to serve as a threshold for people to cross into the circle.

At the altar center, place a pentacle (wood, tile, or metal), a libation bowl, a candle snuffer, and notes for the ritual.

Sweep the circle deosil (clockwise) with the besom, starting and ending at the North (all actions begin and end at the North):

The besom chases away all negative and chaotic energies from within this space that it be cleared and ready for my (our) work.

Light the incense and altar candles; ring the bell three times:

The circle is about to be cast and I (we) freely stand within to celebrate this Samhain sabbat.

Cast the circle deosil with the athame, visualizing light coming from the tip and enclosing the ritual space:

This is the boundary of the circle, around, above, and below, as a sphere is the circle cast and consecrated that only love shall enter and leave!

Ring the bell three times. Touch the tip of the athame to the salt:

Salt is life and purifying. This salt is blessed through the power of the Goddess and the God that it may be used in this sacred circle.

With the tip of the athame, drop three portions of salt into the water and stir three times:

Let the sanctified salt cleanse this water that it be blessed for use in the circle through the power of the Goddess and the God.

Sprinkle the blessed water around the circle deosil:

This circle is consecrated and conjured a Circle of Power that is purified and sealed. So mote it be!

Fanning with a feather, take the incense deosil around circle:

The aroma of incense honors and welcomes visitors, spirits, and helpers, visible and invisible.

At the altar, anoint your forehead with the oil (anoint any helpers in the circle):

I am consecrated by the Goddess and the God, in this, their circle.

(For a group, take besom and sword and cross these on the ground at the entry):

This is the threshold of the circle. Let all who would enter here cross this threshold in perfect love and perfect trust.

Draw a doorway in the circle with the athame to let people in, smudging them with incense as they enter, and greeting them with "Merry meet!" Then undraw the door to close it and return the tools to the altar. Anoint people in the circle on the forehead with the oil:

You are consecrated by the Goddess and the God.

Using the wand, invite the elementals (Earth at the North, Air at the East, Fire at the South, and Water at the West) to attend the rite and guard the circle. Over the altar, use the wand to draw a cosmic lemniscate:

I (we) stand between the worlds with love and power all around!

Set down the wand and raise the athame in both hands straight overhead:

Hail to the Elementals at the Four Quarters! Welcome Lady and Lord to this circle!

Ring the bell three times; pour a libation from the cup into the libation bowl.

I (we) celebrate the dance of life to death to new life and the balance of Light and Shadow in my (our) life (lives)! The last harvest is gathered and stored for the dark months ahead, and the Wheel has turned to the time of the Hunter and the Crone.

Ring the bell nine times:

At this time the veil between the worlds is thin, and the gates are thrown open, so I (we) welcome those spirits who have gone before and who pass between two worlds. This is the time of the Hunter and the Crone. He gathers the dead, but all pass through her from life to life. *The Goddess and the God give a refreshing rest in the continuous turning of the spiral dance of life, death, and rebirth. With them do I (we) move with the dance with the joy of life and knowing that death is only a transition into rest, renewal, and new life.*

Take up the wand and raise your open arms:

The bounty of the land has been harvested and set aside while the Crone and the Hunter rule this season. Soon the Mother will return and the infant God of Light will be born. Until then, I (we) will abide and await the promise of renewal.

Set the cauldron on pentacle. Light the taper from the center altar candle and use it to light the black votive candle inside the cauldron.

Into the burning flame in the cauldron of endings and beginnings do I (we) cast those weaknesses and habits that keep me (us) from attaining my (our) potential. By the death of these things I (we) will live a better life in the New Year. So mote it be!

Drop the paper slip(s) into the candle flame in the cauldron, and pause for these to ignite. Ring the bell nine times as the papers burn. Sprinkle the white votive candle with salt, pass it through the incense smoke, then over the flame of the center candle, and sprinkle with the water. Hold the candle up over the altar:

This candle is consecrated by the Elementals and the Divine, that by its light I (we) will welcome you spirits this Samhain night.

Set the white candle aside for later use in a jack-o'-lantern. Hold the bowl of purple heather over the altar:

I (We) call upon the power of this herb to bless this place and the spirits that visit here. Let the power of the heather clear away the negativity of the past year which I (we) have released.

Drop the heather into the cauldron, onto the black candle and papers:

Through heather is the air is purified and cleansed that the New Year with joy may begin! So mote it be!

Hold the apple or pomegranate over the altar:

I (We) call upon the Hunter and the Crone to bless this fruit to be buried outside to nourish the dead. Let the spirits who visit find sustenance in this food of Underworld, that they move on refreshed. So mote it be!

Place the lid on the cauldron to smother the flames. Later bury the contents. Ring the bell three times. Face the altar with feet apart and open arms raised:

I (We) acknowledge my (our) needs and offer my (our) appreciation to that which sustains me (us)! May I (we) ever remember the blessings of the Goddess and the God.

With feet together, hold the cup in the left hand and the athame in the right, and slowly lower the point of the athame into the cup:

As the blade is unto the God and the cup is unto the Goddess, let their sacred union promote life, love, and joy, that the bounty of the Earth be sufficient for all.

Remove blade and pour a little of the beverage into the libation bowl. Touch the athame to the food:

This food is the blessing of the Lady and the Lord given to me (us). Let me (us) remember to so bless others who are in need.

Drop a piece of food into the libation bowl, which will be emptied onto the ground outside after the ritual. For a Solitary ritual, eat and drink the Simple Feast now. (For a group, touch the athame to the pitcher of beverage):

The blessings of the Goddess and the God pass into this beverage to be shared by all.

Then touch the athame to the plate or basket of food:

The blessings of the Goddess and the God pass into this food to be shared by all.

Take a bite of the food and a sip from the cup. (Announce to the group:

This is the Simple Feast of the Goddess and the God, offered to you. Eat and drink of the blessed meal if you so choose, and feel the Divine Spirit within you.

Pass the food and individual cups of beverage around the circle.)When finished:

As I (we) have enjoyed these gifts of the Goddess and the God, may I (we) always remember that without them, I (we) would have nothing.

Ring the bell three times. Hold the athame level over the altar:

Lord and Lady, I (we) have been blessed by your sharing this time with me (us); watching and guarding me (us); guiding me (us) here and in all things. In love have I (we) come into this ritual, and in love do I (we) depart.

Raise the athame straight up in a salute:

Love is the Law and Love is the Bond. Merry did I (we) meet, merry do I (we) part, and merry will I (we) meet again. Merry meet, merry part, and merry meet again! The circle is cleared. So mote it be!

Kiss the athame and set it down. Bid each elemental farewell deosil, saying:

Depart in peace, my blessings take with you.

Open the circle widdershins (counterclockwise) with the athame, seeing the light drawn back into the blade:

The circle is open, yet the circle remains as the Power is retained.

Notes

Notes

Yule

Winter Solstice

Raven Grimassi

THE SEASON OF YULE is marked by the Winter Solstice, the shortest day of the year. From this day forward, the daily period of sunlight increases until it reaches the Summer Solstice. Related to this experience is an ancient belief in the rebirth of the Sun God at the Winter Solstice. The idea of a renewed Sun God is at the core of the spiritual message of the Yule celebration.

The Yule season is a time to renew and refresh relationships. This includes the relationship with yourself as well as with family and loved ones. The primary message of Yule is a hope that cannot be denied. This is symbolized by an important figure known as The Child of Promise. I will provide more on this later, but for now it is the message itself that is our focus.

The message of hope is represented by the inclusion of evergreens as decorations for the Yule season. The addition of holly berries symbolizes the life force that is present even in the decline of nature as the seasons pass from fall to winter. A wreath of evergreens (decorated with holly berries and hung on the door or an interior wall of the home) serves as a reminder of the unending circle of life. A traditional Yule log works well to connect with the principle of renewal and rebirth.

The colors associated with the Yule season possess mystical symbolism. Green is the color of renewal, the gestation of the seed that assures new life in the spring. Green candles can be used in ritual and spellcasting to create personal alignments to this principle. Red is the color of blood, the liquid essence of life that flows from generation to generation. Therefore, red candles can be used to connect with relatives, ancestors, and loved ones. White is the color of death, the bones that are left when the soul has departed the body. It is memory of what came before. The winter snow that covers the land symbolizes death—but a death that provides for new life in the seeds that sleep beneath the cold blanket. White candles can be used to acknowledge that death is part of life, and that all endings are but new beginnings.

Scented candles, oil, or incense can be used to help connect with the rich symbolism of the Yule season. Bayberry is a popular fragrance, and it is associated with abundance, prosperity and fertility. It can be used in spells and rituals that are designed for gain and growth. Cinnamon is another scent that can be used to attract money or career opportunities. Candles or oils scented with apple spice are useful in spells or rituals for a peaceful home or a harmonious relationship.

If you're interested in syncing up with the inner mysteries of the season then you can obtain some of the traditional characters linked to the Yule season. One pair that stands out is the Oak and Holly King. To represent these you can find a Santa Claus figure among the rustic designs that are available. Look for a Santa dressed in brown or green to represent the Oak King. A Santa dressed in red represents the Holly King. If you're very imaginative you can use a snowman figure to represent the living winter spirit of nature. Reindeer figures can be used to symbolize spirit allies that carry off the wishes generated through spells and rituals. All of this magical imagery can be incorporated into the design of your spells and rituals or even a personal altar for the Yule season. When working with these connections, consider burning frankincense and myrrh as a spiritual and magical scent to enhance spell and ritual work at this season.

To fully embrace the season, create an altar setting that can be left standing in your home or office. On the center of the altar you can place the Yule log, set with three candles. A silver bell can be set in front of it to call the good spirits of the season. On the altar you can make an arrangement of figurines, snow globes, decorative snowflakes, and other symbols that have personal meaning or attachment. Don't forget to include some pine cones, evergreen clippings, and holly.

A popular inclusion in the Yule celebration is the solstice tree, now called the Christmas tree. The tree is a symbol of the sacred groves of Pagan traditions that venerated deities believed to reside in trees. Every grove was home to one particular tree that was honored above all others. Charms and ribbons were often hung from its branches as offerings, and as requests for special favors.

The popular modern tradition of placing gifts under the Yule tree reflects the ancient practice of grove veneration. This is also reflected in the decoration of the tree with various ornaments. The tree can be decorated with symbolic ornaments associated with individual Neopagan traditions. In this way the décor will reflect the unique spiritual focus of your individual Neopagan beliefs and practices. Arranging gifts beneath the tree for family and loved ones helps connect to the sense of community or tribe.

Gift giving has long been associated with the Yule season. As a spiritual tradition, this symbolizes an acknowledgment of the divine spark that dwells within all of us. We all bear within us the essence of that which created us. This is the spirit or soul that animates our physical bodies. In this sense, we all originate from the same source. Sharing feelings of love and closeness helps to brighten the light of our souls. In this sense we renew this force in the same spirit as we stir forth the newborn light of the Sun at Yule.

Yule: The Rebirth Of Light

The sabbat known as Yule is reflective of ancient Pagan themes related to the Sun in myth and legend. The foundation of most modern practices associated with Yule comes primarily from traditions commonly associated with northern Europe. However, due to Roman occupation and conquest, we do find many influences that were carried in from southern Europe and took root in Celtic and Germanic lands. Therefore the celebration of Yule is not unique to any one region or culture. It can be equally embraced by anyone.

At the core of Yule is the idea of sacred light. In many cultures, this sacred light was viewed as a savior, redeemer, or rescuer. This notion likely arose from ancient and primitive fears of the darkness. For our most distant ancestors, the darkness hid predators and enemies. In the darkness, a nightmare might well oppress the sleeper. With the rising of the Sun came protection, safety, and hope. The world of our ancestors was saved each day by the arrival of the Sun God.

In Neopaganism, Yule marks the rebirth of the ancient Sun God who renews the light. He is viewed as the newborn god of light who is often called the "Child of Promise." In the Christian mystical tradition this child is the infant Jesus, whose "light" will save the world from sin (darkness). This general theme has very deep and distant origins. Neopaganism mixes modern elements and perspectives with the ancient beliefs and practices of our ancestors.

In a long-standing tradition, the Sun God is intimately connected with trees, particularly evergreens. Some old customs also connect the Sun God to the oak tree. Mistletoe, which grows primarily on oak, introduces its symbolism into the Yule celebration, which in modern times elicits a kiss from anyone standing beneath its sprig. This is a remnant of its former role in the ancient fertility rites that renewed nature during its fall and winter decline. As a result of the Sun God's link to trees, we find two very important things in connection with the celebration of Yule. These are the Yule tree (Christmas tree) and the Yule log.

The Yule tree symbolizes renewal of the life force and the divine principle of eternal life. The Yule log represents the embodiment of the Sun God held within the form of nature. The log is traditionally a sacred oak or evergreen pine log used to call for the return of the Sun's warmth and light on the Winter Solstice. The tradition itself may have evolved from the ancient fire festivals of the Winter Solstice that were once celebrated in many regions of Europe.

On the eve of the Winter Solstice, tradition called for the burning of the Yule log to release the living spirit of the Sun God and to usher in the renewed power of the Sun. The ashes of the log were stored and later dispersed over the plowed fields in spring to ensure a future fruitful harvest. As part of the Yule tradition, a piece of the log was saved and used to start the fire for the next year's log. Dried holly was placed under the log to help kindle the new fire. People who gathered around the fire would toss in a sprig of holly symbolizing the troubles of the past year. This removed the old connections and purified the coming year.

In modern times, instead of burning the Yule log, it is drilled with holes to fit three candles, which are lighted for ritual use. The light of the candles symbolizes the waxing forces of nature. Placing three candles on the Yule log symbolizes the principle of manifestation. This reflects the concept that three elements are required in order for manifestation to take place: time, space, and energy.

In Neopagan practice, lighting the Yule candles and reciting a chant can serve as a simple spell for prosperity and abundance. For increased symbolism, a green candle can be set in the holes at each end, and a red candle in the center. In such a case, the first candle can be lit a few minutes each day (beginning fourteen days prior to the Winter Solstice). The second candle is then lighted seven days later and burns for a few minutes each day. The center candle is lit on the morning of the Winter Solstice and all three candles are allowed to completely burn down together. This is similar to the Jewish practice of lighting the Menorah at Hanukkah.

One ancient tradition that incorporates all the sacred traditions of Yule together is known as the hearth wreath, which was adopted by the Catholic church and transformed into the Advent wreath. Traditionally, the wreath is made of four candles in a circle of evergreens. Three candles are purple and the fourth is rose colored, but four green candles can be substituted if desired. Each day at home, the candles are lighted, perhaps before the evening meal—one candle the first week, and then another each succeeding week until the day of the Winter Solstice. A short prayer accompanies the lighting, and small offerings can be made as well.

In Neopagan tradition, the principle of the Child of Promise enters into both ritual and magic. On one level, the Child of Promise is the assurance of the coming year and the renewal associated with new beginnings. On another level, the Child of Promise is the manifestation of personal wishes and desires. But at the core essence lies the ancient spirit of the plant kingdom. In myth and legend, this figure also appears as the Harvest Lord.

Associated with the plant kingdom, tree worship appears to be among the earliest "formal" religious acts performed by humans. Elements of tree worship include the Green Man figure, spirits known as dryads, and various deities connected to the oak and other sacred trees. Eventually the spirits and deities of the forest and woodlands of our hunter-gatherer ancestors were venerated in the seasonal crops by agrarian society. Some examples of this are John Barleycorn, the Corn Mother, and the Harvest Lord.

The evergreen plants associated with the Yule season are symbols of the Child of Promise, who is the future Green Man and the eternal Sun God. The Yule wreath symbolizes the unbroken wheel of the year, the promise of life's endless cycle. The holly bough and its red berries speak of the vitality and tenacity of life. Mistletoe, as a symbol of freedom and liberation, announces the end of the waning darkness and the return of the waxing powers of light. The pine cone, as the seed bearer, perhaps best symbolizes the Child of Promise in its potential form.

One aspect of the Yule season that is often overlooked pertains to the ancestral connection, although this inner tradition is now quite obscure. The only remnants of it appear in the traditional inclusion of the chimney/hearth, the hanging of stockings, and the placement of food for the "gift-giver" figure (who in modern times is personified as Santa Claus). But there is a very ancient theme behind all of this popular tradition.

In ancient mystical tradition, the hearth was viewed as the entrance to the realm of the dead, where the ancestors dwelled. This portal connected the past and the present generations. The memory of this tradition is reflected in the modern practice of placing family pictures on the mantel over the fireplace.

Stockings are symbols of the Fates, who are the ancient weavers of the patterns of life and death. Suspending them from the hearth symbolizes a request to the Fates for good fortune. Waking to find a filled stocking is a sign of assured future blessings from the divine Fates. In other words this is a granting of wishes by the Fates.

The modern practice of placing a plate of cookies and a glass of milk for Santa Claus is reflective of an older tradition of offering food and drink to the ancestral spirit. In the inner Italian traditions this is personified as Befana, the good Witch. Although modern tradition has transformed and reduced her to a mere gift-giver (much like Santa Claus), Befana is actually the mediator between past and present generations. Some anthropological studies link her to an obscure ancient goddess associated with fertility and the harvest. Several nineteenth-century engravings depict her seated amidst the gathered harvest, and others show her dispensing bounty to people on the streets.

Another figure associated with the Yule season is the figure known as Santa Lucia. Her veneration began in Sicily and was carried to Scandinavia where its popularity has overshadowed its origins. Santa Lucia appears in a white gown wearing a headdress of lighted candles, and her festival day is December 13, which heralds the Yule season. Many Neopagan traditions associate Santa Lucia with the season of Imbolc which follows the Winter Solstice (although in old folk tradition the festival of Santa Lucia was called "Little Yule").

A popular song that appears in oral tradition is sung to welcome Santa Lucia:

Night goes with silent steps
round house and cottage
o'er earth that sun forgot
dark shadows linger.
Then on our thresholds stands
white clad, in candlelight
Santa Lucia, Santa Lucia

In an old Swedish tradition, the prettiest girl in the house stirs before sunrise, dresses in a white robe with a red sash, and wears a crown of lighted candles. She then awakens the household for a special breakfast. In Sicily the tradition included a procession of people carrying torches through the villages, which culminated in the burning of a huge bonfire. Such traditions fall under the category of the festival of lights, which are rooted in ancient Pagan practices designed to encourage the return of the Sun.

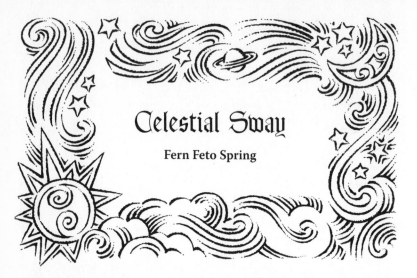

Celestial Sway

Fern Feto Spring

THE WINTER SOLSTICE MARKS the time of the year when we celebrate the return of the Sun and the slowly returning light. Solstice 2009 is shaped by several powerful planetary influences that serve to make this year one to remember.

After the transiting Sun moves into Capricorn on December 21, it comes into a tight conjunction with the planet Pluto. Pluto in Greek mythology is the god of the underworld, and in astrology Pluto represents the power that comes from energy exchange and transformation. In this capacity Pluto symbolizes death, but also rebirth. Pluto is a planet known for its intensity and strength and also its capacity for endurance and depth. In Capricorn this Plutonian energy is amplified, allowing for a unique form of change to occur.

Pluto is known as a "collective" or "transpersonal" planet, because its movements from sign to sign shape the energy of an entire collective or group, as it spends roughly fourteen years in each sign.

Pluto has newly entered the sign of Capricorn, so we are in the midst of experiencing the Plutonian breakdown phase rather than the rebirth or initiation time that comes later. The solstice coming so close to Pluto in Capricorn indicates that the returning light of the Sun will shine on the traditions and structures that we are currently witnessing die away and disappear. We may be offered a powerful confrontation with reality now that asks us to reveal who we are under intense and transformative conditions.

There may also be a certain amount of frustration during this time as Mars, the planet of will, action, and forward motion, goes retrograde in Leo on December 20, making an opposition to the Moon, Jupiter, and Neptune conjunction in Aquarius that is almost exact on the December 21 solstice.

This Aquarius stellium contributes to an overall "stop and start" feeling that can make us wonder if we are ever going to make progress, both at an individual level and also collectively. Patience is the antidote here, and the more of it we cultivate, the better off we will be during this period.

This solstice 2009 planetary energy can best be used by clarifying and intuiting what our visions for the future are, while at the same time taking a long, hard look at our current reality.

Mercury goes retrograde on December 26, further influencing us to slow down, retreat, and reassess our goals, plans, and desires.

Since the Winter Solstice is traditionally a time for divination and reconnection with our inner light, we can use this introspective energy to look into the darkness for the light of the future we want to create.

Solstice Divination

On Solstice Eve, gather the divination tool you feel most comfortable with, whether it's tarot, runes, scrying, bone tossing, astrology, or something else. Alone or with a group of people, make an offering of food, wine, or a candle to the planet/god Saturn. Saturn rules the sign of Capricorn and time, cycles, patience, persistence, and long-term goals. Focus your question around issues related to your own long-term vision or purpose in the world. As you ask your question and proceed with your divination, try to remain unattached to the answer, receiving it with an awareness that there are missing pieces to your vision, which may come slowly and over time.

If you are exchanging readings with a friend or as part of a group, help each other interpret how the reading relates to your goals and life intention, staying focused on a bigger picture. Remember to record your reading so you can refer to it later for insight.

Solstice Season Full Moon

The big energy that starts on Solstice Eve builds to a peak with a partial lunar eclipse at the Full Moon in Cancer on December 31. This Full Moon activates the signs Capricorn and Cancer, and concerns the opposition between home and work, public and private, our inner reality and the external world. The Full Moon is further amplified because it takes place in the Moon-ruled sign of Cancer. Prepare for emotionally surprising events or interactions to occur up to a month before and a month after this lunar eclipse on December 31.

Look to where the Full Moon falls in the houses of your chart for a more specific interpretation of how this lunar event will affect your life. Notice which house cusp Cancer rules, and also which one Capricorn rules for an understanding of the house pairs to be activated.

Full Moon in Cancer Through the Houses

1st and 7th: Self-Identity/The Other, partnerships

2nd and 8th: Personal skills and resources/Shared energies and resources

3rd and 9th: Communication and the immediate environment/ Meaning and expansion of consciousness

4th and 10th: Home, Family and Deep Self/Public persona, career, and destiny

5th and 11th: Self-expression, creativity, and spontaneity/Community, humanity, and the future

6th and 12th: Service to others and in the world/Service to spirit and retreat

New Moon in Capricorn

January 2010 brings us a New Moon in Capricorn on January 15, followed by Mercury's direct motion later that day. The New Moon conjuncts Venus and the North Node in Capricorn, and Mercury also goes direct in Capricorn. These interactions indicate there is a chance for fresh starts and new possibilities in relationships, particularly if we are willing to keep our communications direct, diplomatic, and fair. The emphasis on Capricorn energy shows that this is a time to be realistic and patient in our dealings with others, focusing on what we can do, rather than what we hope for. The Sun and Venus are also in sextile to Uranus, adding a touch of creative innovation into our love connections. Now we might find a possibility for new ways to relate to long-term partners, or an unexpected and welcome spark between us and someone we might have previously thought of as "bland" and "boring." It may be helpful to let go of old patterns we have around our ability to be patient and persistent when starting new relationships or when maintaining ongoing ones. If we can carefully shake things up and change our awareness in little ways, we may find that the rewards are satisfying, even if they may not be as dramatic as we want.

New Moon in Capricorn Ritual

Find a rock or stone that is special to you, or that just feels good. Then, on the night of the New Moon, light a candle for Venus, the goddess of love and relationships. Meditate on your hopes for change and growth in your love life or on a particular relationship with a partner or close friend. As you hold the rock, focus your positive intent for change in this relationship and breath your energy into your rock. You may choose to keep the rock on your altar or bury it so the earth can grow the seed that you started. Notice the changes that unfold as the Moon grows throughout the month. Because this New Moon is in Capricorn, which calls for patience, it may take more than a few months to notice results, but you can rest assured that they will come.

The Old Ways

Dan Furst

THIS FIRST, AND BY far the most important, of the four great solar feasts is the day on which the daylight begins to get longer and the nights shorter, until the White Nights of June, when days are longest and the male has waxed to the peak of his power just before the year turns female at the Summer Solstice.

Here at the Winter Solstice, the solar Boy-Child who will grow into the virile young man of spring is born. Before he can come in, the universal change of year must be played by the Old Man—the old year—who goes out in both senses of the term, as he exits from the stage and runs out of light like a sputtering lamp on Mother Night (December 20), the longest, darkest night of the year. The Old Man may appear in different forms. As Father Time, with his long white beard, hourglass, and scythe, the Old Man is Kronos, or Saturn, ruler of the month of Capricorn that now begins. Before modern pop culture replaced his severe black robe with a white sheet and pasted on his face a kind grandfatherly smile over his lordly scowl, Saturn was an august figure whose staff and lantern proclaimed his dignity as the agent of spiritual knowledge and keeper of ageless wisdom.

Saturn can enjoy playing against type, though, as he is also, curiously, the patron of comedy, still visible even today in the black-clad figure of *Il Dottore* (the Learned Man) in the *Commedia dell' Arte*. He especially likes to impersonate his son, the irrepressible Jupiter, by dressing up as the Holly King: a still virile, mature man with abundant gray hair and beard, richly dressed in red and green, adorned with berries of holly and mistletoe. Before the twentieth century, when his greenery was airbrushed out and he became Santa Claus, the Holly King was Father Christmas. Before that he was as Dickens drew him as the burly, cheery, booming Spirit of Christmas Past in *A Christmas Carol*. In this most jovial, generous form, the hearty, fun-loving older man is Father Yule. His name comes from *Geola*, meaning "yoke," for his critical role, which he must perform before he passes on, is to yoke the chariot of the Solar Child to the old, receding year.

The pop cartoon of the Holly King and Father Yule is well known now as Santa Claus, the sanitized, official Father Winter figure for an era of global branding and packaging. Today's American Santa Claus first appeared in the 1920s, without all those messy leaves and berries, when Coca Cola reinvented him as a synthetic myth without greens and dressed only in Coke's colors of red and white. New myths have flowed from the Coke Santa. Some Japanese, for instance, believe that Santa Claus is the father of Jesus. But in his truly august role as Father Yule, the Old Man at the end of his year brings the cycle to a prosperous, joyous close by invoking the true Spirit of Light: the Solar Child who is born in this radiant season as the Old Year happily moves on. Before he makes his exit, whether he goes out in resplendent Jovian fur and gold or dressed in Saturn's black and white, it is the job of Father Yule to open the festival, and lead its rites until the moment when the community sings in the Solar Boy.

Our ancestors probably played this ritual the way some earth religionists and Neopagans do today: with a blend of reverent awe and exuberant joy that has room for comedy. As Father Yule's chant of welcoming the Sun reaches the birthing point of sound and fervor, the new Solar Child is carried in on the back of a horse (as in the Sun card of the Rider-Waite tarot), in a solar chariot pulled by clowns in Sun colors, or on the backs of elders—including wise women representing Mother Night—who retire as the Boy enters and guides the feast, and leaps into rulership of the new year that now radiates from him.

The light is reborn, and with it the crucial soul question that we began to sing long before we could write it: if the New Sun is reborn again each year as the Old Sun dies—then is it also possible that the same thing may happen with us? That as our mortal body ages and comes closer to extinction, our soul makes ready to be reborn in a new realm of light? If the Sun is immortal, coming to rebirth every Yuletide just as he appears ready to flicker out, can we also do that? Does the promise of rebirth await and fulfill us, just as it does our Father—and Mother—Sun, and all those sacred beings from many traditions who are reborn each year at Yule?

This, clearly, is why so many famous solar deities—Babylonian Bel or Baal, Egyptian Horus, Greek Helios Apollo, Persian Mithras, Roman Sol Invictus (the Unconquered Sun)—were all born on December 25. So in the fourth century, when Christianity was established as the state religion of the Roman empire and the faithful had to decide when to celebrate the birth of Jesus, the choice for Christmas was customary and clear. What day could be better than December 25, what season better than the Winter Solstice, for the birthday of the one who was called, like many others before him, the *Lux Mundi*, the Light of the World?

What is less well known, amid all the rejoicing as the Prince of Peace is reborn, is that the Winter Solstice is not exclusively a male festival. On December 22 the Japanese honor the Sun Goddess Amaterasu-no-Mikuni, heroine of one of the world's great myths of the retreat and return of the Sun. Insulted and ridiculed by her unruly brother Susanoo, the storm god, Amaterasu withdraws into a cave, casting the Earth into such bitter cold and darkness that the other gods, fearing the end of all life, come to sing and dance outside her cave until the goddess relents, and allows the others to charm her back out. The Cherokee celebrate a similar rite as they use the innocent songs of children to lift away the Sun's mourning for her daughter. And the day of Santa Lucia ("St. Light") is but one of this season's many invocations of feminine light.

For all the new solar children who are born now, and for all the awe they inspire, the season's main attractions, and the evergreen customs that are still fresh today, all surround the kindly green god of holly and mistletoe. Just as the Norse God Baldur (also born December 25) was pierced by a holly wand thrown by Loki, so that his blood stained the white holly berries red, the Holly King symbolizes the incandescent moment in which pure spiritual love (white) and passion (red) flame in glorious crimson at "the coming of the Sun and the running of the deer, the singing of Robin Redbreast as merry Yule draws near." It's no wonder that before he became the commercial actor Santa Claus, Father Yule—and Pére Noel, and Father Christmas—were so loved for so long.

Nor is it any wonder that sweethearts still kiss under the mistletoe, though they may never know how explicitly sexy this little ritual was for our ancestors. Mistletoe is an oak parasite that was long called "oak sperm" because its berries resemble male genitalia. Druid priests harvested mistletoe with golden sickles for people to hang in their homes at Yule. The point of this ceremony was to bless couples with the oak tree's vitality and firm sexual power so that the oak's strength would help them get through the Great Cold before the quickening comes at Imbolc.

Feasts and Treats

Kristin Madden

THE BIGGEST OF THE holiday seasons, Yule is jam-packed with feasts, parties, and other gatherings. On the year's longest night, the power of the Dark Times is at its height, but with the promise of the rebirth of light and life. The foods of this season are warming, rich, and colorful, but keep the time constraints of the busy Yule chef in mind.

Tagine Stew

Based on a traditional Morrocan dish, this hearty and spicy stew will keep you going through even the busiest of Yule seasons. Combining meat with what might have been leftover from early harvests, this is something our ancestors may well have appreciated before all our modern conveniences. Appetizing and warming, it is the perfect meal for après snow and ice play and is easy enough to take to a potluck feast.

Prep Time: 15 minutes
Cook Time: 45 minutes
Serves: 6–8

½ onion, chopped
3 cloves garlic, chopped
3 tablespoons olive oil
2 chicken breasts, chopped
1 small squash, chopped
1 carrot, chopped
1 small turnip, chopped
1 can chickpeas, drained
1 can tomatoes, diced
1½ cups chicken broth
1 tablespoon lemon juice
1 teaspoon salt
1 teaspoon coriander
1 dash cayenne pepper

In a large sauté pan, cook the onion and garlic in oil over medium heat until transparent. Add the chicken and cook until browned. In a large bowl, combine the squash, carrot, turnip, chickpeas, tomatoes, broth, lemon juice, salt, and spices. Add squash mixture to the pan and bring to a boil. Reduce heat and simmer for 30 minutes.

Yule Bruschetta

A unique addition to any holiday potluck, crunchy bruchetta in red and green is the ideal Yule appetizer or snack. Quick and easy yet delicious and hearty, this will keep your energy high through all that holiday shopping.

Prep Time: 10 minutes
Cook Time: 5 minutes
Serves: 10

1 loaf Italian bread
3 tablespoons olive oil
1 red and 1 green bell pepper, whole
3 cloves garlic
1 tomato, chopped

½ cup basil, chopped
1 red onion, chopped
3 teaspoons balsamic vinegar

Preheat the broiler to high. Slice bread into 1-inch rounds. Brush with oil and broil until golden. Remove and allow to cool. Roast peppers: coat each one with oil and broil about 5 inches from heating element for 5 to 7 minutes until they start to blister and blacken. Turn peppers over and repeat. Place them in a sealable plastic bag for 20 minutes until cool enough to handle. Remove the stems and peel off skin. Slit each pepper in half, remove the seeds, and slice.

In a medium bowl, mix together garlic, tomato, basil, and onion. Place a slice of pepper on each piece of toast and top that with some of the garlic mixture evenly. Drizzle with balsamic vinegar and serve.

Cranberry Nut Pastries

Cranberries and nuts are traditional foods for the Yule season. Dried to preserve them throughout the winter, you can find cranberries in all sorts of foods at this time of year. They can even be seen strung together with popcorn for cute decorations in some homes. Brought together in these fantastic, easy-to-make pastries, they should be a hit at your holiday celebrations.

Prep Time: 30 minutes
Cook Time: 10 minutes
Serves: 10–12

½ cup walnuts or almonds, finely ground
2 tablespoons baker's sugar
1 teaspoon cinnamon
½ teaspoon nutmeg
8 ounces puff pastry dough
2 eggs
¼ cup cranberries

Preheat oven to 425 degrees F. In a large bowl, combine the nuts, sugar, and spices and mix well. On wax paper, roll out the dough to

⅛-inch thick. Lightly beat the eggs on medium speed. Lightly brush the pastry with the egg. Sprinkle ½ of the nut mixture and then ½ of the cranberries on top. Fold dough edges into center and flatten. Apply another coat of egg onto the pastry and sprinkle the remaining nut mixture and cranberries on top. Pinch edges together along the middle and brush with the remaining egg. Cut into small squares and bake on greased and floured cooking sheets for 5 minutes. Turn over and bake for another 5 minutes until golden brown.

Spicy Wassail

Said to have been shared during winter holiday celebrations since the 1400s, wassail is synonymous with Yule gatherings. Made from the remaining fruits of the earlier harvests, it brings the promise of harvests to come in the new year . . . plus it is a wonderful drink for lively winter gatherings.

Prep Time: 5 minutes
Cook Time: 20 minutes
Serves: 6–8

2 quarts apple cider
½ cup orange juice
¼ cup lemon juice
2 teaspoons whole cloves
1½ teaspoon nutmeg
4 cinnamon sticks
Optional: 2 bottles of ale, 2 ounces dark spiced rum

In a large saucepan, combine all ingredients and bring to a boil. Reduce heat and simmer for 15 minutes. Serve warm.

Crafty Crafts

Silver RavenWolf

Deva of the Season: Unity

Scents/Aromas: Bayberry, Mistletoe, Nutmeg

Energy: Faith

Visualization: Fill a bowl with seasonal greenery. Add a bit of scented herbal aromatherapy oil to heighten your visualization experience. Each evening, focus on the center of the bowl. Visualize your desires (one at a time) as you look into the bowl. Imagine each thing you desire floating up from the bowl and into your hands (or close enough to touch). Practice this visualization every day for twenty-one days beginning on December 1. Envision yourself happily sending out and receiving the things you desire. Always end your visualization with a smile. For a more magickal meditation, add the glowing enchantment of bayberry candles, specifically attuned to good fortune.

Affirmation: I believe I can manifest all the wealth and prosperity I desire. I have faith in myself and the universe. Good fortune comes easily to me.

Going Green for Yule!

Country Prim Scented Paper Bag Ornaments

These easy-to-assemble magickal decorations are not only enchanting, but cost effective! Try using as many supplies as you can from your crafting stash! As you are making your ornaments, intone the affirmation given, or use one of your own. You can even write your affirmation on a small slip of paper and place it inside the ornament.

Supplies

Used brown paper bags

Strips of cloth—12 to 18 inches long, ½- to ¼-inch wide

Template shapes (squares, stars, circles, etc.)—These can be as large or small as you like; larger shapes are easier to stuff

Sewing machine or sturdy needle and thread

Batting

Dried magickal herbs of your choice (even potpourri)

Scented magickal oil (optional)

Embellishments—ribbon, lace, buttons, decorator papers, cloth, beads, small mirrors, etc.

Ribbon or twine for hanging (you can sew the ribbon or twine into the seam at the top of your ornament, or wait until the ornament is completed and punch hole with hole punch to insert ribbon or twine.

Craft glue

Instructions: Cut out two of each shape from the paper bags, making sure the shapes are of equal size and edges will align. Using a ¼-inch seam, sew the two shapes together with machine or hand whipstitch leaving at least 1 to 2 inches open at bottom for stuffing. Stuff paper bag shape with a mixture of batting and herbs. Do not overstuff as the shape will be difficult to close and hard to decorate. Add 1 drop of scented magickal oil to the center of the batting (too much and the oil will bleed into the paper bag). Magickal charms can also be added to the inside the ornament, as well as small spell papers, if you like. Sew shut with machine or hand whipstitch. Sew,

73

or glue, the strips of cloth to the bottom of the ornament so that they dangle. You can add as many or as few as you like. Decorate your ornament with lace, buttons, beads, cloth, stickers, bells, etc. Empower ornaments on the Winter Solstice to bring peace and prosperity into the home. Ornaments can even be strung together to make a great, decorative garland to hang on the Yule tree or over a doorway!

Cost of this Project: If you use items from your crafting stash, less than $3.00 per ornament.

Time to commplete: Approximately 30 minutes, including cutting, stuffing, decorating, and sewing.

No-Stress Holiday Shopping Magick Talisman

The lines, the prices, the traffic . . . and then, finding just the right gift . . . no wonder we get anxious over the holiday season! Here's a great little talisman that I make every year to banish the shopping gremlins and open the way to great deals.

Supplies

One small chipboard shape (packages of variously sized circles, rectangles, stars, squares, etc., can be found at most craft stores)

Embellishments—decorative papers (Yule wrapping papers will do), glitter, beads, etc.

The words "Always a Blessing" and "It Always Works" printed off your computer in a size that easily fits on your chipboard shape

Craft glue

Liquitex Gel (matte or glossy)

Paintbrush

Heavy duty paper punch (to punch hole in chipboard shape)

One key ring

Paper and pen

One small, red, gris-gris bag filled with lavender and chamomile herbs with drawstring tie

Bayberry candle

Lavender-scented magickal oil

Instructions: The focus of this project is to bring prosperity and great shopping deals toward you while experiencing limited stress; so while you are working, you may wish to repeat as a magickal mantra, "Always a blessing. It always works. Thank you." Decorate the chipboard shape with the Yule wrapping paper. Glue the words "Always a Blessing" on one side, and "It Always Works" on the other side. Finish with chosen embellishments. Seal talisman with Liquitex Gel. When completely dry on both sides, punch holes near the top of the shape, just far enough in from the edge to slide the shape onto the key ring. If you punch the hole too far in, you may not be able to insert the key ring properly. On a small piece of paper, write the affirmation given (or choose your own). Place the paper inside the gris-gris bag filled with lavender and chamomile herb. (You can use other herbs, if you so desire.) Tie bag securely shut and add to key ring. (If you really want your talisman to stand above the rest, you can add ribbons, bead strings, and other items to the keychain. The choice is entirely yours.)

To empower your shopping talisman, cast a magick circle and take three deep breaths. Light a bayberry candle (or substitute a gold or white candle) and say, "Peace with the Gods, Peace with nature, Peace Within" three times until you feel calm and peaceful inside. While holding the talisman, reach out in your mind, and touch the deva of unity (that all-encompassing spirit of total peace, balance, and happiness). Think about this connection as long as you can. The talisman might grow warm in your hands, or your fingers may tingle. Repeat the above affirmation three times, then draw an equal-armed cross in the air over the talisman to seal it. Set the talisman beside the candle. Release the magick circle, remembering to say "thank you" when you are through. Allow the candle to burn as long as possible. Take your talisman with you everywhere you go during December. When the holiday season ends, you can cleanse the talisman in moonlight for one hour, then put it away with your other seasonal decorations to reuse next year, or burn the talisman on Candlemas in a ritual fire. To save the talisman, empty the gris-gris bag back to the earth and wrap talisman in a red cloth before storing.

Before leaving the house or apartment on your shopping trip, sit quietly and think specifically about what you wish to find this day. List the things you are looking for aloud and clearly. For example, "I want to find the perfect tie for Uncle George today on sale." You can even say, "I want to find something unique and unusual for my sister—something she will simply love at a price I can afford." Touch the edges of the talisman with the lavender-scented magickal oil to banish thieves, bad deals, and negative people and make way for great sales and a happy experience. Before you walk out the door, hold the key chain in your hand, and say, "I want to have a safe and happy shopping trip today." If you run into a particular problem while shopping, hold the keychain in your hands and like a mantra, repeat, "Always a blessing. It always works. Thank you." You will be amazed at how quickly problems are resolved! From finding parking spaces to breezing right through that crowded mall, you'll be delighted at the ease of shopping with your personally designed holiday talisman!

Cost of this project: Approximately $20.00 (which includes the price of the bayberry candle, magickal herbs, and magickal oil).

Time to complete: Around 30 to 60 minutes depending on drying time and number of embellishments used.

Fostering Family

Lydia M. Crabtree

FOR FAMILY COVENS, YULE is the time to reflect upon all that has begun. Just as the Sun rises to begin again the journey to its fullness, so is this the time for families to reflect upon all the beginnings of their lives: when the partners first met, when the children were first conceived, when the familiars (animals) in the family coven were brought into the household. These beginnings within the family coven should be brought out at Yule and talked about around the Yule log or while sitting in the living room with some hot chocolate. This is a reflection of what this time of year means to Pagans past.

Traditionally, many Earth-based practitioners stay up all night and wait for the rising dawn. A family coven could incorporate this tradition with the practice of reflection. Turn off all the lights and have the family room lit by fire light or by candles or soft lamp lighting. Have the father priest(s) be in charge of knowing the time the Sun will rise and have them prepare a tarp, many blankets and have picked out a good place to watch the new Sun rise.

Back at the family covenstead, in the quiet of night, sip hot chocolate and other eye-opening drinks (hot cinnamon and apple cider or lemon zinger tea) and pore over old photos. Have the partner(s) recount how they met, what it felt like. Recount for the family coveners these stories and let the children ask questions. Don't forget to remind them that we reflect upon these things at this time of year because this is about the new beginnings and celebrating them, just as you will celebrate the sunrise, when it comes.

Then talk about when the partner(s) found out they were expecting the various children. How did they feel? Were they scared? Now is a great time to talk about sex if the children are of appropriate age (parents should determine this on a case-by-case basis). Talk about those beginnings in detail, focusing on emotions and feelings. Children long to know things like how they got their name. The answers to such questions shape the way they view prospective partners and prepare them for a future that might include having or adopting their own children.

Then ask your family coven what new beginnings happened during this past year that should be toasted or celebrated. Did you buy a new car? Did you move into a new house? Did you change jobs? Did you find out you were expecting or start the journey toward adoption? Did you give birth or adopt? Did someone in the family coven commit to a spiritual journey, dedicate to a spiritual path, start a new hobby, career, or extracurricular activity? Talk about these new beginnings and how they affected your family coven. Talk about the negative and the positive.

While all this talking is going on, you could have your family coven be painting or making the year's ornaments. They should reflect your ongoing conversation about new beginnings. You can use foam ornament packages bought at the craft stores, or fill clear balls with images that remind you of the stories you told that year. You could use a simple salt dough ornament recipe to make, bake, paint, and seal ornaments reflecting the discussions.

You can also string popcorn and cranberries while you talk. This activity should remind you that in the darkness of winter, our brothers and sisters outside that need us to help sustain them, just as they have been sustaining us through the majority of the wheel of the year.

When the father priest(s) indicates, bundle everyone up and take them out to watch the sunrise. Use the tarp to protect against snow or dew, and the blankets to help keep warm. Don't forget those hats, gloves, and coats! Watch the sunrise, and when it is fully risen, shout, "Happy Birthday Sun God!"

Rush back inside to open presents. Try to take the edge off the holiday blues by encouraging children and yourselves to have a budget and stick to it. Better a few well-picked presents than a tree stuffed with things that reflect our egotistic desires and crush our spiritual development. Make at least one present for each member of the family coven. They don't have to be fancy; however, a functional gift is a good reflection of this time of year. Then eat a warm and hearty breakfast, taking your popcorn and cranberry strings out to the yard and decorating a bush or tree with them, leaving some of the breakfast there for nature to retrieve and enjoy.

Then, as a family, make a big bed in the family room and sleep together. Start the new beginning with the whole family coven. Let the magic of the season fill the room and breathe into your family coven the surety that new beginnings will always come and will always pass while you sleep. Let the knowledge that through working together, a family coven can overcome any upheaval a new beginning may bring.

In the quiet and stillness of the longest night of the year, you have an opportunity as a family coven to create memories that will last a lifetime while planting within your children comfort with change and new experiences. As you celebrate the changes and new things in your life, you are sending the signal to your charges that life is change, and change is good. Even death is a beginning of a life that is different, a life without. It may be sad; however, it is also an opportunity to learn, grow, and start anew.

Yule Ritual: Child of Promise

Raven Grimassi

Items Needed

Evergreen bough cuttings (enough to form an outline of your ritual circle)

Four pine cones (to mark the directional quarters of the circle)

Four pieces of mistletoe (to set with the pine cones)

One Yule log (with three holes drilled in it to hold candles)

Two green candles

One red candle

One gold or yellow candle (known as the God-flame candle)

Four white candles (for the directional quarters)

One small reed or wicker basket (the Child of Promise's cradle)

One totem to represent the Child of Promise (this can be a gold colored ornament, an egg, or a small figure of a baby, etc.)

One small wreath (to place on or around the basket)

Incense and incense holder (frankincense and myrrh)

One ritual bell

One cauldron

One vial of oil (scent associated with the Sun God)

Create sacred space by using evergreen cuttings to mark out a ritual circle on the ground. At each of the four quarters, place a pine cone with a sprig of mistletoe. In the center of the circle, place your altar. On the surface of the altar, set the Yule log. The three holes in the log will hold the candles: red in the center, green on each side. Place the basket with child figure in front of the Yule log, and set the wreath aside, next to the altar. Orient the altar so that you when you're at the altar, you're facing East. On the eastern oriented side of the altar, place the incense. Decorate the rest of the altar with seasonal items of your choice.

1. Begin by lighting the quarter candle at the east. Ring the ritual bell three times and then say the words of evocation:

I call to powers of the east to renew the light of the Sun.

Light the candle at the south quarter, ring the bell three times, and say:

I call to powers of the south to renew the light of the Sun.

Light the candle at the west quarter, ring the bell three times, and say:

I call to powers of the west to renew the light of the Sun.

Light the candle at the North quarter, ring the bell three times, and say:

I call to powers of the North to renew the light of the Sun.

(For group work, assign four people to take separate positions, one at each quarter. The facilitator stands at the altar and rings the bell to signal the recitation of the quarter evocations.)

2. At the altar, light the incense. Next, light the three candles on the Yule log, and say:

Bring evergreen wreaths for the Pagan's brow,
They're wearing the brightest laurels now;

Another year's conflict has passed away,
By strength from on high they've gained the day;
They've placed from their heart the bright things of Earth,
To gather a wreath for the promised Child's birth.

Lay the wreath over or in front of the basket.

3. At the altar, recite:

I mark now at this sacred time, the rebirth of the Sun God. It is the Great Mother who gives him birth. It is the lord of life born again. From the Union of the Lord and Lady, hidden in the Realm of Shadows, comes forth now the Child of Promise!

4. Carry the basket with child figure from the East quarter and recite:

I call forth now into the Portal of the Eastern Power. I call to the Ancient God, he who brought forth the beasts of field and forest. I call upon the Ancient God, he who was beloved of the ancient tribes.

(For group work, four members separately stand at the quarters, and the basket is passed from quarter to quarter.)

5. Walk around the circle, starting and ending in the East, holding up the basket (symbolizing the Sun's journey). As you walk, recite these words:

My Lord, I greet You. O Horned One, horned with the rays of the Sun, by whose blessings and grace shall life always be born again.

(For group work, everyone recites as the facilitator walks the circle.) Basket is returned to the altar.

6. Set the cauldron at the East quarter and place an offering within it. (For group work everyone separately makes an offering)

7. Stand in front of the cauldron and recite:

O most ancient provider, Lord of Light and Life, I (we) pray you grow strong that I (we) may pass the Winter in peace and fullness. Emanate Your warmth and Your Love that the cold and harshness of Winter not diminish Your followers.

O Ancient One, hear me! Protect and provide in the harshness of these times. I (we) give You adoration and place myself in Your care. Blessed be all in the God!

8. Anoint yourself (everyone in group work) with oil, saying:

Blessed be in his care.

9. Read the Myth of the Season text out loud:

Now the time came that the Goddess would bear the child of the Lord of the Hidden Realm of Shadows. And the Lords of the four quarters came and beheld the newborn God, he who is the Child of Promise. Then the Goddess spoke to the four Lords, saying "Take my son to the mortal realm that he might bring Life to the world above. For the mortal realm has grown cold and lifeless." So the Lords of the four corners departed to the world above, bearing the new Lord of the Sun. And the People rejoiced, for the Lord had come that all upon the Earth might be saved.

10. Place the God-flame candle in front of the cauldron and light it. With both hands, lower the candle into the cauldron and then slowly raise it (symbolically give it birth through cauldron).

11. Once born, take the flame to the East quarter. Present it and proclaim: (For group work, everyone shouts the proclamation):

Hail, to the newborn Sun. Hail Child of Promise, hail Lord of the Sun.

Repeat this at each quarter.

12. Take the God-flame from the East quarter and make one full pass around the circle (holding up the God-flame). Upon returning to the East, raise the flame to this quarter. Then set it on the altar.

13. Recite at altar:

Let the spirit be joyful and the heart to despair not. For on this sacred day is born He whose Light shall save the World. He has come forth from the Darkness and His Light has been seen in the East. He is Lord of Light and Life.

Lift up the God-flame candle, and recite:

Behold the Sacred One, the Child of Promise! He who is born into the World, is slain for the World, and ever rises again!

14. Take the wreath, the Yule log, and the God-candle to the East quarter. The Yule log is set on top of the wreath. Remove the red candle and replace it with God-flame candle (extinguish the red candle and set it aside). The placing of the God-flame candle symbolizes the Lord of Light and the Lord of Vegetation (the Harvest Lord), being as one and the same. (For group work have different members carry the items to the east quarter.)

15. Extend palms out above the God-flame, and recite:

Behold the God whose life and light dwells within me (each of us). He is the Horned One; Lord of the forest, and the Hooded One; Lord of the Harvest, and The Old One; Lord of the Clans. Therefore do I (we) honor Him.

16. The ritual is then concluded with a celebratory meal. For group work, members may wish to exchange presents. When finished gather up the items and declare the circle undone.

The items that were used in the Yule ritual contain magical energy through absorption. They can be used in spellwork associated with renewal, gain, and enlightenment. You can use the dried pine needles from the evergreen boughs and add them to powdered incense. Wax from the candles can be melted and poured into bottle caps, which when dried can be used as charms inscribed with etched symbols. The wax charms can be melted to release the power into the spell. One example is to etch a dollar sign symbol into the wax to attract prosperity.

One ancient practice involved spreading ashes from ritual debris over the soil of the spring planting field. This practice can be modified to influence career and business opportunities. Instead of spreading ashes on a field, the debris can be placed inside a small pouch with symbolic charms. The pouch can be discreetly carried to job interviews or business meetings. It can also be set on top of your résumé in order to pass energy into it before submitting the résumé.

Save some of the pine needles in a small pouch for the next Yule celebration. In this way the undying "light" is carried and passed from Winter Solstice to Winter Solstice. The reed or wicker basket can be reused each season as can the Child of Promise figure. Store these with the pine needle pouch to help keep the solstice alignment active between celebrations.

This ritual is an update of an old favorite that first appeared in Raven Grimassi's 1999 publication, Hereditary Witchcraft: Secrets of the Old Religion.

Notes

Imbolc

Imbolc

Michelle Skye

IMBOLC IS THE FIRST of the three fertility sabbats (along with Ostara and Beltane) and the first of the four Celtic fire festivals or Greater Sabbats, which also include Beltane, Lughnasadh, and Samhain. In short, Imbolc is the seed that starts the whole wheel of the year turning once again. After the spark of Yule, the hard work of beginning another year occurs at Imbolc. Possibilities are endless and eternal at this time. The whole year stretches before you and you have the power to mold it into whatever you desire. Imbolc is a good time to perform spells concerned with the gaining of inspiration, releasing the old to bring in the new, creating and/or increasing the warmth and love within a household/relationship/family, creating prosperity, and welcoming personal growth.

Imbolc, or Oimelc, is a name which refers to the lactation of ewes and to the milk they provide for their newborn lambs. It is essentially an Irish and Scottish holiday, with little evidence that it held as much significance in Wales or Britain, according to historian Ronald Hutton. Of the four fire festivals, Imbolc is given less attention than Samhain and Beltane in the information left us by our ancient Pagan forebears. Imbolc serves as an "opening" of a season (as is the case with all the fire festivals) and, as such, reminds us that spring warmth is on its way. Therefore, many of the activities and symbolic actions taken at Imbolc help to sweep away the old in order to welcome the new. One such tradition holds that keeping up your Yule decorations after Imbolc will bring you bad luck. So, be sure to pack them all away! During this sabbat of new beginnings and growth, you don't want to be left behind, shackled by your tinsel and Santa hat!

Other Imbolc traditions center on the Goddess Brigid, an Irish goddess (borrowed and altered slightly by the Scottish folk), who oversees transformation, inspiration, healing, and personal growth, and whose holiday is February 1. Daughter of Morrighan and the Dagda, Brigid is one of the immortal Tuatha dé Danann, who retreated into the mists (or into the mound, depending upon your preference of otherworld entrances) when the Milesans invaded and occupied Ireland. A Triple Goddess of sisters of nearly equal age, Brigid is goddess of the fire of the forge, goddess of the fire of healing, and goddess of the fire of inspiration, referred to as Imbas in old Irish Gaelic and Awen in Welsh. She is often invoked at the birth of babies, to help the laboring mother and the child within awaiting entrance to the world. She is also a favorite goddess of bards and poets, serving as a divine muse for them to channel thoughts, words, and songs.

Brigid has undergone trials and tribulations within her lifetime, having experienced the overthrow of her husband Bres as king and the death of her young son Ruadan. Her pain over her loss resulted in the first example of *keening* (ritualized vocalizations of grief) in Irish mythology, according to the Second Battle of Mag Tuired. As a goddess of transformation, healing, inspiration, and personal growth, Brigid fits in perfectly with the energy of the first fire festival. Activities that correspond with her are: crafting a corn dolly (representative of Bride or Brigid) and having a parade in her honor; making a fire the night before and, the morning of Imbolc, checking it for bird footprints or other signs that Brigid has blessed the house; crafting a Brigid's cross; baking a special bread or cake; and churning (or, in our case, making) butter.

While intimately united with the Goddess Brigid, Imbolc is also connected to the Catholic holiday Candlemas, which is celebrated on February 2, the day after Brigid's Day. Candlemas is a celebration of the fortieth day after Jesus' birth (Christmas), when mother and child were free from self-enforced seclusion. It was celebrated with candle-lit services that included parades (with statues of the Madonna and child) and a blessing of candles. These candles would then be either kept at the church or brought home to be lit, "enlightening" each individual home. In modern Catholicism, Candlemas has been included in the Feast Day of Saint Blaise (February 3), a rather obscure saint who has nothing to do with fire or candles, despite his name. However, on his feast day, candles are placed at the throat or over the head of those attending mass, conferring a blessing against throat trouble and evil. While it is intriguing to consider the similarities between Brigid's Day and Imbolc with Candlemas and Saint Blaise's Day, they each originated in different areas of the world and, thus, are not really derived from each other. However, the fact that they all have an element of fire at their base indicates that the season of Imbolc is, indeed, a period of energy and passion, perfect for leaving behind the old and beginning the new.

Imbolc Correspondences

Colors: white, red, and yellow

Stones: rutilated quartz, snow quartz, ametrine, charoite, fire agate, sunstone, goldstone, moss agate, nephrite, and Connemara marble

Plants: snowdrop, birch tree, and rowan tree

Animals: lambs and sheep, cows, goats, and any winter birds such as blue jays, cardinals, and chickadees

Looking Back, Moving Forward

It is difficult to move forward when you're holding on to the past. The past is good; don't get me wrong, I love the past. It gives us stability in an unstable world, tradition in a nontraditional society, foundation in a culture ever reaching for the stars. But sometimes we cling a little too tightly to the past. We're like the ivy that grows on the bricks and cement of old Ivy League colleges, holding, holding, holding onto the old, comfortable, and secure mortar, never reaching for the newly budding, green tree just across the quadrangle. We accept our situation, our place, our role in life, even if it doesn't fit us anymore, even if it chafes around the edges. Imbolc, as a holiday, gives us the time, once a year, to assess our lives and do something about it. Change the future, embrace the present, resurrect the past —you have the power, bolstered by the seasonal shifts all around you, to construct a new plan and to evolve into a new life.

Imbolc is exciting and scary and fascinating and terrifying all rolled into one staid holiday, tucked into the wilds of winter. It's hard to image a season so full of potential, as the snowflakes fall outside your window and the temperatures plummet. Yet, what better time to take stock and to evaluate your life than when curled up in front of a cozy fire? I imagine these scenes of winter wonderland because Imbolc was, traditionally, a holiday of the Celtic Isles, particularly Ireland and Scotland. And, as we all know, it can get pretty darn nippy in Glasgow and Dublin in February. They don't make kilts and Irish sweaters out of wool for nothing! So while Imbolc is, on the surface, a sabbat of possibilities and outward actions, all of these new beginnings need to start in the dark, in the womb, in the center of the self. So, Imbolc is both a sabbat of internal reflection and outward action. Balance is important.

Inner reflection can take many forms. In New Age and Pagan circles, gurus and priestesses would recommend meditation, divination, journeywork, and journaling. And while I think all of these are valid and wonderful activities to pursue around Imbolc, these actions leave out a whole host of people who, maybe, are not versed in traditional metaphysical pursuits. As a Witch, don't you want to help your community as well, your family and friends who may not be interested in metaphysics but who would benefit from Imbolc's once-a-year cleansing breath? And let's not leave out the children. Ever try to get a five-year-old to meditate? It's just not happening.

So, how to take stock in a way that could include all members of your life? Easy. Pay attention. The problem with our hurried, fast-paced world is that we never leave ourselves time to just be. We race here and there and back again, never disentangled from the life-wire of our technological devices. Leave the cell phone at home? Horrors! Sit in the living room without the TV blaring? Unthinkable! Ride the bus or in the car without iTunes? Insane! Yet, we are missing so much of the divinity and sacredness of the world because we are distracted. We distract ourselves in an effort to constantly be entertained and amused.

This is not a new problem. Consider the Romans and their bloody games in the Coliseum in Rome and in numerous mini-Coliseums across the empire. "Are you not entertained?" roared Maximus in the movie *Gladiator*, standing on blood-soaked sand. And while we're not killing people for our pleasure, the purpose of all the distraction is the same. Chariot races, wide-screen TVs, gladiatorial death matches, and MP3 players all serve to delight and stimulate the senses in order to distract us from our own true, inner voices. The noise serves to divert our attention from the real wonders, the real entertainment right outside our windows and deep inside our hearts. We are the real amusement and the world is our stage.

So, for the weeks leading up to Imbolc, consider choosing one day a week to simply unplug. This might be a huge shock to your system so start slow at first. Turn off the devices for an hour and see which birds fly over your house. Notice the lone tree poking up through the sidewalk. Listen to the sounds of your neighbors and your neighbors' dogs or cats . . . or guinea pigs. Look at the weave of your shag rug or flip through a pile of old pictures. Pretty soon you'll begin to grow accustomed to the serenity of silence. Now, while gazing at your shag rug may be fascinating for you (and who could blame you?), it's not going to necessarily help you take stock of your life over the past year. Once you've found contentment in the space needed for inner revelation, it's time to reflect. Big time.

As the winter storms howl and the fire crackles, consider all aspects of your life—your work, your interests, your family and friends, and, especially, your emotional core. I like to use an adjective to describe each aspect of my life. Boring, complicated, fulfilling, frustrating—don't limit yourself in describing your life. After all, your life is your own and no one will see your assessment, except you. If you're not a word person, use pictures or colors or movie titles that really speak to the core of your life. Be completely honest! This is not the time to gloss over things and put on a happy face!

Do this for weeks, taking one week to focus on each aspect of your life. During that week, pay attention to things that may happen. Signs, omens, coincidences, serendipity, call them what you will—the universe will be sending you information concerning your chosen life aspect. Let's say you choose to focus on your work one week. It just so happens that all hell breaks loose at work and you have to work 50 gazillion hours for no increased pay and with no recognition from your boss. In fact, your boss never even shows up at work (preferring a week in the Bahamas) and so never even realizes any of the work you just performed. This would be a sign, a serendipitous moment, in which to pay attention.

If you turned on your Sirius radio, you might lose the message in an '80s Guns N' Roses anthem or a diatribe of epic proportions from Howard Stern. You'd relax into someone else's babble and never take the time to listen to your own. But, having reflected on your actions of the past and your personal desires for the future, Howard Stern and Guns N' Roses don't have an audience in you. You are starting to realize that you want something more. You're ready to make a change—whether taking a college course, moving to Hawaii, or finally asking out that cute co-worker down the hall.

You're beginning to create a plan to achieve your goals and live the life of your dreams!

And here comes Imbolc, peeking her sunny little head over the horizon to help you, reminding you that spring is coming and growth is inevitable. New buds huddle just under the fallen snow, safe and warm in their cocoon of darkness deep in the soil. The time is ripe for you to discover what buds, what seeds of possibility await to blossom for you. Imbolc is the perfect time to make plans and take action to change your life, based on the findings from your inner reflection. Work, relationships, location, situation—all can change. Life is transient and fluid and flexible. We all allow ourselves to get boxed into "this life," our life, as if it's a foregone conclusion. It isn't. Imbolc reminds us that our opportunities are endless if we just embrace them and allow our lives to transform.

Welcome the season of Imbolc with open arms as it is the sabbat of many firsts—first fertility holiday, first of the fire festivals, first holiday of new growth and new beginnings. Imbolc is a wonderfully freeing, cleansing sabbat. It allows us to sweep away the old for the excitement and opportunity of the new. Nothing is holding you back. In the end, after all the assessing and omen-watching, Imbolc is a celebration, a sabbat of awakening! With a burst of frenetic energy, the flowers bloom, the trees blossom, and life begins again. Ever renewing, ever growing, Imbolc reminds us that the world will become green again, despite cold, harsh weather. Your life will become green again, despite periods of drought and turmoil. Imbolc gives you the space to realize that the world is open for you. Imbolc provides the energizing push to reach and achieve your dreams. All you need to do is access your truth in order to step into your glorious future.

Celestial Sway

Fern Feto Spring

IMBOLC IS THE SABBAT of growing light and brings us an awareness of our own inner spark of creativity, passion, and power. Brigid's Day is the first, almost imperceptible breath of spring, which encourages hope of new life and fresh possibilities. As the goddess of smithcrafting, poetry, and healing, Brigid awakens us to the power of fire and the myriad possibilities that occur when our blood and bodies began to warm with the ever-increasing light of the Sun.

The stars align for 2010 around themes of justice, balance, and right relationships. The waning Moon on February 2 is emerging from the Full Moon in Leo on January 30, emphasizing the polarity between the individual and the collective. The Brigid Moon occurs at the first degree of the sign of Libra, and is in a close conjunction to Saturn in Libra and squared by Pluto in Capricorn. Libra themes of partnership, fairness, and balance are tested and emphasized at this time. Questions arise as to how we can express our own creativity and spontaneous selves in ways that include others and also engage in the transformation of collective rules and structures.

Because Libra also rules beauty, Saturn in Libra conjunct the Moon may find us working hard to create beauty and harmony in our own homes and in our everyday emotional environments. We may feel bound or trapped by old or outdated aesthetics or ideas of what emotional peace entails. Pluto in Capricorn is in a square to the Moon and Saturn in Libra, and this challenges us to create new models that encompass our changing patterns and allow us to express more current concepts of Libra qualities that fit us better.

Mercury has gone direct and is out of its retrograde "shadow" phase as well, giving us full permission to move forward and take action on any changes we might need to make now. (The shadow phase is when a formerly retrograde planet retraces the degrees that it just went through backward. This allows us to revisit those retrograde lessons with more perspective and a sense of forward motion.)

The New Moon that follows Brigid takes place on February 13 conjunct Neptune, and is also moving toward a conjunction to the planet Venus. Mercury in Aquarius is conjunct Neptune in Aquarius February 27 near the same degree as the New Moon in Aquarius on February 13. Now is the time to communicate to others and gather more information on the dreams we envisioned at the New Moon.

Whether or not you celebrate Valentine's Day, you can still use this New Moon energy to plant seeds that can help relationships grow in new and interesting ways. The visionary qualities of Aquarius, combined with the imaginative, dreamy potential of Neptune, bring a reminder of our hopes for a new way of being in the world. Venus has also just transitioned into Pisces, awakening our ability to love unconditionally, and transpersonally. Our personal vision will be more powerful if we can also ground it in what can best serve the group or the collective. How can we make the personal, if not political, at least relevant to the collective as a whole? We will be motivated to broaden our perspectives on our personal relationships now, and find ourselves stretching beyond our individual needs to more clearly see our place in the collective dream.

Ritual for Brigid Season

On Brigid's Day, or on the day of the next New Moon, February 14, take a walk in your neighborhood, or in some nature spot that calls to you. As you walk, notice any signs of new life—a bud, a baby animal, a blade of green grass. Meditate on how you as an individual fit into the greater whole of life. What are your wishes and dreams for your future? What do you hope for the future of those you love? Of humanity? For the Earth? What do you want to create to express your passion and fire in this life?

Leave an offering (the Earth usually welcomes offerings more on the biodegradable end of things) near the spot where you notice these signs of new life. When you return home, write or collage any answers that came to you on your Brigid walk, or just write about the direction your thoughts went during this meditative process.

Full Moon–February 28

The February Full Moon in Virgo asks us to become aware of how we manifest our spiritual beliefs and make these real in the practical, everyday, physical realm. How do we use our inspiration from the God or Goddess, nature, and the spirit world to serve in the "real" world? The Sun in Pisces is conjunct Jupiter, expanding our idealism and dreams for the future. The Moon in Virgo wants the details of these dreams, a plan, a map, or a system. We can use this Full Moon in Virgo to take a closer look at our vision, connect with others, and learn more about what we might do to take the next steps toward making our dreams real.

Look to where the Full Moon falls in the houses of your chart for a more specific interpretation of how this lunar event will affect your life. Notice which house cusp Virgo rules, and also which one Pisces rules for an understanding of the house pairs to be activated.

Full Moon in Virgo Through the Houses

1st and 7th: Self-Identity/The Other, partnerships

2nd and 8th: Personal skills and resources/Shared energies and resources

3rd and 9th: Communication and the immediate environment/ Meaning and expansion of consciousness

4th and 10th: Home, family, and deep self/Public persona, career, and destiny

5th and 11th: Self-expression, creativity, and spontaneity/Community, humanity, and the future

6th and 12th: Service to others and in the world/Service to spirit and retreat

Mars Direct in Leo

Mars goes direct on March 10 at 0 degrees of Leo. Now we can begin to reconnect with some of the courage, passion, and desire that may have evaded us since Mars went retrograde at the Winter Solstice. Mars in Leo reminds us that courage comes from the heart, and when we are centered in our heart's desire, we have the ability to defend and protect what we love. As Mars moves forward and through its "shadow" phase, we will have the chance to revisit the lessons we learned about love, bravery, passion, and desire, but with a faster pace, and a greater sense of progress.

Mars Direct Ritual

This ritual works with the waning Moon and helps to clear out and release old patterns related to Mars energy in your life.

On the night that Mars goes direct, light a red candle to honor this fiery planet. Then, on a piece of paper, write or draw everything that is holding you back from feeling and fulfilling your passion in life. Keep writing or drawing until you have nothing left to express. Ask Mars to help you reconnect and fully embrace your passion for your art, work, relationship, or life in general. Set an intention that as Mars picks up speed and moves forward in direct motion, you will also find your way back to your heart's desire.

The Old Ways

Dan Furst

THE PEOPLES OF ANCIENT western and central Europe celebrated the next great turning in the year on what we now call early February. This is the moment of quickening that is called Imbolc because the lambs are stirring "in the belly" (Celtic *'mbolg*) just before birth, and the ewes are heavy with milk. That's how we know the ground will start to thaw a Moon cycle from now, and in the second Moon cycle after that, following Beltane, the world leafs out and blooms again. The main thing that must be done again now, just as we did it at Samhain, is to purify our houses and our souls so that we carry love into the time of spring planting and new birth.

As all four crossquarter sabbats feature rites of purification, the style of these at Imbolc is predictable. We've just endured the icy, dismal month of Saturn's own Great Cold in Capricorn month, and we're ready for some comic relief. Symbols of new life bursting up again from the blackness of January begin to appear now, like the white plum blossoms in countless paintings from China and gardens in Japan. The Sun has entered Aquarius the Water Bearer, and with him the promise that the worst of the cold is over, and the water of life will flow again as winter melts into spring. This is why, at the Aquarius New Moon, the Chinese didn't always wish each other *Gung Hay Fat Choy,* "May the Year be Happy!" on their lunar New Year's Day, as they do now. They greeted each other with *Guo Nian,* "We've Survived the Year!" There is a strong sense among the Celts, and other Northern Hemisphere peoples living far east of them, that we've come through nature's roughest ordeal, and it's time to celebrate—after we've cleansed our houses and protected ourselves from harm.

Whom do we ask for protection? The Triple Goddess, of course. She completes her transition to Wise Woman now in the air month of Aquarius, just as the other air months host her evolution into Maiden (Gemini–June) and Mother (Libra–October). This is why the greatest goddess festival of the Celtic year comes now in the renewal rites of the beloved mother called Brigid, Bridhe, Brighid, Brigantia, and other names. Her feast cycle runs twelve days, from January 23 to February 3. As usual, there's a dramatic build to the rites.

The first major ceremony gives thanks and praise to the Wise Woman in her beneficent aspect, as the protector of the eternal life flame of the world, and the bringer of light to those who master her crafts of augury and prophecy, along with plant, stone, and star lore. Nine days later—one day for each month in the woman's gestation cycle—the Goddess puts on her dark mask for the vigil of Imbolc. On January 31, peoples all over the ancient Mediterranean world sacrificed to Hecate, the Moon in her terrifying aspect as purifier and destroyer, beseeching her to cleanse them of all negative, fear-inducing emotions.

The day of renewal would then come at dawn on Bridhe's feast, also called St. Bridget's Day among Irish Catholics, when young women would weave green reeds into spiral and swastika shapes that symbolize the endless whirling into birth of the new life that is not just to come, but to come now, because the crop of new babies who were conceived last spring at Beltane are coming to birth here at Imbolc. The little ones had best be born in houses that are swept, aired, and ready. And blessed with the right offerings.

These votive rites are the source of our word *February*. It comes from *februa*, meaning expiatory offerings that were made in very ancient times to a goddess whom the Greeks and Romans later identified with Hera/Juno, protector of the family and home. After the house was cleaned and the hearth fires blessed, it was showtime for those who felt that if we're going to drive dark forces away, we may as well have fun with it. That's why, in the miracle play cycles that were enacted in the Christian Middle Ages, raucous boot-the-devil comedies would come on February 2, the eve of Candlemas. Their scenario is always the same: the unbeatably ugly Satan roars into the town square, scattering the pious folk like ducklings until they realize that one by one, they have no chance against him, but united in faith and courage, they can beat the Bad One. And they do, chasing him with pitchforks, mallets, and tongs until the climactic moment when one small boy kicks the devil actor's well-padded tail and sends him yelling out the door.

Much the same thing happens on February 3 in Japan at Setsubun, the happiest Shinto festival of the year. The fun begins in the morning, when families cast evil spirits from their homes by throwing dried beans out the door while shouting *Oni wa soto, fuku wa uchi*, "Out with the devil, in with the good." In the afternoon, everyone goes to the shrines for the Oni wa Soto farces, in which devils in grotesque masks run about with huge weapons and menace the people until the children pelt the demons with dried beans and drive them out. The ancient meaning of this *matsuri*, or festival, comes from the older Chinese *Ta Nuo* ("field cleansing") ritual, of purifying the ground before the spring thaw and the planting season. This transition from the sleep of winter to the awakening of spring is enacted in many lands by weather rituals such as Groundhog Day, in which sunshine or rain, light or shadow, indicate whether winter will continue to rule or soon yield to spring.

The children throw beans because there's a miraculous vital power in the bean plant, which sprouts so soon and grows so fast that Jack climbing up a giant beanstalk is almost plausible. If one is going to chase away the evil one, what better weapon to use than nature's own little green bio-bomb? This is why other peoples have used beans to drive dark forces away, as did the Greeks—they'd spit beans to keep ghosts away—in feasts like the Great Dionyseia. The feast was held in ancient times over the fourteen days from the Aquarius new Moon to the Full Moon, but was later fixed in the solar calendar to start on February 1 and run through February 14.

The Dionyseia began by enacting the rising of Dionysos from the underworld, where he has spent the cold months in his winter role as the aged Hades/Plouton. He now begins to grow from a sinuous boy into the god of wine, sex, dance, and all ecstatic experiences—provided, yet again, that the rites of purification are done well. In the early days of his feast, the vines are pruned and sprinkled with the best of last year's wine, so the vine of life is renewed in time for spring, when Dionysos becomes irresistible again in his shining black beard and grape leaves, ready to sing, drink, dance, and love them all. His rites climaxed on the day that doves were seen to mate for life, on what is still the Feast of the Lovers, St. Valentine's Day.

As rollicking as this season can be, the main point is rooted in serious sympathetic magic, and the premise that as healthy and strong as the human beings are—in our actions and speech, intentions and habits—so will the fields and flocks be. If the people are cleansed of rancor and fear, and use feasts like Imbolc to teach their children cleanliness and order, then the soil and the womb will be wholesome and ready for seed. This is why the Christian rite of Candlemas on February 3 has Imbolc written all over it, as the priest holds unlit crossed candles at each child's throat, asking St. Blaise to protect them from illness—and to keep their words sweet. Babies are coming now, and we intend that their home be harmonious and kind.

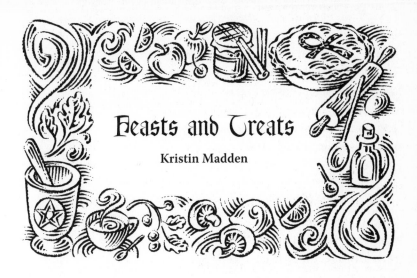

Feasts and Treats

Kristin Madden

THE FOODS OF IMBOLC are rich and hearty. The frozen ground is giving way to warmer, more fertile seasons, but there is still a chill in the air in many regions. So we create celebratory foods and beverages that warm our bodies and invigorate our minds. These foods are crafted as our ancestors might have but with a modern twist, with the best of remaining stored meats and vegetables along with cream from the newly lactating sheep. Seeds, nuts, and breads are traditional additions at this time of year, as are red and white foods that honor the Goddess Brigid.

Lamb Stew

As their ewes began to lactate in preparation for birthing, our ancestors must have relished the delicious milk and promise of fresh meat to come. This tasty adaptation of the traditional Irish lamb stew recipe comes complete with a "secret" optional ingredient that your adult guests will love.

Prep Time: 20 minutes
Cook Time: 2 hours, 20 minutes
Serves: 6–8

2 pounds lamb

4 tablespoons olive oil

2 pounds potatoes, peeled and chopped

2 large carrots, peeled and chopped

1 small turnip, peeled and chopped

2 large onions, peeled and chopped

4 cloves garlic, chopped

½–1 cup barley

1 teaspoon thyme

1 quart chicken or beef stock

Salt and pepper to taste

Optional: ½ cup Guinness® Stout

Cut the lamb into chunks and brown it in olive oil. In a large stock-pot, combine all ingredients and bring to a boil for 1 minute. Reduce heat and simmer for at least 2 hours. Serve with whole grain or sprouted bread and butter for a truly traditional experience!

Sweet Nut Muffins

Life may be starting to show itself, but it is still cold outside in many areas. Imbolc feasts need something sweet and celebratory, but sustaining and solid too. Perfect with your meal or as a dessert, these muffins bring you the best of both worlds and they are just the sort of thing our ancestors may have prepared for this special festival.

Prep Time: 20 minutes

Cook Time: 25 minutes

Serves: 12–16

1 cup sweet potato, finely grated

1 cup cream

1 large egg

⅓ cup butter, melted

3 tablespoons brown sugar

1 tablespoon honey

1 teaspoon vanilla extract

1 cup all-purpose flour
1 cup oat flour
2 teaspoons baking powder
1 teaspoon cinnamon
½ teaspoon nutmeg
¼ teaspoon salt
⅓ cup raisins
¼ cup walnuts, chopped

Preheat oven to 400 degrees F. Lightly beat the sweet potato, cream, and egg on medium speed. Mix in butter, sugar, honey, and vanilla.

In a separate bowl, mix together the flours, baking powder, cinnamon, nutmeg, and salt. Fold dry ingredients into sweet potato mixture just until moist. Then add raisins and walnuts and gently fold in. Spoon into greased muffin tins and bake for 25 minutes.

Brandy Panna Cotta

Pregnant ewes are beginning to lactate, reminding us that life is returning to the world. What a gift this must have been to our ancestors after a long, hard winter! In honor of life renewed and the Goddess Brigid, take the time to create this rich cream custard topped with a tangy brandy syrup in the colors of the season. It really is worth it. This will certainly warm your cockles after a Candlemas feast!

Prep Time: 25 minutes   *Cook Time:* 15 minutes
Chill Time: 2+ hours   *Serves:* 8

1 envelope unflavored gelatin
2½ cups buttermilk
½ cup heavy cream
½ cup sugar

4–5 blood oranges
1 tablespoon brandy
¾ cup sugar
10–12 cherries or strawberries

Panna Cotta

In a small bowl, gently mix gelatin into 1½ cups of the buttermilk and allow to stand for 2 minutes. In a large saucepan, bring cream and ½ cup sugar to a boil, stirring frequently. Reduce heat to low and add gelatin mixture. Cook until gelatin dissolves completely. Remove from heat and add the remaining 1 cup of buttermilk, mixing well. Pour into 8 custard cups. Cover with plastic wrap and refrigerate overnight.

Slip a cold butter knife around the edges of each custard. Turn each one upside down over a plate and tap it to release the custard. Serve topped with brandy syrup.

Brandy Syrup

Remove peels and pits from the oranges. Squeeze out 1 cup of juice into a measuring cup. If you don't have enough, add regular orange juice to bring it up to 1 cup. In a medium saucepan, bring juice, brandy, and remaining ¾ cup sugar to a boil. Reduce heat to medium and cook until it thickens into a syrup. Pour into a medium bowl and add cherries or strawberries. Cover and refrigerate for at least 2 hours.

Candlemas Cocoa

Hot cocoa is a favorite at any winter sabbat but this cocoa is truly something special. Fresh cream, dried spices, and heavenly chocolate combine in one warm mug to deliver a combination of tastes that will revitalize your senses and invigorate your mind. This is a beverage fit for a god or goddess!

Prep Time: 5 minutes
Cook Time: 20 minutes
Serves: 4–6

1 teaspoon dried fennel
½ cup water
½ cup sugar
⅓ cup unsweetened cocoa

½ teaspoon cinnamon
3 cups heavy cream
½ teaspoon vanilla extract
Optional: shot of licorice liqueur

In a small bowl, gently crush the fennel with the back of a spoon. Combine water, sugar, cocoa, cinnamon, and fennel in a medium saucepan. Cook over medium heat, stirring constantly until cocoa dissolves completely. Reduce heat and simmer 5 minutes, stirring occasionally. Add cream and simmer 5 minutes, stirring frequently. Stir in vanilla and simmer another 2 minutes. Pour into mugs and add a shot of liqueur, if you like. Serve immediately.

Crafty Crafts

Silver RavenWolf

Deva of the Season: Light

Scents/Aromas: Wintergreen, Frankincense

Energy: Flow

Visualization: Fill a bowl with water and floating candles. Each evening light the candles and focus on the center of the bowl. Visualize your desires (one at a time) as you look into the bowl. Imagine each thing you desire floating up from the bowl and into your hands (or close enough to touch). Practice this visualization every day for twenty-one days beginning on Imbolc Eve. Envision yourself happily sending out and receiving the things you desire. Always end your visualization with a smile.

Affirmation: I know the shining light of Spirit flows in, around, and through everything I think, say, and do. I am filled with the Divine Light of Spirit.

☙

February is absolutely the month of the Goddess with feasts and celebrations dedicated to Her many forms in various cultures. Here are just a few:

February 1: Brigid (Celtic)

February 2: Vesta, Juno (Roman), and Nut (Egyptian)

February 7: Artemis (Greek), Diana (Roman)

February 14: Vali to honor Vara (Norse)
February 16: Victoria (Roman)
February 26: Neith Festival of Light (Ancient Egyptian)
February 27: Selene (Greek)

You may wish to honor the Goddess on any or all of these days, filling your month with the magickal light of the feminine divine.

Imbolc represents the Feast of Mother Light, a celebration of water and fire to honor the light of spirit as well as the light of individuality within all things. A perpetual flame (or spirit light) can be lit to bless the home and property. Spells and charms are intoned over gardening and farm tools to ensure a profitable and abundant growing season ahead. Before Imbolc, the entire house should be swept with an old broom and dustpan. One magickal country custom includes filling a gris-gris bag with lavender, chamomile, and lemongrass, tying it securely, and pushing the bag around the floor with the broom to dispel any negative energy hiding in corners or under tables and chairs. When you are finished, the gris-gris bag is swept out the back door (not the front), and then thrown into the trash. Both the old broom and dustpan should be thrown in the trash as well and replaced on February 2, but hide the new ones so that your luck will not be swept out of the house that day. An additional country custom includes empowering nine coins for attracting prosperity into the home and placing them under the rug in the four corners of the main room of the home (two coins in each corner and one in the center).

The Spirit Light

The spirit light is a simple, perpetual flame that needs only a heat-resistant bowl, olive oil, and a votive wick. This simple, inexpensive light is used for meditation, in ritual, spellwork, or to honor the Spirit of All Things and can be lit on Imbolc Eve. Scented oil and powdered herbs can be added to the olive oil for a more fragrant offering. The spirit light can also be used for all types of magickal workings throughout the year.

Supplies

⅛ cup olive oil

Glass or metal, heatproof bowl

1 new votive wick with large base

Small amount of powdered herbs of your choice

5 drops of frankincense fragrance oil (optional)

Instructions: Pour ⅛ cup olive oil in a small bowl (approximately 3.5 inches in diameter works best). Cut one new votive wick with large base to about ½ to ¼ inch above base. The amount of wick required depends on the level of oil in the bowl. The wick should stick up just a bit above the oil line. A very small amount of powdered herb can be added to the oil. For more fragrance, add a few drops of aromatherapy oil. Light the wick carefully, intoning your prayer, affirmation, or incantation nine times. Your spirit light can burn a long time, so be sure that the flame is always monitored. If the dish is bumped or spilled, a fire could result. I usually place my spirit light in a metal bowl, out of the way of busy family life. (Note: When working magick for a sick friend, surround your spirit lamp with white carnations to boost the herbal power of the spell.)

Cost of this project: $4.00 (estimated)

Time to complete: 5 minutes

Lucky Draw Magickal Oil

To celebrate the holiday, bless a bowl of water and a white candle in sacred space. Dress the white candle with Lucky Draw Magickal Oil. Light the white candle from your Spirit Light. Carry both candle and bowl of water in a clockwise direction around home and property, sprinkling a bit of the water as you walk. Intone your own chant, or use the affirmation given.

Supplies

1 dark glass jar or bottle with mouth wide enough to insert magnet
1 ounce of jojoba oil (other carriers of choice may be sweet almond
　　oil, saffron oil, or olive oil)
1 drop of lavender essential oil
1 drop of pine essential oil
1 drop of lemongrass essential oil
2 drops of patchouli essential oil
2 drops of french vanilla fragrance oil
1–3 drops of honeysuckle fragrance (optional)
1 magnet
1 mint leaf

Instructions: Place all ingredients in bottle. Cap tightly. Shake several times to mix thoroughly. Store in a dark place for nine days, shaking the bottle twice a day. On the ninth day, remove the mint leaf. Refrigerate for longer-lasting oil if you do not use the jojoba carrier. Do not ingest. To be used to dress candles, poppets, in potpourri, to draw the luck of the universe and to request special favors.

Cost of this project: Essential oils and fragrances can be pricey, especially if you want to make just one formula. Cost could be reduced if oil is made as a group project and everyone shares the expenses.

Time to complete: 5 minutes

Fostering Family

Lydia M. Crabtree

IN THE LIFE CYCLE of relationships, Imbolc is the time from the formal commitment ceremony or handfasting through the first three years. For children, it is all about the time they are/were in the womb. This is when the light is growing stronger and stronger, getting ready to warm the Earth and give birth to all the wonders of spring. In the same way children in the womb grow stronger and eventually will be born, so will the flowers and first foods at the Spring Equinox find strength and birth from Mother Earth.

Because Imbolc focuses on the hearth and home and is heavily associated with Brigid, the goddess of hearth and home, this is an excellent time to direct your family coven's attention inward to the covenstead. Focus on cleaning up and clearing out anything that might impede the planting that will soon begin.

For family covens, the physical stock-taking of your covenstead represents the kind of reflection that occurred while you prepared for the birth or adoption of a child or while you weighed the pros and cons of a commitment ceremony or handfasting. You are physically reliving the spiritual events in your life.

After having cleared an area of your covenstead on Imbolc morning, plan some activities your family coven can do together.

Traditional Imbolc activities include making candles, spiritual cleansings, and setting wards on a home. The physical work should have already been accomplished in the weeks leading up to the Imbolc. Start the morning with a good breakfast to ground and center your family coven, then smudge sage or otherwise cleanse your house thoroughly. As you move through your home, collect and cleanse any old wards you may have set in the previous year. When the cleansing is complete, burn the old wards in your family cauldron or fire pit outdoors.

Now you can start creating the new wards for the family coven—mine prefers the matchbox wards, Bres' Crosses, and house traps. However, there are other wards. You could set out specific types of stones in the four quarters of your house for protection (hematite works especially well for this; last years' hematite should be destroyed by crushing and then thrown away. Smoky quartz also works well for grounding and cleansing a covenstead); invite specific magical creatures to guard the four quarters of your home (renew this with an offering of food or other appropriate items for the work they did in the past year and entreating them to continue their work in the coming year); buy Witches' balls and hang them strategically throughout the house (every year at Imbolc, wash and cleanse the balls to ensure their potency); use wind chimes strategically located to cleanse the energy flowing into the homes (wash and spiritually cleanse these chimes at Imbolc); if your family coven uses a grounding stone, Imbolc is the time to cleanse and recharge the stone for its purpose. Family covens are limited only by their own creativity when it comes to setting wards for a covenstead's spiritual protection.

After setting the wards, remake potions related to banishing and protection. My family coven is partial to banishing powder and the Four Thieves Vinegar. These are fun to make, and you should be sure to make enough for the entire year.

Then move on to candlemaking. The use of gel candle products can eliminate the need for the melting of wax, which can be messy. Make at least one candle to use during your Imbolc feast.

The making of grain dollies to lie with the family coven wand is another excellent idea, especially if you are dealing with children in their tweens or older. Again, this offers another opportunity to discuss sex as the sacred act that it is and move the issue of safer sex practices into a sacred space and time.

Before the Imbolc feast begins, have the children run through the house and turn on every light, inside and out. Then light the candle you made and use it as the centerpiece on the feasting table. Make your favorite dishes of grain and root vegetables—the foods most likely to have survived winter. My favorite dish uses pureed carrots to create a Sun.

During the meal, talk about the strengthening Sun and if your children are of age, how the corn dolly and her wand are used as sympathetic magic to create a bountiful spring. This talk should include discussions of safer sex practices and the idea that sex is a sacred magical rite in and of itself. Talk also about what it was like to be pregnant and the anticipation of the birth of your children. Discuss what the first few years of your marriage was filled with. Did you fight a lot or were these early years easy for you and your partner(s)? By discussing these very important issues, you are giving your child some valuable insight into their own future relationships, what is "normal" and what to look for.

After the feast, set the new wards before you turn in for bed and leave your one candle lit (in the family coven cauldron or kitchen sink) all night to symbolize the returning Sun.

Banishing Powder

I was first introduced to banishing powder by Judika Illes in *The Element Encyclopedia of 5000 Spells*. Banishing powders can be used by family covens to help protect their homes from neighborhood mischievousness and to keep bullies away (put a pinch of banishing powder in a pouch and have your child carry it in his/her pocket). These powders last a long time and are very strong, so only small amounts are needed to work effectively. I once had problems living in an apartment complex with some naughty children who were harassing my family and my son. After the children began to throw rocks at our door, I put banishing powder around our door. As I laid the powder, I chanted that anything that might harm my family could not cross the barrier and would be repelled from this place. Within a week, our upstairs neighbors, who only moved in a few weeks before, suddenly moved out. I secretly worried that I had caused their sudden move, when my fears were confirmed. One night officers came looking for some fugitives who had fled—the ones who used to live upstairs above my family. Within three months of casting this spell, all the families who were causing us problems were moving.

To make banishing powders, you will need a glass container with a good lid (ideally a colored container so light doesn't affect the potion). Use warding herbs, such as sulfur, black pepper, cumin, pepper powder of any kind, salt, graveyard dirt, and anything else that carries the energy of banishing. Mix well and store in a cool dry place.

Four Thieves Vinegar

Another family coven must-have, courtesy of Judika Illes, is Four Thieves Vinegar. This vinegar can be added to mop water in small amounts to help cleanse and banish on a regular basis. Further, it is a good anointing oil for those who are ill. Take apple cider or red wine vinegar. You may need to pour some of it out in order to make room for the other herbs you are going to put into it. Pour the excess vinegar into a spray bottle for general organic cleaning—just a little will do. Add garlic that has been peeled and sliced the long way—slicing with the grain releases more the garlic's aromatic and healing properties. Choose four ingredients that represent healing and cleansing properties you want to induce. I use a whole red habanera pepper in the jar, ground lavender, several rosemary twigs, and some crushed wormwood. Illes suggests you let the concoction sit for four days before use, shaking once daily. I have found the potency of this cleansing agent grows with time and that the herbs and garlic can rise to stop up the neck of the bottle. Shake vigorously before use.

An Imbolc Elemental Ritual

Michelle Skye

IMBOLC IS A BEGINNING—a wondrous, beauteous, life-affirming beginning. And beginnings herald new thoughts, new ideas, and new situations. They remind us that life is about moving forward, up out of the ashes of the past, into the endlessly shifting possibility of the future. The beginning is wonderful and should be celebrated with verve and gusto, for you never know where it will lead; you never know what paths will open before you. The following ritual serves to remind us, through celebration, of that sublime truth.

Items Needed

4 small, many-tined sticks

A cauldron of any size

Lighter or matches

Newspaper or shredded paper

4 ribbons, 3 inches long—one each of indigo (West), crimson (South), gray or pink (East), and black (North) to represent the elements

Your favorite incense

Your favorite beverage

A libation bowl

CD player or MP3 player and the song "Alive" by Omnia
Percussion instruments, such as drums, tambourines, rattles, etc.
(optional)

Prepare your ritual space as you normally do, by cleansing and clearing it of any negativity using sage, sweet grass, Florida water, or your own favorite cleansing incense or spray. I personally think this ritual celebration is best done at night; however, feel free to conduct it whenever appropriate for you. If done during the day, consider closing the curtains and drapes to create an intimate, womblike environment. Gather all of your items and, in the partial darkness, tie one ribbon on each stick. These will represent the elements of our Earth and of ourselves, so place them in the appropriate positions around your sacred space—grey or pink in the East, crimson in the South, indigo in the West, and black in the North.

Return to the center of your space and light your incense. Take a few moments to relax, ground and center, and find your inner peace. When you feel ready, begin welcoming the elements to your celebration, starting in the East and continuing in a clockwise motion to South, West, and North. At each direction, pick up the stick with the ribbon and use it to gather the energy of that element. Do not put the stick down—carry it with you to the next direction so by the time you are welcoming North, you will be holding four sticks in your hands. At each direction, say the following:

East/Air

Feather of bird and breath of voice,
Airy thread that binds all together,
East of Air and Air of East,
By the power of the frightful storm, I call thee to me.

South/Fire

Flicker of flame and pulse of heart
Fiery thread that binds all together,
South of Fire and Fire of South,
By the power of the brilliant burn, I call thee to me.

West/Water

Surge of wave and tear of eye
Watery thread that binds all together,
West of Water and Water of West,
By the power of the midnight sea, I call thee to me.

North/Earth

Black of cave and blood of bones
Earthy thread that binds all together
North of Earth and Earth of North,
By the power of the darkened deep, I call thee to me.

Return to the center of your sacred space and begin to prepare the ritual cleansing fire by placing a fairly large portion of paper into the cauldron. Make sure your incense is still smoking and, beginning with the East/Air stick (and continuing through South, West, and North), break the sticks apart and place them in the cauldron. The cauldron represents your connection to the divine as well as your own intuition, sense of self, and internal power. This is your deep Goddess (or God)-self that is often trampled down by the limitations and expectations of society and culture. The cauldron is the true you, pure and untainted by others.

Be sure to not overstuff the cauldron with the sticks as the fire will need space to breathe and grow. (An exacting metaphor for all of us, to be sure!) You may need to make a small pile of sticks to add to the fire as the flames die down. As you break up each stick, think about your relationship to each element and the skills and attributes it possesses. With these in mind, vow to release anything connected to the element that is not working for you in your life. Perhaps you want to get rid of your stifled voice (Air) or you less-than-passionate approach to sex (Fire). Perhaps you have the opposite problem and you want to channel your sexual appetite into a more serious relationship. Or maybe you want to release emotional blockage and conditioning (Water). Really take your time with each stick, concentrating as you break them up into small pieces. Place the ribbons off to the side and save them until the end of the ritual.

Now burn the sticks. Take your lighter and ignite the paper, making sure the lighter, thinner twigs are added to the fire first, followed by the slightly heavier and thicker sticks. You may need to add more paper throughout the burn so be prepared with extra. As the sticks burn, concentrate on the aspects of your life that you want to change. Know that, as they burn, the smoke and ash of the elemental sticks are rising up to the sacred divine and the universe is listening to your plea. You are being heard.

Once the sticks and paper have all burned to ashes, it is time to celebrate the beginning of the fertile season, the exciting prospects that await you just around the bend. You have removed aspects of your life that no longer serve you, in order to make room for the possibilities of the future. It is so exciting! No longer are you stagnant and still, but growing and surging with energy and the promise of tomorrow. It is time to celebrate! Chant:

> *The deadfall of winter has burned.*
> *Imbolc is here once again*
> *Round and round the wheel turns*
> *Enemy is a sacred friend.*
>
> *A sacred friend for all to see*
> *Reminder of a powerful me*
> *The future awaits, clear and bright*
> *Beginning this eve, this blessed night.*
>
> *Happy Imbolc! Happy Imbolc! Happy Imbolc!*

If the celebration is done in a group, all should hug and kiss each other as they wish each other a happy Imbolc. Music or percussive instruments can be added to the above chant and it can be sung/chanted as many times as you feel is necessary, deciding on a sacred number that resonates with you.

Now it's time to celebrate! Moving from the power built during the chanting, put on the "Alive" song and begin to sway, drum, dance, skip, and cavort to the music. Enjoy the rhythms of the song. Listen to its powerful message. It is a reminder of how wonderful it is to be alive, right here, right now, on this Earth. The song allows us to recall how we should relish each and every minute of this life path. Don't settle, the song tells us, for we are a part of this Earth and can make our own magic.

After you've played the song once (or twice or three times or twenty!), collapse on the floor in a sprawling heap. Pour your favorite drink into a glass and then into the libation bowl, offering it to the spirit of Imbolc, your favorite goddess and god, your ancestors, spirit guides, faery friends, and animal helpers. Say whatever comes to mind as you offer your libation gift. This should be a personal, intimate message to your individual spiritual guides. In a group setting, this can be done aloud, with everyone taking turns. Then, put some more drink in your glass and take a big gulp. (You'll probably need it after all that dancing and chanting!) Relax in the space you have created for yourself, both externally and internally. If you are performing this ritual with a group, feel free to chat naturally among yourselves.

When you are ready, gather yourself and say farewell to each of the elements, starting in the North and continuing in a counterclockwise circle to West, South, and East. Hold all four ribbons in your hand as you bid farewell to each element, saying:

North/Earth
Black of cave and blood of bones
Earthy thread that binds all together
North of Earth and Earth of North,
By the power of the budding leaf,
I honor thee and bid thee farewell.

West/Water

Surge of wave and tear of eye
Watery thread that binds all together,
West of Water and Water of West,
By the power of the streaming river,
I honor thee and bid thee farewell.

South/Fire

Flicker of flame and pulse of heart
Fiery thread that binds all together,
South of Fire and Fire of South,
By the power of the warming hearth,
I honor thee and bid thee farewell.

East/Air

Feather of bird and breath of voice,
Airy thread that binds all together,
East of Air and Air of East,
By the power of the stirring breeze,
I honor thee and bid thee farewell.

Take the libation bowl, the cauldron, and the ribbons outside. In a sacred manner, in a place that feels right to you, offer the contents of the libation bowl and the cauldron to the elements of the Earth, pouring them onto the soil. Untie the knots on the ribbons (signifying your release of the elemental issues holding you back from your growth) and place them under a rock, log, garden gnome, or any other bit of paraphernalia that has accumulated nearby. Do not tie the ribbons onto anything as you want to continue to release your issues and dead weight throughout the season of Imbolc. Your ritual is complete. You have taken the first step in this year's sacred turn of the wheel! Huzzah! Blessed be!

Notes

Ostara

Spring Equinox

Deborah Blake

OSTARA, ALSO KNOWN AS the Spring Equinox, is the Pagan holiday that falls on or around March 21 in the Northern Hemisphere. (The date can vary from March 20 to the 23). Pronounced *Oh-STAR-ah*, this sabbat gets its name from Eostre, the Saxon goddess of spring (as does the Christian holiday of Easter). But don't be misled by the Anglo-Saxon name; Pagans from Egypt to Greece (and far beyond) have been celebrating this holiday in some form for thousands of years, and our modern version of Ostara often draws on elements from many different cultures and traditions.

For instance, while some call on the Goddess Eostre, others are more drawn to her Greek counterpart, who was called Eos or Aurora. These ladies are not only goddesses of the spring, but of the dawn, as well. Other Greek goddesses associated with the Spring Equinox are Demeter and Persephone, the mother and daughter featured in a well-known tale that explains why we have winter.

In Celtic lands, Ostara was referred to as Lady Day, and it celebrated the return of the Goddess after her winter hibernation. In fact, many of the early myths reflected the feeling of abandonment that people felt during the dark, cold months of winter, and their joy at the return of the light and warmth, which they associated with their gods.

Speaking as someone who lives in the snowy Northeast, I can certainly sympathize!

In modern Pagan mythology, in what we often call the wheel of the year, Ostara marks the transformation of the Goddess from Crone back into her Maiden form, and the God—reborn at Yule—is now a virile young man. They begin their courtship, which will culminate in their marriage at Beltane. (Well, or just plain culminate, depending on how you look at the mythology. Beltane is another fertility festival, after all.) Their youthful energy is part of what we are tapping into when we celebrate this holiday.

Ostara is one of only two days in the year when the day and the night are equal (the other being Mabon). At Spring Equinox, the dark and the light are in perfect balance, with exactly twelve hours of each. From then on, the light grows ever stronger, increasing every day until it reaches its peak at the Summer Solstice, the longest day of the year.

Because of this unusual state of symmetry, balance is one of the magickal themes for this sabbat. Not just between darkness and light, but balance between male energy and female energy, and the physical world and the spiritual world. Ostara is also a fire festival, in honor of the return of the Sun, and a fertility festival that celebrates growth, rebirth and new beginnings. These aspects of the holiday make it one of my favorites. To me, Ostara is all about potential: the potential for balance, within and without, and the potential for growth, renewal, and the possibility of a new start.

For what is being a Witch about, if not these things?

If Samhain is the sabbat that allows Pagans to acknowledge the darker side of life, then Ostara is one in which we embrace the light, opening ourselves to the energy of a reawakening Earth.

This is also the time to plant the seeds for the magickal and spiritual work we will do in the year ahead. If you made magickal plans or goals at Imbolc, now is the time to start implementing them, a little at a time.

At Ostara, we throw off the lethargy and quiet of winter and move forward into the blooming of spring—hoping that we too will blossom and grow.

How we go about doing this can vary from Witch to Witch, but most of us use at least some of the following tools that are often associated with this sabbat:

Colors: All pastels are suitable, especially yellow, pink, pale green, and robin's egg blue, but also lavender and white.

Stones: Again, the pastel colors predominate, including rose quartz, moonstone, aquamarine, amazonite, lavender amethyst, aventurine, citrine, and clear quartz. I especially like to use the stones that have a mixture of soft purple, green, and clear, like tourmaline and fluorite.

Herbs/flowers: All early spring flowers are suitable, especially daffodils, snowdrops, crocuses, jonquils, violets, and forsythia. My favorite for this holiday is the simple daisy, whose name comes from "day's eye" to show its association with the Sun. Like the egg (which we'll talk about later), the daisy combines the yellow of the God's Sun with the white of the Goddess' Moon, in perfect balance and harmony. What better flower to use for this particular sabbat?

Incense: Any light and floral scent will work, as will any citrus, such as lemon, orange, or lemongrass. This is not the time for heavy incense like sandalwood or musk; I prefer to use an incense that is delicate and subtle, like lilac or lemon balm.

Animals: Everyone is familiar with the animals associated with this sabbat . . . even if most of us were first exposed to them is conjunction with Easter! Chicks, lambs, and rabbits are probably the best known: the first two to represent new life, and the rabbit symbolizes fertility. For a more Pagan twist, you can use the snake, which sheds its skin in a form of rebirth, and therefore symbolizes healing and renewal.

Whatever symbols or tools you use, this sabbat is the perfect time to work on bringing balance and clarity into your life, and planting the seeds for new beginnings in the year ahead.

Neopagan Traditions

There are no right or wrong ways to observe Ostara, or any other sabbat for that matter. Some Pagans have in-depth rituals for all eight, while others have one or two that they consider to be more important (Beltane and Samhain, perhaps) and don't really pay much attention to the rest. To some extent this may depend on how "formal" your practice is; there are Witches who follow an organized path including New Moons, Full Moons, and all the sabbats, while others rarely do anything more ceremonial than a walk in the woods.

How ornate and complicated a ritual you do may also be determined by whether you practice alone, as a solitary, or in a group with other Witches. I lead a group called Blue Moon Circle, made up of about ten eclectic Pagan women. Because we gather for the holiday, we tend to do a formal, written ritual and invite family and a few selected guests. Therefore, the ceremony I write is considerably more involved than one I might do if I were by myself.

But whether you are a solitary or a group Witch, the basic focus of how you celebrate the sabbat is up to you. Even if you are in a coven or circle, you may want to take the time to do some work on your own before gathering for a group ritual. For me, Ostara is the perfect time to do just that.

I tend to have two major goals or points of focus at this time of the year, and these are reflected in how I observe the holiday. My first focus is on celebrating the end of winter. This can be a bit tricky where I live in upstate New York, since winter can still be making its presence felt with a vengeance in mid-March. We have been known to hold our Spring Equinox ritual with more than a foot of snow sitting right outside the window. (My advice in this situation? Just close the curtains and pretend it's spring!)

But even when it still looks and feels like winter, Ostara is the signal to me that the end is near and spring is on its way. This means that it is time to clear away the debris and stagnant energy left over from the cold, dark months, and prepare myself mentally, physically, and spiritually for a fresh start in the spring.

This leads to my second focus, which is figuring out my magickal goals for the year and planting the seeds for positive growth and change during the warmer, lighter months ahead. I used to just work on the last part of this equation, but I found over the years that if I made the effort to clear away the old crap before starting on my new goals, I made much better progress in the end.

While my exact rituals and magickal workings vary somewhat from year to year, the basic approach has settled into a fairly dependable pattern. Generally, I do some serious cleansing work on my own, followed by a ritual shared with Blue Moon Circle that integrates aspects of both clearing away the old and inviting in the new.

Spiritual Spring Cleaning

Even if you are lucky enough to live in a temperate climate, without the snow, ice, and the chronic lack of light that us north dwellers get to deal with, you will probably notice that the energy of winter is different than that of the other seasons—quieter and more sedate.

This is not necessarily a bad thing.

Our bodies need to have a slower period; a time when we can focus inward instead of outward, ease our frantic pace, and rest a bit. Unfortunately, in the artificial world most of us live in, we tend to be out of touch with the normal cycles of nature and to force ourselves to keep up the same frenetic rush year-round. Between that and the lack of fresh food and fresh air during winter, many of us build up toxins in our bodies, and often, in our spirits as well.

Spiritual spring cleaning is the name I use for the act of clearing away all that winter nastiness and leaving body, mind, and spirit ready for the new season. There are a few ways to achieve this, and you can do one or all of them, depending on your needs.

Clean your house—I know, you're saying, "What's so spiritual about that?" Well, the first step to clearing away mental and spiritual clutter is to remove the physical manifestations of that clutter. Put on some music that inspires you (even if you normally clean to rock and roll, you might want to try chants or drumming for this) and clean your house from top to bottom. Don't forget to throw out stuff you no longer need (or donate it for extra karma points). If you want a magickal touch in your mundane housecleaning, try adding a few drops of a magickal oil to your mop water, or spray some on your broom before you sweep. I like to make up a cleansing and protection oil from rosemary, lemon, and geranium essential oils. And be sure to visualize a pure, cleansing light filling up each space as you clean.

Clear away negative energy—Now that your house is physically clean, you can clear away any remaining negative energy. I like to do this once a year, preferably right before Ostara. You will need a few basic Witchy tools: a sage smudge stick, salt, water, and of course, your own will and intent. If it is warm enough, open all your windows. If not, try just opening one at the top of the house or apartment. Starting at the bottom (or farthest from the front door, if you live on one level), walk through each room with your lit smudge stick and a container that holds the water and salt mixed together. Waft the smoke from the sage along each wall, paying special attention to any places where energy can come in, such as doors, windows, and even chimneys. Sprinkle the salt and water as you go. (If you find this too difficult, you can do one at a time, or just use the sage by itself.) Visualize the smoke, salt, and water clearing away any negative or stagnant energy, leaving your home safe, healthy, and protected. When you reach the last room, send any remaining negative energy out the open window and then shut the window. Visualize your entire living space filling with light and positive energy.

Cleanse your body—You've cleaned and cleared your home; now it's time to do the same for yourself. I like to do this step before performing the Ostara ritual so that I go into it as pure and open as possible, but any time will do. Again, the main difference between this kind of cleaning and what you would normally do is your will and your intent. Try to focus on your desire to rid yourself of anything physical or energetic that no longer works for you. If possible, it is best to do this in a bathtub, but a shower would suffice. Make or buy a magickal cleansing oil. (The easiest way to do this is to find a body oil you like and add a few drops of any pure essential oil that has a magickal quality of protection or cleaning. You can also just take olive or sesame oil and add essential oils, lemon juice, salt, or even honey, if you're okay with a bit of a mess.) If you have a bathtub, throw in some herbs. Set the room up as sacred space in whichever way you prefer: cast a circle, call the quarters, and set candles up if it is safe to do so. Then bathe yourself thoroughly, visualizing all the toxins and negativity leaving your body. When you are done, anoint yourself with your magickal oil, and see yourself as reborn—a clean slate, ready to embrace the potential and abundant energy of spring.

Planting the Seeds for Growth and Change

Once you have cleared away the old stuff, you have room for the new. What do you want to bring into your life? What elements are needed to balance what is already there? (You remember that we're working on balance, right?) What part of your life do you want to grow and blossom?

The answers to these questions are numerous and will vary widely from Witch to Witch. Some people want to work on bringing in more prosperity; others seek love, peace, or healing. You can work on whichever goal you choose. My only suggestion is to be as specific as possible: do you want prosperity in general, or do you want a great new job? Try to focus on the essence of what you really want to attain, not just the abstract concept.

I like to sit down and make a list of my goals for the coming season. Then I figure out which ones I can achieve by purely mundane means and which goals need a little magickal help to bring into being. This is the point at which I finally start writing the ritual for Ostara.

We can (and do) work on our magickal goals all year. But the Spring Equinox gives us a special opportunity to tap into the energy of the Earth as it awakens from its winter sleep, and stretches out in hope and renewal. Ostara marks not only the beginning of spring, but the beginning of the astrological year as well, making it the perfect time to do magickal work for new beginnings, fertility, prosperity, creativity, and anything else that requires a connection to the light and warmth of this particular season.

So take some time out to cleanse and reenergize yourself, and make your list of magickal goals for the coming year. Then wake up early on the morning of Ostara and light a bonfire at sunrise. (A candle will do, if you can't have a fire.) Greet the spring with joy and enthusiasm, and do your best to tap into the potential of the new season that lies ahead.

Celestial Sway

Fern Feto Spring

THE SPRING EQUINOX CELEBRATES new life as the Sun moves into 0 degrees of Aries on March 20. Aries is the sign that initiates the story of the zodiac, and it aptly symbolizes this time of first steps, growth, and fertility. At Eostre we honor the fragility and the courage of life, symbolized by how the thin shell of an egg can contain and protect new beginnings. This is the season of the hero or heroine, as we once again plot out our own hero's journey through the wheel of the year.

The equinox is also considered the official start of spring, when flowers begin to blossom, and color returns to the earth. Though this can get off to a slow start in the eastern climates, there is often some sign now of winter's thaw and the hope of warmth to come.

The planetary landscape of Spring Equinox 2010 is strongly shaped by the planet Saturn, which is now in the early degrees of Libra. The normal Aries feistiness, and "me first" going "head first" approach is tempered by Saturn's more careful approach. Saturn forms an almost exact opposition aspect to the Sun in Libra, emphasizing the need to take others into account as we head off in search of new adventures, plans, and activities. Pluto in Capricorn continues to square these critical early degrees of the Cardinal signs

(Aries, Cancer, Libra, and Capricorn), adding a certain heavy or intense tone to this usually exuberant time.

Aries can have a tendency to act first and think later, but with these planetary influences, it would be wise to draw on the lessons of the Strength card in tarot, and work with gently guiding our instinctive animal self, rather than letting it have free rein. It is important now to learn how to integrate a note of self-discipline and patience with our need to take risks and explore.

Mercury in Aries is in a loose conjunction to the Sun, and also part of the Saturn opposition and Pluto square. This mercurial influence adds to the need for a more careful approach in our dealings with others, particularly in our communications. We may have a tendency now to speak in the heat of the moment, and later come to regret it. The more we can try to integrate truthfulness and heartfelt communication with a diplomatic tone, the greater benefits we will receive from important dialogues now.

Venus is also in Aries during the equinox season, though it does not make an aspect to the Sun or Mercury. The planet of love and relationships is in a challenging place in the feisty sign of Aries. There may seem to be more conflict than relating happening at this time, with our need to express who we are outweighing a gentle or thoughtful approach in dealing with others. If you have waited until now to truly let a partner know what you want or who you really are, give them some time to get used to your new self before holding them accountable for any wrongs you think they may have committed.

Spring Equinox Comic Book Ritual

Plot out your own hero's journey with a graphic story, or a comic book. On or near the Spring Equinox, gather art supplies and your ideas for the story of your inner hero or heroine as you travel through the rest of the year. Light a yellow candle in honor of the first day of spring, and put a bouquet of spring flowers on your altar. What new steps or new beginnings are you initiating now?

Tell the story you would like to see unfold using words and images. You can cut pictures from magazines and write captions beneath, or draw your own images. Imagine that you are the superhero of this story. What great feat are you trying to accomplish? What are your challenges? What villains might you encounter? What are your superhero skills? Let the story unfold naturally, without a need to come to an ending right away. You may find that you work a little on this story every month, or even finish it near the end of the year. Let this time focus on making a strong beginning to the story, as you take the Fool's Leap into a new time.

Full Moon in Libra

The Full Moon in Libra on March 29 amplifies the opposition between Aries, representing the self, and Libra symbolizing the other or relationships. This Moon asks us to look into the mirror of those we encounter to see the qualities in ourselves that we may find challenging or attractive. How are those in your life reflecting back to you the parts of yourself that you might need to learn more about now? Pluto continues to be in a square relationship with the Sun and now the Moon as well, bringing a depth and intensity to our self-understanding and our relationships with others.

Look to where the Full Moon falls in the houses of your chart for a more specific interpretation of how this lunar event will affect your life. Notice which house cusp Libra rules, and also which one Aries rules for an understanding of the house pairs to be activated.

Full Moon in Libra Through the Houses

1st and 7th: Self-identity/The Other and partnerships

2nd and 8th: Personal skills and resources/Shared energies and resources

3rd and 9th: Communication and the immediate environment/Meaning and expansion of consciousness

4th and 10th: Home, family and deep self/Public persona, career, and destiny

5th and 11th: Self-expression, creativity, and spontaneity/Community, humanity, and the future

6th and 12th: Service to others and in the world/Service to spirit and retreat

Saturn Retrograde into Virgo

Saturn makes a final retrograde back into the last degrees of Virgo a few weeks after the Spring Equinox. This gives us a final opportunity to address issues related to health and wellness, day-to-day work, and the service we perform in the world. Any lessons we have learned during the last 2½ years as Saturn moved through Virgo may be particularly relevant during the next four months. Saturn only visits a sign once every twenty-eight years, so we will not have the opportunity to work on Virgo issues in this way for quite awhile. If there are routines or habits that you have been working on changing, now is the time to make that final effort.

Saturn in Virgo Ritual

Find some symbolic or real items that represent personal habits or patterns you want to change in order to encourage a more healthy and human version of you in the world. Arrange these items on an altar and surround them with herbs and flowers that you have gathered. You may want to include rosemary for remembrance and lavender to help encourage a stress-free and relaxed mind. Put a mirror on your altar and light a white candle. As the candle burns, gaze at yourself in the mirror and feel or imagine that you have the self-love necessary to address the habits that you want to change. Gaze as long as you can, or as you need, repeating aloud or silently any positive words that arise, encouraging you in your new self-care routines.

The Old Ways

Dan Furst

As THE WHEEL OF the year turns past Imbolc and into mid-February, the festival calendar has time to laugh along for a few more weeks. This is why the Pisces month, especially early and mid-March, abounds with colorful festivals like the joyous Jewish feast of Purim, that elicits in raucous folk comedies the cleverness of Queen Esther in saving her people from persecution by the wicked Babylonian police chief. There's much to celebrate, and people do tend to get their fill of wine and hilarity now—at the famous Carnevale festival, too—because soon enough it will be time to get to work again under the plowing and planting Moons of Aries month, after the sabbat of Ostara at the Spring Equinox.

This is one sabbat that tends to "play against type." As the aggressive heat and drive of the Aries month break through what's left of winter—warrior metaphors are unavoidable in this month when, as the Bible puts it, kings go forth to war—the point of the ritual calendar is to make sure that the fields and flocks are tended. This is why the beautiful male divinities honored now are lovers, not fighters, who give their lives to the grain and their blood to the new wine just as they give their seed to the Goddess, so that she blooms in spring as he attains a miracle of rebirth—leafing back into life so that both lovers can bring again the green surge of spring at Beltane.

The month of Aries, ruled by Mars, has few festivals in his honor. Instead, many of the rites held now celebrate the feminine deities whose care and devotion hold the community together and affirm the magical core premise of our relation to the Earth year: the more we act in love and service to one another, the more fruitful our fields will be. This is why we hold Maiden Goddess festivals like the Roman Fornicalia, honoring the patroness of ovens, whose mysterious art turns grain dough into bread. And we also invoke the Lady of Love as Astarte, Aphrodite, Venus, and many others. Her festival of peace, which the Romans called the Veneralia, came as an esbat after Ostara and a Moon before Beltane. The rites of Venus the Lover, coming as they do weeks before the Venus-ruled month of Taurus, affirm each year that she is triumphant even in the month of Mars, and reminds us that *Amor Vincit Omnia*, "Love conquers all." The Love Goddess also promises that no matter what sorrow may fall along with the spring rains, Earth's vitality will prevail. This is why the festivals of the Spring Equinox have always included games of hunting for eggs, pine cones, rabbits, and other emblems of new birth.

Ostara or Eostre is better known to most people today as Easter, which is always celebrated in Aries month on the Sunday after the Full Moon following the Spring Equinox. The rites were not hard to devise, as peoples all over the Roman world held similar ceremonies in which the young god is violently slain—Adonis and Tammuz by a boar, Attis by castration, Osiris by dismemberment—so that he gives his blood to promote the growth of the new wine and fecundates the Earth with the vegetation that will flourish in spring. The rites normally begin with the ceremonial sharing of the old year's wine, the death and mourning of the god, and his resurrection after three days.

The Pagan ritual that is closest in form to what would become Easter was the spring festival of Cybele and Attis, from Phrygia, in the south of what is now Turkey. The rites began on March 22, when young devotees of Attis cut a young pine tree and fastened to it the god's image, which was covered in violets to symbolize his blood. The next day, to the sounds of solemn music, the faithful would bear Attis' effigy to the sacrificial ground and raise it to stand upward—yet again, the dying god hangs on a tree—for rites of mourning that would be enacted the next day. On March 25—the third day after his entombment—the god returned to life, and his revival was marked by scenes of music and revelry at which other sensual events were known to occur. Now that the miracle of resurrection had been accomplished, the god would wax in power toward the harvest, two sabbats from now.

The ancient world abounded with such festivals, and some still survive. Among the Yoruba and Santeria peoples of Africa and the Americas, March 25 is the feast of the Orisha Oshun, the male principle of sexual vitality and fertility. Many other male love gods and principles appear now at Ostara time. But long before early societies got more patriarchal in the Middle East, eastern Europe, and lower Africa, and began to sing the tale of spring in the death and rising of the male green god, the Spring Equinox was actually a Goddess festival, as unimaginable as that may seem in the "developed" Western world today.

The ancient Celtic and other western and central European peoples called this sabbat Alban Eilir or Ostara from Eostre, a mysterious figure who is mentioned in Old English literature only once, by the Venerable Bede. He wrote in the early eighth century about a goddess of dawn worshipped by the Angle and Saxon Pagans, especially in late March. Her coming again, and her warming of the year after the Great Cold, heralded the return of life in the green season.

However, as Eostre does not appear in other Norse or Teutonic myth, it is likely that she was in Britannia long before the Germans came, though whether or not she was honored at this time of year is unknown. The Celts did not have a multiplicity of goddess figures, as they saw the Triple Goddess behind all the operations of nature. So Eostre may not have been a dawn goddess, but could instead mean "easting," as in the rising and beginning of new life in the symbol of sunrise. In these terms, Eostre's feast of Ostara was not a feast of mourning the dying god, then rejoicing when he rises again. Rather, Ostara was a feast of conception as the Goddess begins to turn in her cycle again from Maiden to Mother.

To the Celts in Ireland, Ostara was the moment when the Earth Goddess Bridhe (Brigid), who had married the sky god at Imbolc, conceives the Sun Child who will be born nine months from now at the Winter Solstice. This is why, in so many mythic streams and religions, so many divine conceptions come now. In the Roman Catholic feast day cycle, St. Gabriel's Day on March 24, and the next day, when he delivered the Annunciation to Mary, are relics of earlier pre-Christian rites sacred to the divine female who will give birth to the New Sun when winter comes again. This is why the Spring Equinox sabbat has been called Lady Day, and still is, in many traditions of Earth-based spirituality, for it honors and beseeches the love and nurturing of the one who will be the Divine Mother of God.

The fertility of the Goddess, and her power to renew the Earth, appear in other Ostara customs besides hunting for baby rabbits and brightly colored eggs. The hot cross buns that have traditionally been baked and eaten in this season have been said to represent everything from an amulet of dough for protection against illness to the cross of Jesus to—more plausibly—the four quarters of the year, and the intersection of female and male in the act of conception. But look through a book of signs and symbols sometime, or some other bag of ancient designs, and you'll see that the universal symbol of the Earth is a circle divided in quarters by a cross. The world is a hot cross bun, and at Ostara we celebrate her bounty yet again.

Feasts and Treats

Kristin Madden

SPRING HAS OFFICIALLY ARRIVED and foods of this sabbat center on the fresh and the new. We luxuriate in the blessings of fresh eggs, spring greens, and beautiful colors. But let us not forget the wonderfully balanced energies of the equinox. Dark and light in delectable balance may also be found on holiday tables, bringing joy and perhaps helping us bring some of that celestial balance within.

Eostre Frittata

Omelets and frittatas developed from ancient dishes that were not only relatively simple to create but also combined eggs, meats, fruits, and vegetables in a never-ending feast of creativity. Perfect for your Ostara breakfast, this one brings through the colors and balance of the season, all in one egg-filled package.

Prep Time: 5 minutes
Cook Time: 20 minutes
Serves: 4–6

¼ small onion, chopped
2 tablespoons olive oil
2 cloves garlic, chopped

½ red bell pepper, chopped
½ green bell pepper, chopped
1 can black beans, drained
6 eggs
⅓ cup water

In a large frying pan, cook the onion in oil over medium heat until transparent. Add garlic, peppers, and beans and cook for 5 minutes. In a medium bowl, beat the eggs and water until mixed well. Pour egg mixture over vegetables in frying pan. Cover and cook for approximately 10 minutes, until eggs are nearly set. Broil about 5 inches from heating element for 2 minutes.

Blackberry Scones

In the deep darkness of blackberries nestled within a rich oat scone, you can find a luscious balance that truly celebrates Ostara. Even though blackberries are not in season in March, this is still a lovely snack or dessert to share with warm tea or mulled wine at an equinox gathering.

Prep Time: 25 minutes
Cook Time: 35 minutes
Serves: 8

1 egg
1 teaspoon vanilla extract
⅔ cup yogurt
2 cups all-purpose flour
1 cup oat flour
4 teaspoons baking powder
½ teaspoon baking soda
½ cup butter, cold
½ cup baker's sugar
½ cup buttermilk
1 cup blackberries, cut in half

Preheat oven to 375 degrees F. Beat together the egg, vanilla, and yogurt. In a separate bowl, mix together the flours, baking powder, and baking soda. Cut in butter to the flour mixture. Add sugar and buttermilk, then mix well. Gently fold berries into the mixture. Spoon out rounds of ice cream scoop–sized batter onto buttered cookie tins. Bake for 35 minutes or until tops are golden brown.

Blueberry Peach Crisp

This mouth-watering dish not only delights the senses with sweet tartness, but the dark berries and light peaches are reminiscent of the equinox. Even better, this dessert is high in antioxidants and vitamin C. What a lovely offering to share at your Ostara celebrations . . . or to indulge in all on your own!

Prep Time: 20 minutes
Cook Time: 40 minutes
Serves: 6–8

4 cups fresh peaches
1 teaspoon cinnamon
3 tablespoons oat flour
1 cup blueberries
1 cup all-purpose flour
½ cup oats
½ cup brown sugar
¼ cup butter, cold
½ teaspoon nutmeg
¼ teaspoon allspice

Preheat oven to 375 degrees F. Peel and pit the peaches (or use canned peaches). In a large bowl, mix the cinnamon and oat flour with the peaches and blueberries. Pour into the baking dish.

In a medium bowl, mix the all-purpose flour, oats, and brown sugar. Cut in the butter. Spread this flour and oat mixture over peaches and berries. Sprinkle with nutmeg and allspice. Bake for 40 minutes in a greased baking dish.

Ostara Coffee

The addition of real vanilla and sweet crème fraîche turns everyday coffee into a blessed event. This beautiful blending of dark and light, sweet and tart is the perfect finish to an Ostara feast. Pair it with Blueberry Peach Crisp or Blackberry Scones to delight your senses and enchant your guests.

Prep Time: 13 hours plus 25 minutes (just before serving)
Cook Time: 10 minutes
Serves: 8

1 cup heavy cream, not ultrapasteurized
1 tablespoon buttermilk
1 vanilla bean
1 cup rich roast coffee beans
1 tablespoon confectioner's sugar

Combine the cream and buttermilk in a glass jar. Seal the lid tightly and keep it in a warm spot for 13 hours. This is your crème fraîche. Grind the vanilla and coffee beans together. Brew as you normally would in your coffee maker. Pour crème fraîche into a medium bowl and whisk in the sugar before serving. Pour the freshly brewed coffee into mugs and top with a dollop of crème fraîche.

Crafty Crafts

Silver RavenWolf

Deva of the Season: Motivation
Scents/Aromas: Lemon, Lime, Orange, Pine
Energy: Cleansing
Visualization: In the center of a blank, white piece of paper, visualize the item or circumstance you desire. Practice this visualization every day for twenty-one days, beginning on the eve of Spring Equinox. Envision yourself happily motivated and busy doing the things you love to do. Always end your visualization with a smile.

Affirmation: I am motivated and associate myself with motivated people, places, and ideas to improve my life.

❧

The spark of Spring Equinox! From planning the garden for the coming season to assessing your property and projects for the days and weeks ahead, there's so much to accomplish! One of the most difficult problems we all face at this time is the feeling of being stuck, especially when cloaked with the cold temperatures of a winter that just doesn't seem to want to break loose. We look at a problem or a situation and sometimes we only see the amount of effort required—not the hoped-for end result. This looming effort sometimes makes us feel lethargic and can feed emotions of hopelessness.

The universe knows that humans can get this way, so She provides us a very special Deva at this time of year—motivation.

The month of March is all about cleansing and preparation for new growth in our lives. Cleaning your house or apartment breaks up negative chi and allows for the attraction of fresh ideas and wealth, resulting in the overall harmony you desire. As you release old dishes, clothes, decorative items, jewelry, and furniture from your living area as you clean, you are making plenty of room for new and exciting energies to take root and grow. Time to look at cleaning and rearranging your environment in a new light—rather than drudgery, think of your entire living area as a ritual place of becoming! Close your eyes and think of how you would love this space to be, and then start making it that way! It doesn't take a lot of money to create a harmonious space that will draw abundance to you—just a little elbow grease! Remember, you can't welcome the generosity of the universe if your environment is stuffed full of old junk that you refuse to release. Gather up all that old, stuck energy and chuck it out in the trash.

The physical task of cleaning is also a mental task that can improve focus. For example, washing the windows can help you to see your world (or a particular issue) clearly. By physically wiping away the grime, you are mentally wiping away fears, unhappiness, and negative thoughts that can cloud your judgment. Removing junk and clutter helps you to mentally navigate freely through your life. It gives positive vibrations (thoughts, music, etc.) more power—leaving them less likely to be deflected or absorbed by negative influences. The naturally pleasant scents of lemon, lime, orange, and pine are not only uplifting aromas to the mind, they also magickally correspond to cleansing, good health, abundant wealth, and attracting positive vibrations. Washing floors, laundering curtains, and cleaning upholstery lifts and removes ground-in dirt that can actually hold negative memories that you associate with your limitations. By releasing this dirt with the powerful vehicle of water you are allowing the flow of abundance to enter your life.

With the Deva of Motivation, we learn to look at our lives differently. For example, don't view the entire house or apartment and say, "I'll never get this done," or "I don't have the money to fix this." Instead, start at the heart of the house, which is the room where you or the family spends the most time, and do what you can. Work outward from there in a circular, clockwise pattern. As you clean, reorder, and organize, the universe will provide the tools, people, and products necessary to do needed repairs. All you have to do is begin—the energy will flow from there. Don't allow yourself to think about how much work it is or how long it will take you to get your environment ready for the coming good fortune of the year. Instead, view the task of cleaning and refurbishing as one of the most amazing tools you possess in your manifestation arsenal.

Part of spring cleaning is the fun aspect of bringing in new, decorative items that match the season. Once you are finished cleaning, here is a great, inexpensive, hanging decoration to hold your colored Ostera eggs that can also be used as a magickal wind chime outdoors in the coming months. Burn a candle with a lemon, lime, orange, or pine scent while assembling and blessing this great project! Use the affirmation given (or one of your own choosing) as a mantra for empowerment.

Country Magick Egg Basket Wind Chime

Assemble your project on the eve of Spring Equinox. As you tie the torn strips of cotton to the basket, envision the positive energies you wish to bring into your life. When the project is finished, empower the basket to bring blessings into the home. In powwows, magick eggs represent birth energy and are used to draw people, items, and experiences to you. You can empower each egg for something different. The technique is very easy—as you put each egg in the basket, hold the egg in both hands, and whisper your intent three times across the surface, then blow on the egg three times. Draw an equal-armed cross over the egg, saying: "Always a blessing. It always works!" Place the egg in the basket, and move on to the next. If you prefer not to use eggs, you can fill your basket with seed packets for the plants you wish to grow this year in your garden. Empower the seed packets the same way you would empower the eggs. Finally, you could mix eggs, seed packets, and artificial flowers in a pleasing arrangement in the basket. I'm sure there's no end to your imagination!

Supplies

1 metal egg basket with handle
    (style and shape your choice)
8 torn cotton cloth strips
    (17 × 1 inch)
6 metal mini-bundt tins
1 small metal measuring cup
Colored, Ostara eggs

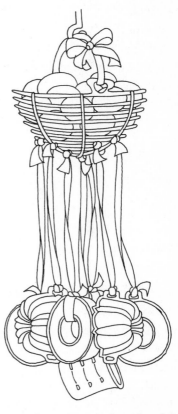

Note: Instead of the mini-bundt tins, you can also use just metal measuring cups, or punch holes in the handles of old silverware.

Instructions: Tie the torn cotton strips to the metal mesh of the egg basket around the bottom edges of the basket in equal distance to each other (as best you can for balance when the basket hangs) leaving about 14 inches hanging on each strip. Tie each of these loose ends to the 6 mini-metal bundt tins. Tie one strip to the center, underside of the basket, and the other end to the metal measuring cup. Use the last cloth strip as a decorative bow on the handle. Place the eggs in the basket and hang. Once the holiday is over, remove the eggs and fill the basket with decorative flowers. Hang outside during the spring and summer months. Write your wishes on small pieces of paper and clip them with clothespin to the wire mesh of the basket, asking the winds of change to manifest your desires. My basket hangs from the rafters of my back porch. I cleanse and re-empower the basket on each of the successive holidays (Beltane, Midsummer, Lammas, Samhain) until Samhain night, when I bring the basket in for the winter.

Cost of this project: About $17.00 with new items; around $7.00 if you purchase used items from flea markets and swap meets).

Time to complete: Approximately 10 minutes.

Fostering Family

Lydia M. Crabtree

IN THE LIFE CYCLE of children, Ostara represents the birth of a child and his or her growth into self-awareness—or, as most mother priestesses and father priests recognize it, the ability to scream, "No!" Children are the epitome of spring during this time frame, exploring and learning at an amazing pace just as the world around us is blooming and defrosting before our very eyes.

Now is a good time to reassess our goals as a family coven, which is precisely what decorating eggs is all about. As a family coven and as partner(s), we should decide what we want to harvest starting in Lughnasadh. Do our desires as individuals line up with the desires we have as a family coven? If not, how can we support the individual goals that coveners create?

You can also harness the power of spring by creating Gloom Bombs. These spells are taken out and utilized when gloom and darkness creeps into your family coven through bad attitudes or psychic attack and they give that extra burst of energy your family coven needs to get beyond the superficial issues that can sometimes trip us up.

Activities

Prepare for Planting

Partners can do this by making separate lists of goals for the coming year or two and then comparing them. Utilizing these separate lists, create one list that all partners can get behind. Then make Ostara eggs that symbolize these goals and plant them in your garden or in a wild wooded area, allowing them to symbolically fertilize the ground you are planting. When you are finished, in essence, the seeds you are going to plant are the ones listed, and there is an egg (fertilizer) for each seed. It isn't the seed, it is the fertilizer that prepares the soil for the seed.

This activity can be done with children as well. Decorating the eggs with the hopes and dreams they wish to harvest this year and in years to come and then burying them will help prepare the Earth for the things you will plant in the future.

Create Gloom Bombs

To create a Gloom Bomb, prick the bottom and top of an uncooked egg and blow out the yolk and egg white. (It is helpful to use a straight pin to scramble the contents before blowing the egg clean.) Save the contents in an air-tight container to refrigerate and use for cooking at the next meal.

Now rinse with cold water to remove any residual egg. Carefully create a hole in the top of the egg large enough to put things inside. Then allow the egg to dry completely.

After the egg dries, fill it with dried herbs and essential oils. Choose herbs for specific bombings against perceived psychic attack, general negativity, tantrums, family fighting, natural disaster, illness, injury, and any other negative force. After the egg has been filled, use any craft glue and some tissue paper (preferably in the appropriate color) to seal the top of the bomb. Now decorate the exterior of the egg carefully to ensure that you know which bomb is which. You can decorate with crayons, markers, stickers—anything to identify the bomb. During your Ostara ritual, charge your bombs. Store in a cool, dry place (like your herb closet) and wait for future use.

When you have a child whose fever won't break, get your Illness Gloom Bomb and throw it to the floor, breaking it in the room with the sick child. Let the herbs and eggshells stay in the area (usually twenty-four hours will do) and vacuum up after the fever has broken. To use for tantrums, have the screaming tot take the egg and tell them that the tantrum will end when the egg is broken. If it doesn't, then some serious consequence will be given. Have the tot break the egg in the manner they wish. Then have them clean up the mess.

For Natural Disaster Egg Bombs, break one in your front yard when pending doom is coming (be sure to take shelter and evacuate as instructed by local authorities). The bomb creates an instant circle around your house and will protect it from the disaster's blows.

Alternative Egg Hunt

An alternative to the egg hunt is one where your "hunt" is for the type of magic you may need in the coming year. Instead of filling the plastic eggs (you can use them year after year) with candy, fill them with stickers or small foam representations of different totem animals. Have the mother priestess or father priest hide the eggs and then send the children to hunt them. When they return, open the eggs and talk about the animals' totemic meanings and how they might assist each family member.

Feast

The Ostara feast should be filled with anything that is fresh and in season. A tasty vegetable soup loaded with fresh herbs or a light meal of fish and salad are great feasts for this ocassion. Be sure you bring your eggs to the table to continue the talk of the totems each child found (choose one child to collect some eggs they designate for each parent). If you can enjoy this feast outdoors, even better. It might be a bit nippy, but the promise of spring is all around.

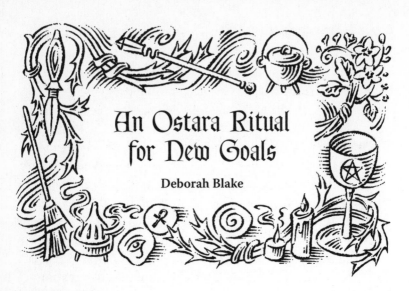

An Ostara Ritual for New Goals

Deborah Blake

Items Needed

Sage smudge stick (or incense if you prefer)

Salt and water (small bowl)

Candles: cream/white & yellow/gold (for Goddess and God), pink, pale yellow, light blue & light green (for quarters), plus one or more tealights if holding ritual inside [You can use the standard red/blue/green/yellow candles if you want, but I like using pastel colors at Ostara]

Matches or a lighter

Hollow plastic "Easter" eggs [available at dollar stores and such—or if you are really crafty you can make your own eggs out of papier mâché by using a small balloon to mold the paper on, then letting out the air so that the egg is hollow after it dries . . . this is nicer than plastic, if you have the time to make your own]

Paper and pen to write with (preferably something nice, like parchment or pastel-colored notepaper)

Small cauldron or fireproof bowl (if inside)

Optional: bowl filled with sand or salt (if you can't have a fire or candles)

Table to use as an altar

Bowl of edible seeds (such as pumpkin and sunflower) or seedcakes

Chalice or glass containing wine or juice

Optional altar decorations: spring flowers (daffodils, crocuses, jonquils, forsythia, daisies), dyed "Ostara eggs" or painted wooden
eggs, chocolate eggs (you can find lots of candy eggs around
because of Easter—I like to use the malted ones that look like
robins' eggs), pastel or flowery cloth to cover the altar

Note: I recommend reading the entire ritual through before starting. It will go much more smoothly if you know exactly what to
expect at each section of the rite.

Where and when: It is optimum to do this ritual outside at dawn,
with a bonfire. Needless to say, this won't always be possible, either
because the weather interferes, or because dawn isn't a good time
for you (or the folks you are celebrating with). You will definitely
want to do this ritual during the day, but if you can't be outside—or
can't have a fire—you can substitute a cauldron or fireproof bowl
with some tealights inside for the bonfire.

Who: This ritual is designed to be used by either a group or a
solitary Witch. I have written it out to include the "welcome and
explanation" speech that would customarily be given by the High
Priest and/or High Priestess leading the ritual, which any solitaries
can just leave out when doing the ritual by themselves. All "group"
instructions will be printed in bold, so that solitaries can spot them
easily and skip over them as desired. As necessary, substitute the
word *we* for *I*. If doing a group ritual, the quarter calls would usually
be read by various group members, and the HP/HPS would invoke
the gods and cast the circle.

Preparation: Do whatever cleansing you desire for yourself and
then gather all your supplies where you will have your ritual. If you
are going to have a bonfire, light it now. (You can also light some
candles around the room if you are stuck inside—they can symbolize
the return of the light, just as a bonfire does.) Set up your altar, and

remember to shut off any phones or anything else that could interrupt or distract you. Now you're ready to begin your Ostara ritual.

Cleanse yourself and your sacred space with the sage smudge stick. As the smoke wafts over you and around the circle space, visualize a glowing golden light washing away all negativity, and surrounding you with clarity and serenity. **Pass the smudge stick around the circle.** Take a few slow, deep breaths to help you ground and center.

Mix your salt and water together in a small bowl. If you want, you can say aloud: "Salt into water, water into salt. Wash away all negativity, leaving only the positive and beneficial." Anoint yourself at forehead, lips, heart, and center, then sprinkle the salt and water mixture around the outline of your circle.

Cast the circle by walking around the perimeter deosil (clockwise) with an athame or your finger pointed at the ground, while saying: "I cast the circle round and round, from earth to sky, from sky to ground. I conjure now this sacred place, outside time, and outside space. The circle is cast, I am **(we are)** between the worlds." Visualize the inside of the circle filled with light.

Invoke the four quarters by standing to face each direction (starting with the East), then lighting the appropriate candle after you have called that quarter.

East (yellow): *I summon the spirit of east, the element of air, and bid you guard me* **(us)** *with the power of the sudden storm and hold me* **(us)** *safe with the gentleness of the evening breeze.*

South (pink or red): *I summon the spirit of the South, the element of Fire, and bid you guard me* **(us)** *with the power of the roaring flame and with the softly fading ember.*

West (blue): *I summon the spirit of the West, the element of Water, and bid you guard me* **(us)** *with the power of the ocean waves and hold me* **(us)** *safe like the waters of the mother we all come from.*

North (green): *I summon the spirit of the North, the element of Earth, and bid you guard me* **(us)** *with the strength of the land* *beneath my (**our**) feet, and hold me (**us**) like soil that nurtures the smallest seed.*

Invoke the God and Goddess by standing in front of the altar with arms upraised. Light the white or cream candle after invoking the Goddess, and the yellow or gold candle after invoking the God.

*Great Eostre, goddess of spring and the dawn, I ask you to join me (**us**) at this Ostara ritual. Help me (**us**) to connect with the potential for growth and renewal that comes with this season, and bless me (**us**) with your healing love. Welcome, and blessed be.*

*Great God Zephyrus, god of the South winds, I ask you to join me (**us**) at this Ostara ritual. From days of old, you have announced the arrival of spring with your warming breezes, blowing away the cold and gloom of winter. Come to my (**our**) circle today and bring spring with you! Welcome, and blessed be.*

For group ritual:
HP/HPS: Welcome to our celebration of the Spring Equinox, also known as Ostara. This is a time of hope and renewal, growth and rebirth. As the wheel of the year turns again to bring us out of the darkness of winter, and into the light of spring, we are given the chance to start fresh, and welcome new beginnings into our lives. Today we turn our energy and the energy of our circle to the goal of opening ourselves to the potential of the season to come—planting the seeds for all of our goals and wishes, and nurturing them with our will and our intent and the help of the powers that surround us.

We will start with a meditation for cleansing, balance, and growth. [Note: This can be read by the HP/HPS or by any group member who reads well. Solitaries can tape this ahead of time and play it back during ritual, read it silently, or read it out loud to themselves, as they prefer. Or they can just use the basic imagery without using the specific words.]

Meditation

Close your eyes. Take a slow, deep breath, breathing in the fresh, clear air of spring. Breathe out slowly, breathing out all the toxins and stresses of the winter. Breathe in the light and breathe out the darkness. Feel yourself let go of the tensions of your everyday life and allow a feeling of peace to fill your body.

Listen to the sounds around you. Hear the birds sing and the trees rustle in the breeze. Listen to your own breathing **(and the breathing of those around you)**. If you listen carefully, you can hear the breathing of the Earth as she stirs and awakens under your feet. Silently send her greetings and welcome her back from her long sleep.

Send your awareness down. Down through the ground below you. Feel the stirring of the seeds, lying dormant in the ground, awaiting the touch of the Sun and the gentle spring rains. Feel the subtle energy of the small creatures that live underground. Reach out with your essence, sending small roots out through the bottom of your feet, down into the ground below. Send all those things that no longer work for your benefit out through your feet, and let them be fed harmlessly into the land. Sense the strength of the Earth flowing back up into you, to help you achieve your goals later on.

Send your awareness up. Reach out with your essence into the sky above, and feel the light and clarity infuse your very being. Take in the bright, powerful energy of the Sun, and let it fill you with unlimited potential for growth, change and renewal.

Feel yourself connected with the universe around you, and sense the new balance in your body, mind and spirit. See yourself glowing with the energy of spring, beginning to grow and blossom, and know that all things are possible.

[Take a moment of silence at the end of the meditation.]

Now take your piece of paper **(pass paper and pens out to all in circle)** and on one half of the paper, write all those things that are standing in the way of your goals, or that you need to get rid of in order to achieve and maintain balance. Be as specific as possible. (For example, if your goal is to lose weight, you might write "eating from stress, not eating a balanced diet, never finding the time to exercise," etc.)

On the other half of the paper, write down your goals for the season to come. Again, be specific, but this time try to leave things open-ended enough to allow for the gods to grant what you want in ways you didn't expect. But be careful how you phrase your goals, so you don't accidentally get something you don't truly want. (For example, if you want to lose weight, be sure to say "in a healthy way" so you don't end up dropping 20 pounds because you got really sick.) Take however much time you need to really think about both lists.

When you are done writing, rip your lists apart. Take your list of things you want to get rid of, and burn it in the bonfire, or in your cauldron of candles, if it is safe to do so. If you can't burn it, you can bury it in a bowl of salt or sand, and take it outside to burn or bury permanently at a later time. **(In a group ritual, each person should take a turn, going around the circle. If desired, people can say aloud what they are getting rid of, before dropping their paper in the fire.)** As you burn the piece of paper, visualize all it contains being lifted up and out of your life. Take a moment to feel how much lighter you are now.

Then take your other half of the list, with the seeds you wish to set in motion for your goals during the upcoming season, roll it up and place it inside your plastic or papier mâché egg. If you are outside, you can bury it to "plant" your seeds within the Earth. Alternately, you can place it on your altar where you will see it often, to remind you of the goals you have set for yourself. Be sure to take a moment to visualize your dreams and wishes as strongly as you can, before releasing them out into the universe.

Now it is time for cakes and ale. Hold up your bowl of seeds or the seedcakes and say:

*God and Goddess, bless these seeds, symbols of the potential for growth and abundance. As I (**we**) eat them, let me (**us**) take in the energy they contain, that I (**we**) might have the strength to work on my (**our**) goals in the months ahead.*

Eat some of the seeds or cake, and if outside, sprinkle a few on the ground. Hold up your goblet and say:

May life be as sweet as this wine (juice), a gift from the Earth and the Sun.

Drink, and if outside, pour a little on the ground. **In a group ritual, this would be the time to pass a speaking stick around the circle, and let everyone say a few words.**

Dismiss the quarters (starting with North) by turning toward each direction and snuffing out the candle after saying thank you.

North: *Powers of Earth, I (we) thank you for being here today and protecting my (our) circle. Stay if you will, go if you must, in perfect love and perfect trust. So mote it be.*

West: *Powers of Water, I (we) thank you for being here today and protecting my (our) circle. Stay if you will, go if you must, in perfect love and perfect trust. So mote it be.*

South: *Powers of Fire, I (we) thank you for being here today and protecting my (our) circle. Stay if you will, go if you must, in perfect love and perfect trust. So mote it be.*

East: *Powers of the Air, I (we) thank you for being here today and protecting my (our) circle. Stay if you will, go if you must, in perfect love and perfect trust. So mote it be.*

Thank the God and Goddess for their help by lifting your hands in the air and then snuffing out each candle after speaking.

Great Eostre, I (we) thank you for your presence here in this circle today, and always. Guide me (us) as I (we) walk the path seeking balance and growth, and help me to achieve my goals. Farewell, and blessed be.

Great Zephyrus, I (we) thank you for your presence here in this circle today, and always. May your wind always be at my back (our backs), encouraging me (us) to move forward in a positive and pro-ductive way. Farewell, and blessed be.

Open the circle by walking widdershins (counterclockwise) around the circle, or simply visualize the sacred space opening up and returning to the mundane world. **For a group ritual, you can all join hands and recite the Wiccan Rede, or simply say: "The circle is open, but never broken. Merry meet, merry part, and merry meet again!" Let go of each other's hands, and the circle is open.**

If you want, have a feast to celebrate the sabbat, featuring spring foods like lamb (if you're not a vegetarian), asparagus, salads made with fresh herbs, strawberries, and such. Don't forget to follow up your magickal work with concrete action in the mundane world. Happy Ostara!

Notes

Beltane

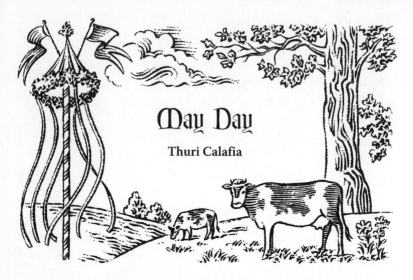

May Day

Thuri Calafia

"Over here, Seamus," the raven-haired young woman called out to her companion, her deep blue eyes surveying the multicolored spring flowers in a small clearing in the trees, "There are hundreds of them! And they're beautiful!"

A tall young man with flame-red hair came rushing to Caitlin's side. "Indeed, my darling," he said, his eyes locked on her breasts, "they are beautiful."

Caitlin giggled, blushing slightly, "The flowers, Seamus," she said, sweeping her other hand to show him the scene before them.

"Those are nice, too," he said, slipping an arm around Caitlin's waist. She laughed and stepped away, then took his hand when his brow furrowed, and led him into the center of the little grove.

"Come on now," she said, setting down the large baskets she'd been carrying, "We have to collect them, for tomorrow's celebration."

"Aye," he agreed, "for tomorrow. Which means we have all night."

Caitlin laughed as Seamus moved closer. "I suppose you're right," she said, her voice becoming thick with emotion as she touched his arm and raised her eyes to meet his. "And with this many, we won't need to look further. These will fill our baskets with much to spare."

"Let's crush a few, then," Seamus said with sly smile, slipping both arms around Caitlin's waist this time. "I mean, how else would we know if they smell good?" She looked into his clear hazel eyes, which were shining with desire for her, as her own body began to sing with an equal desire.

"True enough, my love," she said as Seamus pulled her closer, "For surely it would be insulting to the gods to bring in the May with imperfect flowers."

"And we must bring in the May, sweet Caitlin," he said, leaning in for a kiss, "in the most perfect way we can."

Bringing in May by gathering flowers, couple by couple, like the one in the story above, was one of the most beloved traditions of Beltane in times past. Although it isn't common anymore, those of us with a little silver in our hair may remember a tradition of giving "May baskets" to our sweethearts, friends, and teachers anonymously when we were kids. Those of us with more curious natures would leave the baskets, and then ring the doorbell and go hide so we could watch the recipient of our carefully gathered flowers smile and pick them up from their front porches.

There is some speculation regarding when Beltane actually occurs, ranging from May Eve, April 30, to the first Full Moon after May 1. In *A Witches' Bible*, Janet and Stewart Farrar state Beltane means "May Day," but Raven Grimassi, in *The Encyclopedia of Wicca and Witchcraft*, says Beltane means "bright fire." The Beltane Fire Society says it may also mean "sacred fire." Indeed, this was when farmers drove their cattle between two fires (called "need fires") to bring luck, fertility, and an abundant milk yield for the year, so holding these fires sacred makes sense. In addition, many of our ancestors would walk between (or jump over) these fires for similar blessings. As the ancient Celts only truly acknowledged summer and winter, Beltane heralded summer and the season of fertility. At this time, the very air is charged with excitement, sexual energy, and passion, which affects animals, crops, and more significantly, us humans.

In those ancient times, while the young people of the villages were away gathering flowers, the more adult members of the family would gather in the freshly plowed fields and bring fertility to the land by making love in sacred orgies. Babies born of these unions were often considered blessed, as they brought the energy of fertility, joy, and summer's blessings to their families with their very conception. The king and queen would secretly steal away to celebrate by making love privately. In those days, the queen represented the land, so the energy raised by the royal lovemaking (and that of their subjects) would bless the land and the people with abundance and fertility. The gods and goddesses of love, lust, and fertility were honored on this holiday, just as they are honored by many Pagans today.

One such goddess is the Greek Goddess Aphrodite. The Farrars, in *The Witches' Goddess*, speak of Aphrodite as being, "in the purest sense," a goddess of love, eroticism, beauty, desire, and passion. Unpredictable, uninhibited, and single-minded, "She was all these things without qualm or apology." This purity they speak of is in the sense of this love goddess being unadulterated, undiluted sexual energy; both desire and fulfillment. Even her name speaks of her power to seduce, as the word *aphrodiasic* comes from the word *aphrodisiakos*, which comes from the Greek "Aphrodite," according to *Funk and Wagnells Standard Dictionary of the English Language*. In *The Grandmother of Time*, Z. Budapest says the word *April* is derived from the Roman word *Aprilus*, which appears to be rooted in the verb *aperire*, which means, "to open." This again speaks to the idea of Beltane occurring in April—the month belonging to Aphrodite. Sadly, this incredibly powerful and alluring, often wise, and benevolent goddess is still often seen as little more than a dumb blonde, even in the Pagan subculture. This is a dishonor to her, as well as a perpetuation of the lie that owning our sexuality somehow diminishes, rather than elevates, our power as people.

Whoever our personal gods of fertility and passion are, they can teach us much about our own sexuality if we take the time to listen. Meditations and other inner work designed to discover ourselves in this way can be extremely rewarding and can help us connect to these archetypal energies both within and without, especially at this special and sacred time of year. For Beltane, like Samhain, is a time when the veils are thin, and the truth of self and spirit is easily accessible if only one opens to the energy.

Beltane Traditions

Probably the most popular and common Beltane tradition is that of dancing the maypole, a beautiful symbolic Great Rite that honors the Sacred Marriage of the Lord and the Lady. Other holiday traditions include, but are not limited to: other types of symbolic Great Rites, walking between two fires or leaping fires for blessings and luck, garden blessings, feasting on symbolically and erotically shaped foods (which may or may not be laced with herbs for love, lust, and romance), drinking May wine, adult-themed parties such as the Haloa, love and lust spells, and of course, the actual Great Rite.

The Maypole – A Symbolic Great Rite

A Great Rite is a sexual act done in sacred space. There are many ways to express this energy that do not involve actual lovemaking, however, such as the tradition of dancing the maypole. In the weeks preceding the holiday, and especially on Beltane itself, the energies of fertility and sexual desire are all around us. This is cause for great joy and celebration, as Pagans everywhere will likely agree that we hold sexuality sacred. When lovers come together in passion, the energy between them builds and builds, and becomes a tangible force that is much greater than the sum of its two (or more!) parts. Sexuality is sacred to Pagans because it honors and celebrates life and love, and in doing so, it serves the life force.

The Great Rite is most commonly symbolized by dancing a maypole, a richly symbolic representation of the Lord and Lady's Great Rite, or Sacred Marriage. The pole itself symbolizes the Lord's phallus, pointing up into the sky, a giant monument to his sexual power and potency. In some traditions, the ribbons twined around it represent the Lady. More often, the Lady's yoni is symbolized by a ring of flowers, which is placed atop the pole.

The ring of flowers is easy to make. Simply purchase a good-sized ring of straw from your local hobby shop (if the straw ring is too small it won't slide down the pole smoothly). Then, you can take flowers of the season, love- and lust-inducing herbs, and poke their stems into the straw base until the top and sides are completely covered. Make sure you don't prepare the ring of flowers too far ahead, or they may begin wilting before the ritual starts. You can combat this a little by holding the ring in a big bowl with a few inches of water—deep enough for the stems to get a "drink"—or by "watering" it occasionally throughout the day. Roses are always a great choice, though they would have to be purchased if not in season. Other good choices are tulips (they are also sacred to Aphrodite), lavender, daisies, hibiscus, violets, columbines, hyacinths, jasmine, orchids (though, like roses, can get pricey rather quickly), and pansies. Herbs for the ring can include patchouli, sweet basil, cinnamon sticks, juniper, lady's mantle, peppermint, rosemary, thyme, willow, yarrow, dill, lemongrass, and any other herbs or flowers you find appealing.

Once your ring of flowers is assembled, have three or four people pull their ribbons out to create a "platform" for the ring to rest on until the dance starts. Then, as the dance progresses and the ribbons are woven round and round, the ring of flowers and herbs slowly lowers itself over the pole, symbolizing the Great Rite of the Lord and Lady, woman-superior style.

A refreshingly different variation on this theme is the male-superior style, which is done at the Spiritual Anarchist's Beltane (SAB), a private festival in the Pacific Northwest. Earlier I spoke of Aphrodite's sexual "purity"—if there was ever a gathering of Pagans who speak to that energy, this would be the place, and the people. Unabashed, uninhibited, openly in favor of the joy and sacredness of both human sexuality and the Sacred Marriage of our Lord and the Lady, these people personify and embody the sexual purity of Aphrodite in a beautiful and vital way.

First, the current May King, whose reign started the previous year, at the appropriate time, takes a team of men off into the woods for special mystery rites, part of which includes the "hunting" of the current year's maypole, which can be either a fallen tree or fresh one. Sometimes this choice is dictated by the current May Queen. From the time it is chosen, the pole is imbued with abundant male energy, and is considered the Lord's phallus, so it is never allowed to touch the ground, or it would lose all that energy. The men then spend a day stripping the bark and carving the end into a wonderfully blatant phallic shape, adding symbols and carved pictures as the spirit moves them.

In the meantime, the women gather around the May Queen, awaiting her orders. At her word, they begin digging a hole for the maypole in a spot that has become tradition for SAB. Now, this isn't just any old hole in the ground. The women make it sacred from the very beginning, as it is consecrated to the Goddess and becomes, for the duration of the festival, the Goddess' yoni. Over the course of the next day (or two), the hole is dug out to the correct depth which is marked by the moment the shortest woman in camp can no longer see out. This takes the effort of every willing woman in camp. The finishing touch is just the right-sized rock for the Goddess' clitoris and dozens and dozens of fresh flowers all around, which emphasize the beauty and mystery of the Goddess and all of nature.

About the time the women are finishing up the Earth yoni, the men come back from their mystery, carrying the giant wooden phallus. The women sing songs of enticement and love to the gods of fertility and passion, and thereby the men who personify him and hold his energy with their intent and their actions. The phallus is then placed lengthwise to the earth yoni, with the "business end" closest to the opening in the ground.

The current May Queen then announces that it's time to choose the new queen. Any woman who feels called may step up and join the others in the circle around the current queen. The current May Queen, through whatever method she feels called to use (usually some system of drawing lots), chooses the next queen. The men step up next, and the new queen chooses her consort (which can be a woman or a man), using whatever method she chooses.

The maypole dance doesn't begin yet, however—the Lord must be made ready. Brilliantly colored ribbons, which were pre-dyed magically by the May Queen, the queens from former years (each one affectionately referred to as a "May Ma"), and other women in the local Pagan community, are rolled out. Each woman in camp chooses one, and attaches it to the far end of the shaft. Once all the ribbons are on, they are secured, and that's when Aphrodite really takes control.

One by one, the women in camp all "dance the pole," which consists of dancing their way, straddling the pole, from the far end down to the beautifully carved head. This they do either simply or quite blatantly, stroking the shaft and carved head erotically, sometimes kissing, licking, or even locking their legs around it and . . . well, let's just say they bless it with their own sacred emanations, enticing and delighting the Lord to his great purpose. Finally, amid much cheering, drumming, and chanting, the Lord and Lady are united as the men, as one, lift, push, and thrust the sacred phallus into the deep earth yoni. Shortly thereafter, the new royal couple withdraws from the revelers to prepare themselves. Once they are invoked with the spiritual energy of the Lord and Lady, the maypole dance begins, and colorful ribbons fly on the breeze as they're woven round and round the pole in a dance as old as time.

A little later in the evening, the bel-fire is lit, also in a traditional place in camp, and the evening continues with much of the same wonderful revelry, drumming, and dancing one finds at most other Pagan sabbat celebrations, with one small exception: everyone is deliciously horny. The new May Queen and her consort sometimes do a symbolic Great Rite with a chalice and blade for the crowd before sneaking off to perform an actual Great Rite (one can imagine the other revelers gathering in the woods in the Old Way), sending bright, sacred, and magical energy to the stars and back, blessing the land, the people, and the holiday in the sublime and sacred tradition of our spiritual ancestors.

Other Symbolic Great Rites

If one doesn't want to do an actual Great Rite or a maypole for her Beltane celebration, there are other symbolic ways to express this energy, such as planting something, burying a crystal that has been charged with magical energies, or joining the chalice and blade as is done in a typical Wiccan ritual. Smaller groups or solitary practitioners can braid magically charged ribbons around an "invisible" maypole by hanging the ribbons from a hook in the ceiling, and then tying off and dividing up the braid later for each participant to use as they will. You can also make a "may gad"—a miniature maypole made by a single practitioner, using a small branch or twig, which is then wrapped with ribbons that carry your wishes. May gads look beautiful lining sidewalk gardens, or stuck in a plant pot on an apartment patio or balcony.

If one wants to do an actual Great Rite, it's a good idea to set up the space, preferably outdoors, with as many symbols of love, lust, and power as possible (soft, fresh rose petals on the bed are a nice touch), and, if the person or people involved are very good at holding their focus, they can even chant while raising energy in this fashion, which adds to the magic. At the moment of orgasm, the energy can be sent to any purpose, but a good one for this bright and fertile time of year is to bless plants with the energy. One year, my lover and I surrounded the magic circle with all the baby plant starts we'd just made, firing the energy into the little peat pots. We had a great garden that year! If the people involved want the energy to be extra powerful, they can build it over a period of days (I don't recommend more than ten for beginners), by teasing each other sexually every day, bringing each other almost to the point of orgasm, and then backing off and holding the energy until it subsides. This is more difficult than it sounds! Good communication is key—simple code words, such as "My Lord" or "My Lady" can let your partner(s) know to stop or slow their actions when orgasm is imminent. By the time the Great Rite occurs, the stored up energy that's released is like a sparkling rocket!

Revelry

For the party afterward, one can invite people to celebrate in a blatantly sexual fashion, such as in a Haloa celebration like Z. Budapest speaks of in *The Grandmother of Time*. The Haloa was the Greek celebration of women's free speech, and was for women only. As my rituals and parties are open to both women and men, I wanted to include men in the Haloa-type celebration I did one year. At the beginning of the post-ritual party, I laid down the "rules": People were encouraged to flirt blatantly with each other, to say whatever sprang to mind, and to keep in mind that it was all in fun (couples laid their own ground rules for how far the flirting could go). We also had a sexy-joke-telling and bawdy-song-singing competition. For the contest, I first gave each participant a roll of pennies in a paper cup. As each person told their story or sang their song, each member of the audience who laughed had to drop a penny into the performer's cup. For groans or silence, the performer had to give each member of the audience one of their pennies. This helped keep people from telling sophomoric and disgusting jokes just to hear themselves speak. It worked very well; people don't like getting groans, and so the jokes and songs were hilariously funny and sexy. At the end of the evening, the pennies were counted up and prizes were given, but the best prize for all of us was the freedom to be wholly ourselves, even if for only one evening.

Beltane Foods and Drinks

One very traditional and lovely drink for Beltane is May wine. This is commonly made with white wine, lemon slices, and a lovely fragrant herb called sweet woodruff. I have adapted the recipe a bit, so I use champagne and sliced strawberries in mine. In a large punch bowl, I tear some sweet woodruff (a couple of handfuls per bottle is a good measure to go by), then cover this with sliced berries, then more sweet woodruff and another layer of berries. I pour the champagne over all and let it steep for the duration of the ritual. If the sweet woodruff is in bloom, I reserve the pretty white flowers to float on top. By cakes and wine time, the brew should be perfect—delicately flavored, heady, and sweet.

For the cakes, I like to use what I call "hot peach cakes," which are an adaptation of the Fararrs' Aphrodite cakes, found in *The Witches' Goddess.* These are easy to make: you'll need the pastry recipe for a two-crust pie, about a dozen peach halves, a whole, unblanched almond for each one, and some heavy table cream to serve them with (optional). First, roll out the pastry and cut into circles about an inch bigger than the diameter of the peach. Place the peach on top of it and cover with a larger circle of pastry, pinching the edges to seal them. Then, take a knife and cut from the top down on one side almost (but not quite) to the bottom. Dust the very top of the dome with cinnamon, and then push an almond, tip up, into the slit. They will open slightly as they bake. They are delicious served hot, with plenty of cream!

For those who are not inclined to bake, there are many pastries available that can serve just as well, such as cream horns, cannelloni, and of course, the more blatant pastries available for purchase from erotic bakeries. Another option is to buy rolled wafer cookies that come filled with hazelnut or chocolate cream, and then dip one end into melted chocolate a few times. And strawberries, all by themselves, either sliced or whole, can speak to the most erotic shapes if one only takes a moment to look.

Foods for the feast can include stuffed manicotti, stuffed shells, bratwurst, seafood of any kind, and love- and lust-inducing culinary herbs and foods such as sweet basil, cinnamon, avocado, and ginger, to name a few. There is also a lovely damiana liqueur on the market, which is supposed to help induce female lust, though after most Beltane celebrations, the ingestion of damiana liqueur could be like lighting a match to a box of Roman candles!

Celestial Sway

Fern Feto Spring

BELTANE HONORS THE RISING sap of life-force energy that emerges as the spring season fully hits its stride. The lusty, sensual Earth overflows abundantly with her gifts. As we partake in this feast of life, soaking in the warmth and nourishment of nature, we awaken our senses and connect with others, appreciating the simple joy in being alive.

Taurus is the sign in the spotlight at Beltane, aptly representing the earthy contentment and desire for sensual comfort that mark this time of year. Beltane 2010 finds the Sun in Taurus and the Moon in Sagittarius, just on the waning side of an April 28 Full Moon in Scorpio. With both the Sun and Mercury also trining Pluto, and in a square to Mars, this looks to be one hot Beltane season indeed.

We may find that after a long hard winter, we want to revel in the comforts of the body and fully explore the pleasures of being human. The Sun and Mercury trine to Pluto allow us to express the depth of our intense need to connect with others in a harmonious way, easing our communication and allowing us to just be in the moment. With Mercury still retrograde in Taurus, now might not be the time to have long, process-oriented communications, but companionable silences will play an important and beneficial role in helping us to build intimacy with others.

The Moon in Sagittarius is in trine to Mars in Leo on Beltane Eve, and Mars is just about to move out of its shadow phase (when a previously retrograde planet retraces the degrees that it just went through backward, offering a chance to revisit those retrograde lessons with more perspective and a sense of forward motion) arising from the retrograde period that took place from December 2009–March 2010. This planetary combination brings a certain playfulness and an ability to take action and move forward on our heart's desires. The dreaming and visioning we did earlier in the year may now begin to bear fruit, and we can see some of the results of our hopes and wishes for the future.

Throughout May, Jupiter grows closer to its yearlong conjunction with Uranus (beginning June 2010). This planetary duo is poised to bring exciting new opportunities into our lives, expanding our idea of what is possible and offering unexpected and innovative ways for us to evolve as humans. This conjunction will be a welcome relief from the heaviness created by the ongoing Saturn/Pluto square, and will give us the opportunity to develop a sense of hope and optimism for the future.

Mercury goes direct in Taurus on May 11, days before the New Moon in Taurus on May 13. The direct motion of the planet of communication so close to this Moon indicate that we can use the fertile nature of the sign of Taurus to plant the seeds of new thoughts and ideas. Given the earthy and practical nature of this sign, we may find that our desire to communicate is physical rather than verbal, as we build and shape the world around us into new forms and designs.

This New Moon also continues the good news of the Beltane cycle, with a sextile aspect to Jupiter and a trine to Saturn. This puts the Sun and the Moon in a creative, harmonious relationship with both the ability to expand and the power to contract. We can take practical and grounded action to move forward, enjoying the present and expressing gratitude for the simple pleasures in our lives.

Beltane Feast of the Senses Ritual

Prepare a feast of your favorite foods and invite one or more friends to come, (ask them to bring a dish of one of their favorite meals). Have drinks (alcoholic or not, depending on your preference), and a selection of beautiful glasses. Decorate with spring flowers and create a selection of sensual music to play. Try to create an environment that feeds all five of the senses: sight, sound, touch, taste, and smell. If your budget allows, you may even want to hire a massage therapist to offer hand or foot massages to your guests. As the feast commences, offer toasts of gratitude for all the things that bring you pleasure and comfort in life.

Full Moon in Sagittarius/May 27

The Full Moon in Sagittarius explores themes of education, communication, belief systems, and the expansion of consciousness. What are you learning or teaching about now? How do you make meaning from the world and how do you communicate about what is meaningful for you to others? You may be experiencing a greater sense of optimism and possibility now, and an awareness of new directions and adventures to embark on.

Look to where the Full Moon falls in the houses of your chart for a more specific interpretation of how this lunar event will affect your life. Notice which house cusp Sagittarius rules, and also which one Gemini rules for an understanding of the house pairs to be activated.

Full Moon in Sagitttarius through the Houses

1st and 7th: Self-identity/The Other, partnerships

2nd and 8th: Personal skills and resources/Shared energies and resources

3rd and 9th: Communication and the immediate environment/ Meaning and expansion of consciousness

4th and 10th: Home, family, and deep self/Public persona, career, and destiny

5th and 11th: Self-expression, creativity, and spontaneity/Community, humanity, and the future

6th and 12th: Service to others and in the world/Service to spirit and retreat

Jupiter in Aries

Jupiter moves into Aries on June 6 after half a year in the sign of Pisces. The planet Jupiter expands the qualities of the sign it is in, offering growth opportunities and a greater awareness of that signs particular energy. As Jupiter moves from the watery and intuitive realm of Pisces into the fiery independent movement of Aries (until it retrogrades back into Pisces in September), we will benefit from taking risks and staying true to our own essential nature. This is the combination of the adventurer and warrior, confident and ready to take on the world. Collectively, we may have a renewed sense of courage and a desire to take on challenges and face the unknown. There may be new trails blazed in the fields of education, law, and the media. Stay alert for your own opportunity to try something new and different.

Jupiter in Aries Ritual

(For maximum effect, try doing this ritual on the first New Moon after Jupiter goes into Aries: New Moon in Gemini on June 12)

Pick one area of your life that would be helped by a courageous and bold approach. Possible areas include: love, work, family, travel, goals, money, or health. When you have identified this area, write it down on a piece of paper, and put the paper in a special spot on your altar. Light a purple candle and ask that the energy of Jupiter in Aries infuse this area of your life with its energy. Let the candle burn down and notice how your approach to this area of your life changes as the month goes on. Look for new opportunities, openings, and a growth in your general level of confidence in this area of your life.

The Old Ways

Dan Furst

THE GREAT MID-SPRING FESTIVAL of Beltane is the fifth sabbat of the year. Like the others, it is usually celebrated over several days. While festivities are usually said to run from May 1 through May 3 or 5, it's more accurate to see Beltane as a five-day affair with the structure of a Shakespeare play: Act 1 begins on April 28, and the action rises in riot and intensity from Act 1 to Act 4 on May 1, so that the day we celebrate as Beltane at the top of May is actually the climax of the festival, not the opening of it. It's more likely that the ancient Beltane ran April 28 to May 2, and the main rites came on the next-to-last day.

The day known to us now as April 28, coming three days before the first day of May, began the last great Earth goddess festival of the month. The Romans called it Floralia, the Flower Festival, a heady mix of color, fragrance, music, revelry, and sex to welcome the lusty month of May. There's a sensuousness in late April. We are in the month of Astarte, Freya and Venus right when they are in bloom, soon to grow big with the children they will bear later in the year, because every love goddess expresses herself as the mother as well as the lover. Floralia was timed to peak on May Eve, just before the dawn of the universal spring festival. As flowers were naturally associated with youth, the time abounds with celebrations of beauty, vitality and health.

Early May affirms life in all its gorgeousness, juice, and sensuality. The days that burst at Beltane are exactly across the zodiac wheel from the great feasts of death on October 31 and November 1. So the solemn All Hallows, honoring the dead on November 1, is the opposite number to the sacred play of life on May 1; and the darker, scarier, funnier Halloween mirrors the revels of Walpurgis Night on April 30. The dancing, singing, and ecstasy of May Eve were not sexual; the next night was for that. The true, holy purpose of Walpurgisnacht, as the Teutons called it, was to honor and beseech the Horned God, Cernunnos. One of the two primordial nature gods in central and western Europe, he embodies the vitality of animal life, just as the Green Man, who also appears in festivals everywhere now, represents the surge of vegetation in the spring.

The Horned One's night was originally a hunt ceremony in which the tribe prayed for an abundance of deer and elk to be born now, to grow fat by Hunter's Moon, then feed the people through the winter. The crucial step in the rites of the Horned One was prayers addressed to the spirits of the horned animals who would give their lives in the months to come, to bless their sacrifice and ask their forgiveness for the clan's hunters. This true meaning of Walpurgis Night, which made it essential to the ancient people's survival, has been replaced in the pop culture toy box by a black arts orgy, a night for Witches to drink wine, sing, and roll in the red clover with the wildly nasty predator Satan, who resembles Cernunnos only in also having horns. Before church propagandists in the Middle Ages turned the Horned One's night into a sinuous mosh as immortalized by Dutch painter Hieronymus Bosch, it was really a prayer for food. For the priests, though, whose tonsures were already tingling at all that dancing and singing around a fire in the forest on May Eve night, the next evening's romp in the meadow was even more dangerous, drenched as it was with the most joyous pleasure Venus offers.

The ancient people knew reverence, though, and some restraint. For them, even love in the grass and flowers—with the intent of creating new babies—can be done in a sacred manner only after a proper rite of purification by the fire that gives Beltane its name. The word means "bright fire," the Bel coming, from the ancient Gaulish solar god Belenus, counterpart to Helios Apollo and also related to Baal and Baldur. But the fire that was celebrated on May 1 was not mainly the Sun. It was the hearth flame that was used to light the twin fires that were erected on poles as a ceremonial portal for the cattle, then the lovers. The mid-spring festival comes at the time when the cows who have been sheltered in the barn through the cold time, and have just held their weight by feeding on hay, get to go out in the balmy meadow to feast and fatten on fresh green grass and clover. The people bless and purify the herd before it enters the pasture, leading each flower-garlanded animal between the Beltane fires, and praying that the bull will be dutifully powerful and the cows will bear healthy calves and give sweet milk in the summer.

Along with the horned patron of hunters, Cernunnos, and the horned cows walking through the Beltane fire gate, one more Horned One has always been indispensable to Venus in May: the laughing, stinking great God Pan. Beltane without him is as unthinkable as a party with no music. He comes again on May Day to play his pipes, swing his wineskin, and love every nymph who comes near him. With his leer, his hairy chest, and curling goat's horns, he is so randy that not even Central Casting could design a smellier tempter to excite women and scare pleasure-hating, woman-fearing men. That's why the church copied its alleged devil from Pan. But long before he was misdrawn by priests, Pan was thanked and hymned all over the Greek world as the one whose boundless urge to merge brought new goats and lambs each spring, gave piquant resin to the wine, and invited Earth herself to the dance . . . and to what comes after the dance. By May Eve, he can hardly wait for the cows to get past the fires, and the couples to follow them later, as sunset deepens into night on Beltane.

Lovers who'd been waiting to get outdoors again, with all that that implies, longed for sunset on May 1 and the joys of May Night. Beltane may be the year's best example of a fertility ritual that civil law and religious dogma have starved over many centuries into a whisper of what it used to be. Long before it grayed and quieted down into a workers' holiday, a Soviet army parade, or the unappetizing fabrication of America's Law Day, May 1 was a day when lovers went to the places where, as the Shakespeare song has it, "the wild thyme blows." No one in the Northern Hemisphere, least of all in Europe, had any doubt what they wanted to do on May Night. This was the evening when people would go into the meadows and forests and make love in the clover and the flowers.

Basic courtesies had to be invented, naturally. It was understood that if you were arm in arm with a partner, you were taken for the night, or until you walked the meadow alone later. If you were outdoors alone on May night, you were as available as a human being ever gets, and you had to say yes to anyone who asked you. This is why so many mid-winter babies were born around the following February 1. As there was no institution of marriage, or even any idea of paternity when the Celtic culture first formed, and as a baby's prospects of future success are always brighter when the child is the son or daughter of a god—the little ones who were born at the next Imbolc were said to be the children of Robin Goodfellow, the mischievous wood spirit more familiar to us as Puck in Shakespeare's *A Midsummer Night's Dream*. Robin always loved to frolic on May Night, and that's why there are so many Robinsons today.

Feasts and Treats

Kristin Madden

THE GOD AND GODDESS come together at this time of year to share in all the blessings of body, mind, and spirit. And what is more sensual than a celebratory feast? Set your table with beautiful colors, romantic flowers, and soft candlelight and let the blessings begin! These recipes, filled with spring greens and plenty of berries, will arouse your passions while keeping you feeling energized enough to dance the maypole and jump the fires all night long.

May Day Dandelion Salad

By now, dandelions have taken over lawns across the Northern Hemisphere. Rather than eliminate these healthy, delicious flowers, why not rejoice in their sunny little faces and bring in their sweet, young greens for a truly unique salad? Remember to send your Beltane wishes off on the air and the dandelion fuzz!

Prep Time: 25 minutes
Serves: 6–8

Dressing
½ cup vinegar
1 cup mayonnaise
1 teaspoon mustard
1 teaspoon onion, minced
½ cup honey
1 teaspoon parsley
½ teaspoon oregano
¼ teaspoon pepper
½ cup bacon, cooked and chopped
½ cup olive oil

Salad
½ pound young dandelion greens
½ red onion
¼ cup green onions
2 Roma tomatoes
½ yellow bell pepper
½ carrot
Optional: grilled chicken, cut into small strips

In a blender, combine the vinegar, mayonnaise, and mustard and blend well. Add the onion, honey, parsley, oregano, pepper, and bacon. Blend well. While blending, gradually add oil.

Tear dandelion greens and chop vegetables, then add to a large salad bowl. Top with chicken, if desired. Toss in a small amount of dressing and serve with extra dressing on the side.

Beltane Pockets

Inspired by the Persian Purim Hamantaschen, these sweet pastries are a beautiful twist on a traditional spring holiday dessert. Flaky pastries filled with sweet berry preserves are sure to entrance the senses of your Beltane guests. With two berry preserves side-by-side within the delicate circle, this is a beautiful offering for the Divine wedding.

Prep Time: 30 minutes   *Cook Time:* 25 minutes
Chill Time: 1 hour   *Serves:* 15–20

8 tablespoon butter
3 ounces cream cheese
3 tablespoons confectioner's sugar
1 large egg
1 teaspoon vanilla extract
½ teaspoon lemon zest
¼ teaspoon salt
1⅓ cups flour
Blackberry and strawberry preserves
1 egg
1 tablespoon milk

Cream butter and cream cheese in blender on high speed until smooth. Add sugar and mix on medium. Add egg, vanilla, lemon zest, and salt and blend well. Mix in the flour until sticky. Roll into a ball, wrap in waxed paper and refrigerate for an hour.

Preheat oven to 350 degrees F. Roll out cookie dough to ⅛- to ¼-inch thickness on a well-floured surface. Cut into 3-inch circles. Fill each circle with ½ teaspoon of each preserve, side by side. Pinch the dough up around it into a sealed pocket. For a traditional cookie, pinch it into a triangle. Beat egg and milk on medium, then brush cookies with this mixture. Bake for 20 to 25 minutes until golden brown.

Chocolate Flowers with Strawberry Sorbet

Is there anything that says Beltane more than chocolate and strawberries? Pair it with a rich red wine, roses, and your beloved and it becomes a joyful festival for two. This sinful dessert is actually much healthier than you'd expect, making the indulgence even better for friends, family, and lovers alike.

Prep Time: 1 hour   *Cook Time:* 50 minutes total
Chill Time: Overnight   *Serves:* 12

Flowers

2 egg whites
½ cup confectioner's sugar
½ teaspoon salt
¼ cup butter, melted
¼ teaspoon vanilla extract
⅓ cup all-purpose flour
⅓ cup unsweetened cocoa powder

Sorbet

1 pound strawberries, chopped
½ cup sugar
¼ cup lemon juice

Preheat oven to 400 degrees F. In a medium bowl, whisk the egg whites, sugar, and salt together. Whisk in the butter and vanilla, then the flour and cocoa powder. Drop 2 tablespoons of batter onto a floured surface to create 4-inch circles, ⅛- to ¼-inch thick.

Bake on a greased, floured baking sheet for 5 to 6 minutes, until edges begin to brown. Immediately place cookies over greased custard cups and mold into flower shapes. Cool for 15 minutes before removing from cups. Continue baking and shaping two cookies at a time until you have used all your batter.

In a large bowl, mix berries with sugar and lemon juice. Mash slightly with a fork and allow to sit for 30 minutes. Puree in a blender then chill in the refrigerator until cold. Cover and freeze overnight. Serve sorbet in the flower cookies.

Passion Fruit Mojito

A crisp, clean, and cooling mojito will get any Beltane party started right. But add passion fruit to the traditional mint mojito and you create the perfect drink to accompany those Beltane Pockets for the Divine wedding feast. This delectable Beltane mojito can be made "virgin" or with rum, as you choose.

Prep Time: 10 minutes
Cook Time: NA
Serves: 2

12–14 fresh mint leaves
3 ounces passion fruit juice
4 teaspoons baker's sugar
4 ice cubes, crushed
3 ounces lime juice
Lemon-lime or club soda
Optional: 6 ounces white rum

With a mortar or spoon, crush the mint in a pestle or bowl. Transfer to a pitcher and add passion fruit juice, sugar, ice, lime juice, and rum, if desired. Stir well for 10 to 15 seconds. Pour into a glass and top with soda.

Crafty Crafts

Silver RavenWolf

Deva of the Season: Possibility
Scents/Aromas: Honeysuckle, Jasmine
Energy: Opportunity
Visualization: In the center of a clear bowl of blessed water, visualize the item or circumstance you desire. Practice this visualization every day for twenty-one days, beginning on the eve of Beltane, changing the water every day. Water houseplants or outdoor plants with the old water each day. Envision yourself happily receiving the opportunities you need to succeed. Always end your visualization with a smile.

Affirmation: I always recognize and take advantage of opportunities that are good for myself and my family.

❧

The Beltane deva brings opportunity! She sees no limits and is happy to provide open pathways to guarantee your success. By Beltane, the spring frosts are gone and gardeners galore are planting opportunity with each lovely flower, vegetable, or seed. If you are an avid gardener, use the affirmation above with each bit of greenery you plant.

Two holidays in particular concentrate on the Fairy Kingdom—Beltane and Midsummer. At Beltane, the fairies begin to surface, spreading their magick from garden to forest. Beltane is a wonderful time to send messages to the fairies. Here is an easy, inexpensive magickal project for both adults and children that embodies the joy of the season!

Beltane Paper Fairies

Fairies represent the divine order of the cosmos. They are activated by your positive thoughts, helping bring the central perfection of the thing into physical reality. Many magickal people believe that every physical item on this planet sparks from the pathway opened by deva energy. In essence, people create the thought, but it is the fairy kingdom that follows specific channels to bring the item or experience to you. The collective fairy kingdom, then, is the whole of Mother Nature which lives in, around, and through everything on this planet—including us.

These Beltane paper fairies are a type of petition magick to help you contact the totality of Mother Nature. Each fairy you design should have a specific theme, just as fairies do in nature. For example, you could make a healing fairy, an opportunity fairy, a good-luck fairy, or even an unlimited-possibilities fairy. How you decorate your fairy is only limited by your imagination! As you work on your fairies, they will gather your creative energy, so be upbeat and focused during the creative process. You can use the affirmation given in this article as you work and empower your fairy, or you can choose your own. Remember, your little fairies are a pathway to the divine!

Supplies
Cardstock
Craft glue
Decorative papers
Brads
Glitter
Ribbon

Other embellishments of your choice
Small hole punch
Craft gel (I used Liquitex Medium Matte Gel)
Dried herbs or dried flower petals (optional)

Instructions: Draw on cardstock some generic pieces to represent the fairy body, arms, legs, and wings. The fairy body (with head) should be about five inches long and the other limbs should be proportionate. Cut out all pieces. Cover cardstock pieces with decorative paper, rubber-stamp designs, or pictures cut out from magazines to make your fairy look totally unique. If you want your fairy to be a bit more durable, coat the front and back of your fairy with the decorative paper using craft gel and allow to completely dry before assembling. Punch holes in appropriate spots on the body, arms, and legs. Use small brads to affix the arms and legs to body. (The brads allow you to move the arms and legs.) Add any other embellishments you desire: ribbons, bells, beads, glitter, dried herbs, dried flowers, etc. Glue on the wings. Finally, add to the back of the fairy a spell pocket or envelope. This is where you will put your spell petition papers. (The spell pocket is optional; you can simply empower your fairy for a specific purpose. Also, your fairy doesn't have to have a face, so don't worry about drawing or finding a cool one.)

Dot your fairy with honeysuckle- or jasmine-scented oil or perfume or the fairy elixir from the recipe below. Empower your fairy over a Beltane fire! Your fairies can be hung anywhere in the home, office, or apartment. Just punch a hole in the head, insert an eyelet and string with decorative ribbon. Use them as bookmarks, carry them in the car, or glue them to a thin dowel rod to place in potted plants. When you are done with your fairies, don't throw them away. Cleanse them in moonlight or sunlight and use again. When it is time for you to part, bury your fairy on your property, giving the supplies of nature back to nature. And . . . if your fairy just . . . disappears? Her (or his) job is done. Be sure to state your gratitude to the universe!

Fairy Elixir

Medieval legend has it that one drop of fairy elixir will heal any malady, two drops will open your mind to the power of nature, and three drops will turn any idea into physical matter. What is important is not necessarily the ingredients (which were all standard fare for the times), but the belief in its power. Today, through the study of quantum physics we have learned that belief truly is the key. To make your own enchanted fairy elixir, you will need the following:

A 4-cup Pyrex (or heatproof) measuring cup
1 cup of fresh rose petals
1 cup of fresh marigolds
1 cup of fresh thyme

Instructions: Place rose petals, marigolds, and thyme in heatproof measuring cup. Fill cup to top with boiling water. Allow to cool thoroughly. Then strain, throw out spent the petals and herb, and bottle the fairy elixir. Add glitter to the elixir if you so desire. Cap, label, and empower to touch the heart of Mother Nature. Keep refrigerated. Do NOT ingest. This fairy elixir is for topical use on petitions, tools, conjuring bags, candles, etc. It will last about three weeks if kept cold.

Time needed for fairy project: Approximately 45 minutes
Time needed for fairy elixir: Approximately 15 minutes
Paper fairy cost: If you have many of the supplies, your cost will be minimal. If, however, you do not have a small hole punch (for example) or matte gel, then the cost of one fairy made exactly as indicated here might be more than you wished to spend. You can always use your imagination to cut costs, or make your fairies as a group coven project and share the cost of the tools and supplies.

Fostering Family

Lydia M. Crabtree

FOR FAMILY COVENS, THE mother priestess(es) and father priest(s) represent the May King and Queen of Beltane. The past interactions from Yule to Ostara have taught them a lesson that can be passed on to the rest of the family coven through the maypole. They have learned that as the maypole is danced, what at first appears to be chaos, change, and general ugliness is about to come to order, ruled by the love the mother priestess and father priest have found for one another. They know that as the dance of life continues, the chaos will slowly become order and a beautifully plaited weave of stability will be created.

For children, Beltane represents the time when they are two to five years old. They are no longer screaming masses of organic material taking up space and resources. They have become little persons with personalities that bloom like the May flowers that surround us during the Beltane season. They have opinions and ideas and questions—lots of questions—and they want answers.

The inquisitive nature of children at this age leads them to dream about their own future harvests, what they might like to do or be when they are all grown up. This leads family covens to begin to take financial stock of their lives. Is the financial planning enough to support college tuition and/or retirement? What about the Pagan festivals, concerts, or extracurricular activities that the growing children might be interested in? Suddenly, dance lessons, shoes, and outfits become dollar signs that some family covens struggle to pay for. Money can rule the relationship partners have with one another, and what should be a reassurance of the abundance of the natural world around us becomes a reflection of how little a family coven believes they have.

Beltane is also around the time of the year when school is about to be let out. For the family coven this means a change in scheduling and activities. This is a time of joy for the children, but can become a time of worry and financial strain as a family leaders attempt to adjust the care for their children without breaking the budget.

Beltane, more than any other time of the year, amply reflects the darkness of its opposite on the wheel of the year. Beltane sits directly across from Samhain, the time ruled by endings and fears of having enough to sustain the family coven through the time of darkness that has surrounded them. Family covens must make an extra effort to turn their back on Samhain—for it is not here yet— and turn their faces to the promise of the maypole. Family covens should look around and in nature to seek the reassurance of the God and Goddess. If together through their sacred marriage, the Divine Couple can provide enough for the entire planet at this time of year, then surely the representations of the God and Goddess in a family coven can find a way to provide for their own charges.

Activities

Part of the ritual of this time of year is to reorder the world of your family coven. Where are the family coveners going to go now that school is out? What vacations, if any, are going to be taken? Take time to get a summertime schedule together and plan for your child to participate in some summer camps alone and some with you. Take this opportunity to set limits on playing indoors and encourage playing outdoors. Plan swimming trips regularly so that your children feel that they have had some summer fun. Don't let summer be like the chaos of the beginning of the maypole. Plan summer to be the carefully plaited weave of the finished dance.

Planting

This is the time when family covens plant; however, the family coven should stretch their view of planting beyond the soil of the Earth and into the financial soil created by saving accounts, college funds, and future needs. If a family coven does not have a savings plan for emergencies, now is the time to create one. Find money to set aside, either in a bank account or an envelope in your home. Reserve this money for a time when your need is greatest and the abundance of this time has faded.

Of course, this can also mean planting seeds to watch them grow. You can paint earthenware pots to reflect something you want to harvest (a new job, conception of a baby or idea, a family vacation). Plant seeds in the pot and tend to them as they grow. The growth of the plant may give you a magical indication as to the likelihood of the harvesting of that painted image. It may also give an indication that you need to work on your green thumb. Don't be afraid to buy "started" plants instead of seeds. Sometimes it is easier to tend something that is already started than to try to spring something from scratch. Which is why, by the way, starting a savings account is so important—once started, it is easier to keep up with.

Maypole (Simple Version)

Let's just suppose you don't know any other family covens, and you have an odd number of family coveners. Don't rule out the maypole just yet!

The maypole is representative of the intertwining of persons with the seeds and ideas they want to harvest. So there is an opportunity to teach a family coven about working together.

Purchase a dowel rod and ribbon, either in red and white or your family coven's favorite colors. Be sure to use an even number of ribbons regardless of the number of family members you have. If you have three family members, you will need at least four ribbons. The more ribbons, the more difficult this magic is going to be. Take an appropriately sized earthenware pot and fill it with crafters cement, then place the dowel rod in the center. If you leave room in the pot, you can top it off with potting soil. You can decorate the pot for a nice centerpiece effect, if you wish. Attach your ribbon with wire ties and cover those up with a pole topper of your choice or a small wreath of flowers. Use tape to secure the other end of your ribbon to the edge of the pot or out farther, if you like, onto a plate or table. Now tie strings that represent the seeds your family coven wants to plant in the coming year around the dowel rod.

When you are ready, sit around your maypole and instead of dancing around the pole, work together to create a weave around the pole, the idea is exactly the same, weaving the ribbons over and under and around to create a weave on the pole. Don't be afraid to start slowly and do some trial runs before the "real thing." Have fun with it and practice working together as a family coven.

After you have finished weaving your maypole, plant a climbing vine in the pot and let the pot itself become a living topiary.

Craft a Family Coven

Since Beltane is about abundance—and nothing is more abundant than a family coven—take this time to spend some quality time with your family and make through art a reflection of your family coven. This can be achieved in several different ways.

Mosaic

Utilizing pictures from magazines, you can create a mosaic of your family coven, including the names of the members, and place it in your family coven Book of Shadows. You could even let family coveners draw something to create the mosaic, being sure to include the name and age of each covener and the date of creation.

Modeling Creation

Let each member of the family create a clay image of themselves, then combine these images onto one clay backplate. After it dries, seal the art and keep it. If you do one every year as your family coven grows and develops, then you will have a physical representation of the abundance of change your family coven goes through.

Paving Stone Creation

Together create a paving stone that incorporates the fingerprint and name of each member. Don't forget to give the year. Save these and use them as the stepping stones leading to your outdoor circle. Kits for paving stone creations can be purchased at most hobby stores.

May Day Feast

Pack up the picnic basket and raw veggies and fresh fruits and go outside to enjoy the growing sunshine. Play family games with balls, Frisbees, croquet sets, volleyball sets, or make up your own games. Go fishing together, take a campout, and go hiking. The weather should be beautiful in the day and chilly enough at night for a fire and s'mores! Donate part of your feast to the forest or land you visit, a gesture of giving back to the abundance the God and Goddess have given you.

A Beltane Ritual: Erotic Energy

Thuri Calafia

THIS RITUAL IS WRITTEN for a small group, but can be easily adapted for solitary practice, or for larger groups.

Each covener must bring a spool (10 yards) of half-inch ribbon, in the color that best represents the power of their own sexuality as well as the story of how they came to own such power (who or what influenced them, for example). For the party afterward, each covener must also bring a love- or lust-inducing herb as thank you offering for the bel-fire; bawdy songs, tales, and jokes; and something "sexy" for the potluck feast.

The altar is decorated with crafter's lace, candles, and a bouquet of spring flowers in the colors that remind the practitioners of love and lust. Also on the altar are all the regular Witch's tools. If outdoors, a fire is laid ready in the South (the wood is soaked with lighter fluid for a dramatic quick start), and two tables of candles stand opposite for people to walk between, with the bowl of herbs everyone brought all mixed together. If indoors, two tables of candles are set up, framing the South quarter of the circle, and the thank you offerings will be cast into the air outside instead of into a fire.

The circle is then cleansed, purified, charged, and cast in the usual way.

Coveners Call the Quarters

Blessed East, we welcome you
Who bring the winds of change,
Who open up our minds and hearts
And fan the sacred flames.
We seek you and we call you
To our Beltane rites tonight
That all may free their minds in love
And bring their truths to light.
Blessed be.

Blessed South, we welcome you
Who keep the sacred fire,
Who blaze within our minds and hearts
And lead us to desire.
We seek you and we call you
To loan your passion to our will
That all may feel the primal force
These Beltane rites fulfill.
Blessed be.

Blessed West, we welcome you
Whose emotion crests within,
Who frees our loving discourse,
That romance may begin.
We seek you and we call you
To our Beltane rites this eve
That all may find the courage to dare
To flow where passion leads.
Blessed be.

Blessed North, we welcome you
Who manifest desire,
Who teaches us the power held

When Earth banks passion's fire.
We seek you and we call you
To our Beltane rites tonight
That all may manifest their truth
Bringing Mystery to the light.
Blessed be.

HPS Calls the Goddess: *Foam borne Lady who rides the waves of desire, who burns true in women's hearts, who sparks the libido of women and men, we bid you come! Aphrodite, Goddess of allure, desire, and ecstasy, we welcome you this blessed spring evening. Sweet Lady of Love, whose eyes reflect the deep green sea, whose scent is of the ocean, we ask you to be here now! Come join in our celebration of all that is you. Blessed be.*

HP Calls the God: *Mighty, dark and sultry Horned One of the green and wild places, who touches our core in sweet surrender, who drives the aggression in both women and men, we bid you come! Lord Cernunnos, who gives all in the service of the Lady and the life force, who guides us to her, we welcome your presence and your blessing tonight on these rites. Gentle savage, we ask that you be here now! Come join in our celebration of passion and joy! Blessed be.*

HPS Leads the Group in a Guided Meditation: *Everyone, let's breathe together, ground and center...*

Tonight, we celebrate Beltane, and we're about to embark upon a journey.... Know that what is at the truest, deepest part of you is from the gods, and is therefore sacred. There is nothing to fear here, for it is you whom you are exploring, and only you can see what lies ahead, what lies at the core of your own inner mysteries. You are safe, therefore—safe to explore all that is a part of you, even those things you've never told anyone, even those things you've kept hidden from yourself.

And as you seek this deeper connection, this Mystery, you can see a network of interconnected threads, connecting all . . . to all. And with this visualization, you understand that there is harmony within this individuation, that we resonate with each other, with the world, and most importantly, with all of nature.

Feel the energy on the rise, then, feel the call of all things wild as this season takes hold in your heart, your body, and the deep and vast Mystery far within . . . to your core, illuminating your most sacred, fundamental life force—your passion, your sexuality, your drive, your deepest desires, and know that here, you are safe.

So just take a moment now to explore your truest self . . . it is safe . . . let your mind wander as you feel the circle around you, this bright sphere of light and love protecting you as you explore the depth of your own mysteries . . . and know that when you awaken, you'll be stronger in your convictions.

As you come up from this secret and holy place, hold on to the truths you wish to keep: the truth of yourself, of your ways, your way of loving, knowing that passion and sexuality are good, and healthy, and sacred! Emerge when you are ready, eyes open, spirit awakened, holding fast to the love of the gods you hold dear.

HP Delivers the Ritual's Message: *Here in this place between the worlds, in this sacred time, the air is charged, this circle is charged, and we ourselves, are charged with the intense and erotic energy of Beltane.*

Now, what are we gonna do with that enegy?

In ancient times, our ancestors used this energy in a pointed fertility rite, under the Beltane fires, the fires that beckon to our own inner fires. The spirits of the Lord and the Lady came down into the High King and Queen where they lay together, blessing the land and the people with fertility and abundance.

In other ancient cultures, there was a tradition called the Haloa. This tradition began in ancient Greece, and was the one day every year when women were allowed free speech . . . of course, the talk was blatantly sexual, as women by this time had begun to be robbed of their sexuality. And now, with layer upon layer of cultural baggage upon us, the yoke has fallen upon the shoulders of men as well. But tonight, perhaps we can reconnect a bit with those core beliefs, those inner callings. . . .

Imagine, if you will, a world where the fire in our hearts can blaze freely, where all are valued—woman, man, transgender, gay, straight, bisexual—where all are free to be who we are. Imagine a world where a Haloa would not even be needed, where women and men alike are free to say the things their hearts long to express, where words are neither rewards nor weapons, where censorship of the self is a more serious offense than any acknowledgment of the bright flames of passion within.

Just imagine . . . FREEDOM!

HP lights the need fire.

HPS: *Let this be our challenge then: Now, and for the rest of the evening, try to not just imagine freedom of thought and speech, but to allow that freedom to rule over these rites and the party afterward. The circle will stay up after this ritual, so we'll still be in sacred space as we party, our words and feelings and safe to express. Let's let freedom of speech rule, an orgy of thought, if you will, a dance of life, a Haloa for both women and men, and at the end of the evening, we will part friends, for all that is said here will be held in honor and respect for the courage of those who have spoken.*

HP: *For now, let's share the stories of how we became more sexually free, filling these ribbons with that energy, so we can share the energy with each other when we each take a segment of the ribbon home.*

All share stories as they hold their ribbons, imbuing them with that power. When all are finished, the ribbons are tied together at one end, and looped over a hook in the ceiling (if indoors) or tied to a low tree branch (if outdoors).

HPS: *Since there is no space at this time for a large wooden maypole, let's imagine the God's sacred shaft of light standing here, in this space, a magical maypole. As we twine these ribbons into a braid around it, let's celebrate the life force inherent in our wild side, our spiritual passion, our sexuality, for it is spring, it is Beltane, and it is time to let the veil between the worlds part, that we may touch the power and gifts of the gods yet again. And so we weave . . .*

All chant (from my book, *Dedicant: A Witch's Circle of Fire*):

We weave in love a promise left
In the Lady's keeping
Surround the Lord with passion's gift
Rewards for future reaping.

Power peaks. Energy is fired into the braided ribbons.

Cakes and Wine

HPS blesses the wine: *Wine of May, fragrant and sweet, freshest draught of love, as grail to the lance, let passion's dance fill this bowl from above. May the touch of Aphrodite and Cernunnos flow here, and remind that us we are all as one.*

HP blesses the cakes: *Cakes of May, delicate and rich, symbolic of passion's sweetest gift, may our blessings be sweet, as merry we meet, and the love of the gods merge within.*

Cakes and wine are passed around, and several minutes are allowed for folks to enjoy them.

HPS: *Let's go to our partying then. The circle is permeable, and the gods and guardians are welcome to stay—don't be surprised if they touch you! Because of the nature of this circle, people can enter and leave it at will. But before the first person leaves for the evening, we will stand again in this space to say goodbye.*

Remember that all those you interact with here tonight are aspects of the gods, children of the gods, and their messengers, and are therefore sacred beings. So mote it be with our words and our games. Blessed be.

Throughout the evening, coveners go to the need fire and give herbs to it, saying thanks to their ancestors. Some will jump the fire, and some will merely walk between the fire and the table of candles burning opposite. Later, the fire spent, some will take ashes from it, to bless children and pets with a smear of the ashes, as the ancients did.

When the time comes to say goodbye, all return to the circle. Deity and quarters are all thanked in the same spirit in which they were called, and the HP opens the circle. The HPS hands out the segments of braided ribbon from the ritual to each participant.

HPS: *I ask you all to give the same blessing to every one of your sisters and brothers here tonight: (she takes a covener's hand and looks into her eyes) I honor you, my sister. The words you said and the energy we shared here only served to make us closer. May you go forth in the world a freer woman (or man), and be blessed.*

Notes

Notes

Litha

Midsummer

Ellen Dugan

MIDSUMMER, OR LITHA, IS a celebration of light. This is a solar festival and a fire festival that marks the astrological day of the Summer Solstice. In 2010, this is June 21, when the Sun enters the sign of Cancer, the crab. The day of the Summer Solstice actually has the longest daylight hours and shortest nighttime hours of the year. At this point the Sun reaches its zenith. Magickally, we are at the climax of the Sun's power. But after the Summer Solstice, with nighttime hours slowly and inexorably increasing, the Sun's power gradually begins to decline as the dark half of the year begins. The sabbat of Midsummer is a potent and magickal date. This is a great time for fire magick, bonfires, garden witchery, herbal, and green magicks, and the best night of the year to commune with the elemental kingdom and the faeries.

The magickal correspondences for Midsummer are simple and natural ones. Colors are gold and green: gold to celebrate the might of the Sun, and green to symbolize nature and the faerie realm—all of which are at their peak of influence and magickal power. Some eclectic magickal traditions may choose a celestial theme of deep blue and golden suns and stars.

Also, just to keep things interesting, there is a watery theme to Midsummer as well. People did make journeys to sacred wells for cures at Midsummer. Wells and springs and the life-giving summer rain are just as important to the crops and your own garden as the sunshine—so keep that in mind. If you want to try something different for Midsummer, you could play up the watery summer theme. I have personally seen a "Magickal Mermaid" ocean theme successfully used for Midsummer. It was haunting, ethereal, and gorgeous. Think of lots of starfish and sand dollars cleverly arranged on an altar with iridescent seashells and blue beach glass scattered around the base of off-white candles, and crystal-clear bowls of water. Sounds pretty, doesn't it? I imagine that if you live along the ocean or coast, this would be a gorgeous Midsummer altar decoration, and a distinctive theme for any ritual performed on a beach—or in your own backyard.

Animals that are linked to Midsummer festivals tend to be those associated with the Sun, and the elements of fire and air, such as honeybees, eagles, hawks, dragonflies . . . oh and don't forget lightning bugs. Lightning bugs, or fireflies, have long been associated with the Fey and the elemental kingdom. On soft nights in June, the lightning bugs are out in force putting on quite the show for children and the young-at-heart, and for any magickally minded adults who care to watch.

Corresponding magickal plants for Midsummer include oak leaves, holly, ivy and mistletoe, roses, and all summer-garden herbs and flowers—especially the red rose, St. John's wort, meadowsweet, lavender, and yarrow. Many varieties of yarrow *Achillea* (including my favorite, a yellow-blooming variety called 'Moonshine') are in full bloom at Midsummer. Yarrow is considered to be a Wise Woman's herb and it is also an all-purpose magickal herb, so be sure to work with golden yarrow on this sabbat.

At this time of year, your spellworking themes may include asking for the blessing and assistance of the faeries as well as working green magick with the garden. Prosperity, health, and abundance spells are also appropriate, since the light is at its peak and all of nature is at its most lush, vibrant, and green.

If you like to work with the more traditional fire theme of this sabbat, consider building a small ritual fire in your outdoor fire pit or chiminea. Bonfires on Midsummer have been lit by people from all over the world, from many magickal customs, for centuries. The bonfires were classically lit at sundown on Midsummer's Eve—so set up your fire and get ready to go! If you like, you can toss a few herbs or oak leaves into the flames as an offering to the old gods.

If you are not able to have an outdoor fire safely on the Summer Solstice, light several bright-yellow candles and group them together inside of a cauldron and enjoy the effect of those flickering flames. Using sparklers as a bonfire substitute is an alternative that I started with my coven years ago. They were passed out prior to our rituals. When finished, we lit the sparklers and danced around the gardens on Midsummer's night with the lightning bugs. When the sparklers flamed out, we dropped them into a bucket of water. Hmmm, and there's that water imagery again. Just celebrate the Summer Solstice and put your own personal spin on things!

Midsummer Folklore and the Faeries

Truly there are more labels and names for this summer sabbat than you can shake a golden bough at. Everyone has an opinion and a theory about why there are so many titles for this sabbat and, of course, everyone has an argument as to why the name they choose is correct. Today, many Pagans, Wiccans, and Witches do refer to the Summer Solstice sabbat as Litha or Midsummer. The magickal group probably the most associated with this sabbat would have to be the Druids. The Druids and Neodruids of today have their own titles for the sabbats, many of which are Welsh or Old English. The contemporary Druids call this festival Alban Hefin (pronounced AL-ban HE-vin). The Welsh word *hefin* actually means "summer." This summer solstice festival may also be referred to as Mean Samhraidh (pronounced Mywan Sour-ee).

If you are wondering where the usage of the name Litha came from in more modern times, you can thank the Lord of the Rings trilogy. In J. R. R. Tolkien's classic books, he called a midsummer festival Litha, thus making the term romantically popular. But Tolkien didn't coin the term. According to tradition, the ancient Anglo-Saxons called the month of June Litha.

For myself, it has always felt correct to call this sabbat simply Midsummer. And I encourage you to go with whatever title you you like best. No matter what you call the sabbat of the Summer Solstice, it is a enchanting date in our magickal year and a phenomenal time for faery magick and ritual.

Midsummer is a most opportune time to harvest your June-blooming magickal herbs and flowers for drying, so take a good look around your magickal garden right now and see what can be gathered and stored away for use in your own future spells, enchantments, and charms. Also, keep in mind that any strongly scented flower is rumored to be a Fey favorite, so incorporate your favorite scented summer flowers in your Midsummer rituals and spells with the faeries.

One of my favorite magickal themes for Midsummer is of course faeries. Blame it on seeing the play *A Midsummer's Night Dream* when I was a teenager, many Moons ago! Faery magick and green magick are perennially popular topics and they do go well together. Where else are you going to encounter the faeries but in a Witch's magickal garden?

Faeries in the Summer Garden

Here are a few tips that you'll need to know when it comes to attracting the Fey onto your property and for working successfully with the faeries this Midsummer. How do I know that these will work? I have been using them myself for over twenty years.

Rule number one: Be respectful and polite. Oh yes indeed. A certain amount of reverence and a good dose of common sense is required when working any magick or spell with the faery realm. Be careful what you ask for because you will probably get it. I would recommend adding a tag line on the end of all your faery spells, to ensure that the magick doesn't go astray or that you don't get "pixied" (a term used to describe faery trickery). Sometimes being pixied is silly and harmless, but sometimes it is much darker. I recommend tagging on a final line to your faery spells with something like this:

With help from the friendly faeries this spell is sung,
For the good of all, this magick brings harm to none.

Finally, if you can't take faery magick seriously, don't attempt it. Trust me, you do not want a bunch of ticked-off nature spirits on your property.

Rule number two: Know the faery days and times. To increase your chances of success, work faery magick at a 'tween time. In other words a "between time" such as sunrise, noon, twilight, or midnight. These times of the day are neither one nor the other—this is the quality that links it to the faery realm. Think about it. Twilight is neither day nor night. Undefined transitory times like these are often when you will encounter the most faery activity and sense the strongest faery energy. Other 'tween times include the sabbats (especially Midsummer), the Full Moons, and solar and lunar eclipses. These are all great times to work magick with the Fey.

Rule number three: Keep the spirits of nature, the elementals, and faeries happy by caring for your gardens, and the flowers, trees, and herbs on your property to the best of your abilities. Water the plants regularly and keep them healthy. Pull the weeds and keep up the maintenance on your yard. Use your common sense and keep chemical usage to the bare minimum for ornamentals plants, shrubs, and trees. For your herbs and magickal plants—especially for culinary herbs and veggies—try your hand at organic gardening. Another perk of laying off the chemicals is you'll have more beneficial insects and pollinators such as bees and butterflies in your garden. Better yet, a healthy and natural garden is the best way to encourage the faeries to make their home on your property and to dwell happily in the garden.

Rule number four: Encourage the Fey to come to your property by making it a place filled with birds, butterflies, and bees. Hang hummingbird feeders in the garden this summer. Plant flowers and blooming shrubs that attract the butterflies and hummingbirds with nectar, and the birds with seeds and fruit. (There are many varieties of dogwood and viburnum that produce tiny berries that the song-birds will happily gobble up.)

Plant drought-tolerant native plants and readily available peren-nials such as the purple coneflower, and Brown-eyed Susans. Try planting annual sunflowers. These plants will bloom reliably all summer and into fall and, as September draws near, their cones dry up and the goldfinches and other birds land on the flower heads for a snack.

Also, put up birdfeeders in the garden. Nope, not kidding. Fill up your feeders with a high-quality songbird birdseed—a mix that includes dried fruit, safflower, and sunflower seeds will attract the largest variety of birds into the garden. Also hang a birdfeeder with thistle seeds in it. Goldfinches are sacred to the faery kingdom and thistle feeder will help to bring them into the garden. Once they find your other flowers, they'll keep coming back.

Rule number five: Container gardens, window-boxes, and hanging baskets on a porch, deck, or balcony DO count as a gar-den. When cleverly arranged and lushly planted, these become an enchanting container garden. You can easily add a small birdfeeder out there. Trust me, the nature spirits are everywhere. They are in the city, the suburbs, and the country. If you lovingly tend your mini garden in the heart of the city with magickal intention, they will find you.

Rule number six: Do bless your magickal garden and your property. Stamping your own magickal energy onto the property will only add to the atmosphere and encourage other elementals and faeries to wander through the area and see what's going on in your yard or garden. Here is a spell to do just that.

Midsummer Faery Garden Blessing

Work this spell at sunrise on Midsummer day, or pick another day and time that is equally harmonious to Faery magick (refer to rule number two). You will need only yourself and a small crystal point, which you are going to leave in the garden for the faeries. Stand outside in your garden and hold your hands up and out to your sides. Keep the crystal point in the palm of one of your hands. (You can hold the crystal in place by tucking your thumb over it.) As you cup your hands toward the sky, imagine them filling with your personal power and your desire to invite the benevolent faeries onto your property. Now repeat the spell verse:

I call the kindly faeries into my garden and yard,
If you are friendly, then you are welcome from near and far.
Bless this land, protect these herbs and flowers,
Fill them up with your magickal power.
Now hear my request as these words are spoken,
In thanks, I offer you this crystal token.
By the might of the Midsummer's Sun,
So must it be, and let it harm none.

When the spell verse is finished, turn your hands palms down over the garden and let the crystal fall where it may into the plants. Now envision the energy flowing out from your hands and into the garden. Finally, crouch down and place both hands on the ground. Ground and center yourself. If necessary, you can tuck the crystal deeper into the garden and leave it for the Fey.

Celestial Sway

Fern Feto Spring

THE SUN REACHES ITS highest peak at the Summer Solstice, blazing brightly before it sets and dies, its light slowly waning, to be reborn again during the Winter Solstice. Now we have the ability to notice and celebrate the fullness of our lives in this bright light of summer. This is the time to notice and recognize our accomplishments and successes and appreciate who we are in the world. As a sabbat honoring the peak of the Sun's brightness, we can also celebrate our own solar energy, our sense of self, our vitality, and our essence.

The Sun moves from the information-gathering sign of Gemini into the sensitive and emotional placement of Cancer on the Solstice. As the light of the Sun slowly begins to dim, we can draw on the wisdom of the Moon-ruled sign of Cancer for sustenance. Cancer is known for its deeply nurturing energy, and provides us an opportunity to nourish ourselves emotionally and creatively so that we can come to know more of who we are before we express ourselves outwardly into the world during the upcoming season of Leo.

Summer Solstice 2010 has a particularly introspective quality, further enhancing this already paradoxical time. The Sun at 0 degrees of Cancer trines the waxing Moon at 1 degree of Scorpio. With both the Sun and Moon in watery and intuitive signs, we will be touching the innermost parts of our psyches now, opening to a deep well of inspiration. Because both the Sun and the Moon are at the beginning degrees of their signs, we find ourselves at the start of this inward journey. There is an opportunity to gather intuitive and instinctive information during our travels within our psyches, mining our inner landscapes for support in navigating our life paths.

The Sun in Cancer is squaring the newly formed conjunction to Jupiter and Uranus in Aries, and in opposition to the ongoing transit of Pluto through Capricorn. Though we want to dive deep, we also need to stay aware of new developments and surprising changes taking place in the world around us. We may feel some tension within as we try to integrate our need for depth with our desire for action. This tension between our need for introspection and our parallel desire to break free of old constraints and embark on new adventures can be challenging, but it is possible to navigate. As we witness and integrate these opposing forces, we can build our strength and power, and fully embrace the uniqueness of who we are.

Mars, the planet of action and will, is in Virgo, trining Pluto in an earthy harmony. Our energy level and ability to make change happen is enhanced now, and we are able to take practical steps to patiently move forward on projects and plans. This trine should also ease some of the tension associated with the Sun and Pluto opposition, providing us an external outlet for our internal work.

Summer Solstice Ritual

If you don't already know, find out your astrological Sun sign. On Solstice Eve, plan to honor the qualities of your Sun sign, as the Sun itself reaches the peak of its light. Dress in colors that match with the element of your sign, decorate your altar with items associated with it, and try to become aware of how you live out the qualities of your particular astrological Sun. You may want to ritually release and let go of the more challenging qualities associated with this sign at your time. If you are celebrating the solstice with a bonfire, release what you want to let go of into the fire, or burn it in a cauldron.

Full Moon in Capricorn on June 26

This Full Moon picks up the where the Full Moon after Winter Solstice left off. The Moon in Capricorn opposing the Sun in Cancer reminds us of the polarity between home and family, our inner life and our role in society, and how we grow and change away from our roots into our destiny. A partial lunar eclipse also take place June 26.

This lunar occasion carries a particular intensity with it, as it takes place in almost exactly conjunct to Pluto and is one of a series of eclipses in the Cancer/Capricorn cycle. With this Pluto conjunct and with the eclipse influence, we may experience great inner changes that affect the Capricorn/Cancer areas of our lives. Eclipses can be felt at least a month before and after the actual eclipse date, and planets within 0–6 degrees of Cancer and Capricorn will be particularly affected. Pay careful attention now to how you experience Cancer/Capricorn qualities in your life, and look to see if there are changes that either have already occurred, or that need to be made in response to this eclipse energy.

Look to where the Full Moon falls in the houses of your chart for a more specific interpretation of how this lunar event will affect your life. Notice which house cusp Capricorn rules, and which one Cancer rules for an understanding of the house pairs to be activated.

Full Moon in Capricorn through the Houses

1st and 7th: Self-identity/The Other, partnerships

2nd and 8th: Personal skills and resources/Shared energies and resources

3rd and 9th: Communication and the immediate environment/ Meaning and expansion of consciousness

4th and 10th: Home, family, and deep self/Public persona, career, and destiny

5th and 11th: Self-expression, creativity, and spontaneity/Community, humanity, and the future

6th and 12th: Service to others and in the world/Service to spirit, and retreat

Mars in Virgo

After seven months in the fiery sign of Leo, Mars transitioned into earthy Virgo on June 7. This planetary shift lends a trine of support to Pluto traveling through the early degrees of the earth sign Capricorn. Mars will give Pluto a hand in making practical changes in the physical world that may take time and patience to see through. Mars in Virgo also allows us to complete tasks, organize projects, and make detailed plans for the future. We need to be careful to not let stress and anxiety affect our health now, or allow any backed-up anger turn into criticism of ourselves or others. Mars traveling through Virgo can give us the chance to revamp our approach to our bodies and our health, and also help us find new ways to attend to our day-to-day routines.

Mars in Virgo Ritual

Pick one habit that you can change or adopt that would help you support your health and well-being. This may be one of the habits that you identified during a previous Virgo planetary cycle. Light a green candle and put an image or words that symbolize your old or new habit in front of the piece of paper. As the candle burns, imagine that you now taking action and moving forward, using the energy of Mars to support you in letting go of, or embracing the habits that affect your body, mind, and spirit. Ask for the help of Mars in Virgo in providing a spark of will and energy for this change and transformation you are making.

The Old Ways

Dan Furst

THE SABBAT THAT WICCANS and Pagans now call Litha has been much better known to most people as the Summer Solstice, Midsummer, or St. John's Day. This last, Christian name is one that many celebrants of Earth spirituality are perfectly comfortable with using, as St. John the Baptist is not the only holy John or Jack who flourishes now, in the middle of the solar year. The Sun flares in his virility now, moving in a higher arc through the sky toward the heat of Lughnasadh in August. The Sun's hottest blaze of the year is marked in countless Summer Solstice feasts like the Norse *Sonnenwende*, "Sun's turning," named for the Sun's having reached his northernmost sunrise point on the horizon, from which he must now turn south to the fiery and rapid climax of summer.

The ancient peoples of Europe did not see the June solstice as the beginning of summer, but as the peak of the season, the time when the Oak King is mighty, the Horned God is potent and ready, and many people in northern climes who found the air still chilly at Beltane are apt to make this June festival the giddiest, wildest one of the year. For our ancestors, summer did not culminate in August, the season of intense heat, but in June, the month of the longest light. That's why celebrating the Sun is everything now—at least in daytime. In Russia, June 21 begins the White Nights, which last for ten days. In this and other festivals with fireworks and fire jugglers, people burn off grudges and envy, and wash them away with kvass and vodka—just as Americans blow them out with fireworks and beer bubbles on the Fourth of July.

In the old Celtic cycle of the midseason feasts, June 24 was called Midsummer Day. It marks the opposite point on the zodiac wheel to what the West now calls Christmas, December 25. The night of Midsummer Day—yes, the one on which Shakespeare's play takes place—is still celebrated in fire festivals that purify the fields to keep the crop healthy and ensure that the union of lovers, as in all the marriages that end *A Midsummer Night's Dream*, will be blessed with healthy children. Midsummer Day had to become a feast of high importance on the Christian calendar, so Roman Catholics named it the birthday of St. John the Baptist. This strategic date means St. John announces the coming Messiah exactly half a year before Jesus will be born again in winter. But the priests did not plant a big holy day on June 24 solely for liturgical reasons. For them, Midsummer Day was an issue of public order and safety. Human beings have been known to get so unacceptably happy in late June—to dance and sing and drink and embrace in so many alarming ways—that Midsummer Day may be, over the centuries, the target of more religious persecution and control than any other sabbat, even Beltane. Some of that bouncing, swooning freedom may be in the Wiccan name of the festival.

The word *Litha*—one of the two sabbats named in modern times by Aidan Kelly along with Mabon—means "mild" and "breezy," but also "navigable," because the waters around the British isles are smooth during this season, and one can sail safely again. The Venerable Bede (the only source of Litha or Eostre information we have in Old English literature) called June *Ærra* Litha and July *Æftara* Litha, meaning respectively "before" and "after" the main Litha event that was likely held in late June. The word *Litha* implies mobility, and freedom. If Yule literally means "yoke," and the time of binding the year and locking nature's vitality in winter, Litha can be said to mean "release" (it could be related to lithe) at the time when nature's vital energy is highest, and June calls everyone—humans, animals, and fairies—outdoors for some fire and fun.

Bede did not say what went on at Litha, but another church official, St. Eligius, banned the solestitia (solstice rituals), dancing, fire jumping, and "devilish chants" that were still going on in Flanders in the seventh century, and much too noisily on what was supposed to be the reverent occasion on St. John's Night.

The fire of Litha is unique among all the ritual fires in the sabbats. It doesn't just "set the watch" and repel malign spirits, but it's the only fire the people get to play with, jumping over it alone or as couples or even leaping over wheels of fire rolled down from fires built up a hill. Naturally, the people who were most expected to jump the fire together for good luck were the couples who had just been married at Dyad Moon and were already happily making babies in the season that was sacred to the Green Man, Green George, Pan, Jack o' the Green, and all the other leafy gods who were well-loved long before anyone heard of any baptists anywhere. All of these hearty, happy green lords represent the masculine fire of the year in all its majesty, at the moment when the Oak King has triumphed over his counterpart, the Holly King, who will wax in strength now toward winter as the Oak King fades.

Underneath the tree battle, though, as everyone knew, was a far deeper duality: between the male force of solar fire and the female force of lunar water at the moment when the Sun enters the water sign of Cancer, ruled by the Moon. From this moment, the male power wanes as days get shorter, and the Moon is high and splendid in her silver chariot as the month of watering comes and nights get longer. It is time. The month of the Two (Gemini), when lovers pair in union and the Great Goddess changes from Maiden to Mother, is now just past. Some of our new couples have already planted babies. It's time now for the Lady of the House to manage the tending, ripening and harvesting from the month that bears her name, June for Hera/Juno. She, and Bridhe (Brigid) and all other mother goddesses bless the new homes and hearth fires now, and are themselves honored in rites like the Athenian Day of All Heras, when mature mothers were acknowledged for their achievements in domestic, healing, and spiritual arts. Women spoke their truth on this day, and all listened.

For them, the Litha season was as much about water in the spring and the fields as it was about the Sun in the sky. Midsummer Eve and Midsummer Night, most of all when they are lit by a Full Moon, are the ideal time for women to bathe in sacred waters, collect water from healing springs to sprinkle on the crops, and gather the herbs that were said to have their strongest magic power on St. John's Night. Roses, rue, trefoil, and vervain were all prized and picked, but the plant everyone wanted was the one named for this night: St. John's wort. People wore sprigs of it to ward off dark forces, and this plant had special rules for marriage-minded young women. With this plant teacher's help, they could divine who their future lover would be. But if a barefooted girl stepped on a St. John's wort blossom at midnight on Midsummer Night, then the fairies—they're everywhere tonight—could spirit her away and leave a changeling in her place. Mothers checked that their daughters were wearing shoes before wishing them a good time on their way out for the night.

It's easy to have fun now. Like Halloween, Midsummer Night is a time when the Sidhe run around on Earth and one can see them, but this time they're the happy spirits who are playful and mischievous, not frightful and mean. So Litha has been a costume party since ancient times, full of Morris dancers, fairies and sprites, gnomes, dragons, and unicorns all united and directed by, of course, Pan and the water goddess, the Green Man, and Our Mother the Moon.

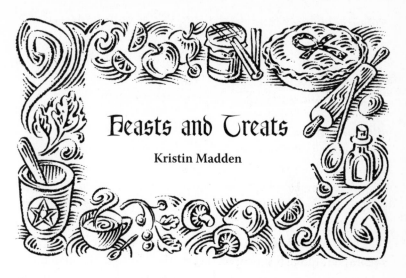

Feasts and Treats

Kristin Madden

ON THIS LONGEST DAY of the year, we celebrate the last hurrah of the light and the Midsummer revelry of fairies. Since herbs and flowers are said to reach the height of their potency at the Summer Solstice, Midsummer meals include them in beautiful combination with other foods. While Beltane brought the Divine wedding, June is often an auspicious time for mortal marriages. Fine, light fare is ideal for a solstice gathering or a handfasting celebration.

Summer Spinach Dinner Salad

Herbs and new greens combine with beautiful colors and textures in this dinner salad. Tastefully healthful, the dressing for this unique salad starts with a tincture rich in B vitamins and antioxidants. This is a lovely start to any handfasting feast or can be a light, yet hearty, summer meal in itself.

Prep Time: 2 weeks, 10 minutes
Cook Time: 5 minutes
Serves: 6–8

Tincture

4–6 garlic cloves, peeled
1 teaspoon basil
1 teaspoon oregano
½–1 cup apple cider vinegar

Salad

⅔ cup olive oil
¼ cup cashews
4 cups baby spinach
½ cup cucumber, sliced
1 cup broccoli florets
¼ red onion, chopped
½ yellow or orange bell pepper, sliced

Gently crush the garlic cloves with a fork. Use them to cover the bottom of a glass jar or clean salad dressing bottle. Add basil and oregano. Add vinegar to cover the tops of the garlic by 3 to 4 inches. Shake well. Seal the container and let it sit for 14 days, shaking occasionally.

In a small sauté pan, heat 1 tablespoon oil over medium-high heat. Add cashews and cook for 1 to 2 minutes, stirring frequently. In a blender, purée the tincture and the remaining olive oil. In a large salad bowl, combine all the vegetables and the cashews. Top with dressing and serve.

Sun-Dried Tomato and Asiago Bread

Ripe tomatoes dried in the sunshine are a perfect Summer Solstice food. Strong and sweet with all the vitamins and minerals of the original tomato, they are both tasty and healthy. Combined with smooth but tangy Asiago cheese, this solstice bread is nearly a meal. It hits the spot on a warm summer day, especially when paired with minty iced green tea.

Prep Time: 15 minutes
Cook Time: 15 minutes
Serves: 6–8

2 cups all-purpose flour
1 cup Asiago cheese, shredded
¼ cup Sun-dried tomatoes, chopped
3 teaspoons baking powder
¼ teaspoon salt
1 tablespoon basil
1 large egg
¼ cup vegetable oil
1 cup milk

Preheat oven to 400 degree F. In a large bowl, combine the flour, cheese, tomatoes, baking powder, salt, and basil. In a medium bowl, beat the egg, oil, and milk on medium speed. Fold the egg mixture into the flour mixture. Bake in a greased bread or cake pan for 15 minutes, until a knife inserted into the center comes out clean. Cool for 5 minutes before removing from pan.

Minty Iced Green Tea

Reputed to protect against cancer and heart disease, green tea has become increasingly popular in the West. By this time of year, mint is ready for picking and brings a delightful aroma to all it touches. Full of life and the revitalizing power of the Sun, mint and green tea make for a harmonious, cooling, and healthy solstice drink.

Prep Time: 5 minutes   *Cook Time:* 10 minutes
Chill Time: 2 hours   *Serves:* 10

½ cup fresh mint leaves
10 green tea teabags
10 cups boiling water
Optional: 5–8 teaspoons honey

With the back of a spoon, bruise the mint leaves and place them in the bottom of a large pitcher. Add teabags and boiling water. Steep for 10 minutes, then add honey, if desired. Allow to cool to room temperature. Remove teabags and refrigerate for at least 2 hours. Serve over ice.

Cream-Filled Apricot Suns

The Turkish people have a wonderful dessert called Kaymakli Kayisi that is reminiscent of miniature Suns. An edible solar disc, in honor of the power of the light, seems to be the perfect dessert for a Summer Solstice celebration. The yang energy of the apricots hides the yin of the cream filling, reminding us that we are about to move from the light, sowing half of the year into the darker, reaping time.

Prep Time: 2 hours, 15 minutes
Cook Time: 10 minutes
Serves: 10–12

1 pound dried apricot slices
2 cups water
½ cup sugar
1 teaspoon lemon juice
1 cup whipping cream
1 cup slivered almonds

Soak the apricots in 1 cup of warm water for at least 2 hours. In a medium saucepan, combine the other cup of water with the sugar. Bring to a boil and cook over medium-high heat until syrupy.

Add apricots and simmer for 5 minutes. Add lemon juice and cook for another minute. Remove from heat and allow to cool. Whip the cream until stiff peaks form.

Fold the almonds into the cream. Place half of the apricot slices on a plate and fill with whipped cream. Top with the other half of the apricots.

Crafty Crafts

Silver RavenWolf

Deva of the Season: Sacred Spiral
Scents/Aromas: Rose, Geranium
Energy: Balance
Visualization: In the center of a flower, visualize the item or circumstance you desire. Practice this visualization every day for twenty-one days with different flowers, beginning on Midsummer Eve. Envision yourself happily sending out and receiving the things you desire. Always end your visualization with a smile.

Affirmation: When I focus on positive energy, it spirals out and back to bring me more of the same.

🌿

"As above, so below" is the theme of Midsummer, when day and night are equal and the world falls into a magickal balance at twilight. This is the time when the fairy energy is thought to be most powerful. Any broken item in the house should be thrown out on Midsummer Eve, or removed from the premises if you plan to have it fixed. The week before Midsummer, you may wish to make needed repairs on those items you want to keep. On Midsummer Eve be sure to set out milk and honey to honor the fairies and the spark of nature within all things.

The Golden Wish Box

The golden wish box combines the power of herbs (dried bay leaves) and a paper box (like a cigar box) or wooden box to create a focus vehicle for your spellwork. Craft stores carry a variety of paper and wooden boxes in different shapes and sizes. If you are more into vintage, pick up a cigar box at a swap meet or flea market.

The box can be used for all manner of manifestation desires. You can make one box with a general theme (like this one) or make several with different themes (for example: love, money, healing, opportunity, protection). Empower your golden wish box with the fairy elixir recipe found on page 186 in the Beltane project, or use the wonderful scents of rose (which symbolizes clear navigation) and geranium (touching Spirit) in the empowerment process.

Supplies

One box
Gold spray paint (spray paint is fastest and easiest to apply, but you
    could also use gold acrylic with a brush)

Gold Glitter

The day before Midsummer, spray the box inside and out with gold spray paint. While still wet, sprinkle with gold glitter. Drying time will depend on weather conditions. When the box is completely dry, it will be ready to use. Next, write your desires or wishes on dried bay leaves with an indelible marker. Put the box and the bay leaves in a safe place until twilight on Midsummer Eve. Do not put the bay leaves in the box—keep them separate.

The Spell
Supplies:

Two golden pillar or taper candles
Dried bay leaves, sunflowers (or local flowers of your choosing),
Milk and honey
Lighter
Bonfire (optional)

At twilight, on Midsummer Eve, sprinkle bonfire logs with crushed, floral-scented incense. Light your bonfire (if you are performing this spell outdoors). Place two golden candles (one on each side of box) on your altar. Open the box. Arrange sunflowers on the altar to symbolize success and good fortune. Place the milk and honey offerings in small bowls anywhere on the altar. Put the bay leaves with your wishes written on them in front of the box.

Envision yourself encircled by white light or use the HedgeWitch circle casting as indicated in my book *HedgeWitch*. Say: "Peace with the gods, peace with nature, peace within." This statement should take you to a calm place. If it doesn't, repeat the statement until you feel at total peace within yourself. Light the golden candles, repeating the statement. Sprinkle the bay leaves with a bit of the fairy elixir or dot with rose or geranium magickal oil (or a favorite Summer Solstice/Midsummer oil). If you feel you need your spellwork to manifest quickly, sprinkle the leaves with a bit of red pepper, vervain herb, or Mars magickal oil. If you like, you can also draw the double spiral on the back of the leaves with an indelible pen.

One by one, place the wish bay leaves in the box. State what you want aloud with each leaf. Be sure you say "I want" firmly before listing each desire, followed by the affirmation listed in this article. When you have stated all your desires, imagine each leaf spiraling up to the heavens, and, in their place, each of the things you want spiraling down to rest in your hands or close enough for you to touch. When you are finished with the visualization, close the box firmly, saying, "Always a blessing. It always works." Allow the candles to burn to completion if you can. Release the circle if you cast one to begin. Be sure to thank the universe.

At any time from now to manifestation, do not try to second guess *how* you will receive what you want. Your primary concern in any spellcasting venture for manifestation is the *what*. Let the universe (Mother Nature) worry about the how. She's very good at filling your orders as long as you don't send her confusing messages or change what you want midstream. Any time you speak a desire aloud (or think it) be sure to be simple, straightforward and specific on the what—not the how. If you try to micromanage Mother Nature . . . well, she doesn't particularly care for that!

Thirty days from the day you put the bay leaves in the box, bring them out, regardless of whether you have received your desire or not. Repeat the "Peace with the gods . . . " statement along with the affirmation in this article, and burn all the leaves. If your desire has not manifested, simply repeat the statement just as you did before while you are burning the leaf. Do not allow any doubt to enter your mind. Remember to thank the universe when you are done. Place the box in the midday sun for one hour to cleanse. Your golden spell box is ready to use again for any spell you desire.

Cost of this project: about $6.00 (the brand of paint and size of box you choose will make the cost fluctuate).

Time to complete (including drying time): ½ to 1 hour, depending upon weather conditions.

Note: You can make your box far more creative than the one listed here by painting Suns, spirals, or other magickal symbols on the lid, and then adding the glitter last. Your box can be as plain or ornate as you desire.

Summer Thunder Water

The months of June and July are often excellent times to take advantage of the marvelous energy of Mother Nature through her delightfully powerful thunderstorms! Thunder water (as the Pennsylvania Dutch called it in powwows) was thought to be a primary ingredient in a variety of magick including banishing disease, removing negativity, and washing away unhappiness; but, it can also be employed in combination with success spells that require quick-moving energies or a fast change. All you need to make thunder water is a clean, glass jar; a piece of paper with the rune *tyr* on it; tape; and of course, a thunderstorm! Simply draw the rune on the paper with the arrow head pointing up. Affix with tape to jar. When the thunder begins to rumble, place the jar outside where it will receive the greatest amount of rain. Don't worry if the paper comes off the jar during the storm or if the rune washes off. In fact, it is believed the more illegible the rune after the storm, the more powerful the water. Once the storm is over, bring the jar inside, cap it, and refrigerate. This water can be used in a variety of spellwork. To activate, simply hold the jar in both hands and say, "I call up the thunder!" (And mean it.)

Cost of this project: FREE

Time to complete: Depends on length of storm

Fostering Family

Lydia M. Crabtree

IN THE LIFE CYCLE of family covens, Litha is ruled by renewal, recommitment, and balance. Here at the time when the light is the strongest, the God's power and energy are felt. However, the cool quiet evenings provided by the Goddess reminds us of the need for both.

With summer in full swing, children begin to get a little hot and bored. Now between the ages of five and eight, their development no longer reflects the sudden burst of energy of Ostara and Beltane. They have leveled off, waiting on the next stage of development. They are totally consumed by childhood and dominated by playing pretend in the complex and interesting ways their developing minds now allow.

The partner(s) in the family coven are rundown to some extent by the heat and looking for relief and renewal of emotions with each other. The heat drives the family coven to the cool and balancing waters of the mother, whether in the ocean, lake, stream, river, or pool—freshness is sought by the family coven during the Litha of their lives.

During this time of renewal, there is also anticipation. As we tend our gardens, our harvests draw near, and the Sun that has grown and developed—urging our plantings to do the same—will now diminish and wane. Growth will slow, then the harvesting of life-sustaining foods can begin . . . but not yet.

Despite the fact that Litha is the time of suspense where the Sun rises to its height, and we wait in anticipation for it to begin its turn to diminish, things are alive in the hills and woods around us, and this time of year is dominated by the special creatures known as the Fae. With them they bring not only magic but healing, for Litha is the time of the harvesting of the herbs—herbs that heal and bring sweet or bitter tastes to our mouths, just like Litha itself, filled with the bitter of heat and the sweet breath of a summer's eve.

Love renews now, because the Fae bring back the magic in full force during this time of the year with their healing herbs, musical laughter, and mischievous schemes. They bring back to us something that might have been lost during the hustle and bustle of preparing and planting—joy, magic, music, love, and a renewal of clanship.

Litha offers opportunities to reunite, recommit, and renew as a family coven in broader and more expansive ways, including the magic of the wild wood that was forbidden during the chill of Yule.

Activities

Camping

Gather the family during June and go camping. Spend the time exploring the woods, looking for the Fae at twilight and seeking the magic of being together. Make the trip as low maintenance as possible and tell stories real and made up together by the light of the stars and Moon. Don't forget the faeries are listening!

Think of this event as the direct opposite of Yule. Instead of sleeping together indoors in the family room, sleep together in a tent (or out in the open) and share that same feeling of togetherness and love.

During your outdoor explorations, find different leaves, twigs, and flowers. Bring these home and using wax paper and some heavy books, press the items over a period of ten to fifteen days. Keep the items in a warm, dry place for best results. Once the items are pressed, arrange them on a primed wooden display using decoupage glue to adhere them to the board. Allow to dry, then use a glossy or matte sealer to seal the project. Put a regular picture hanger on the back to hang up in the covenstead.

Create a Faery Home

Take an earthenware clay pot and (wearing eye protection), gently use a hammer to chip away at the top of the rim of the pot, creating a small doorway. Now utilizing paint, glue, moss, twigs, leaves, and other Earth-friendly and found materials, turn the pot over and decorate it to become a faery house. To make it especially inviting to the faeries, be sure it blends in with the surroundings in which it will be placed and has a bit of sparkle to it. A little glitter is very attractive to faeries. The interior walls can be done in a mosaic of rhinestones or small mirrors glued like decorations.

When you are finished, choose the place outdoors where you are going to put your faery home. Make sure it has some cover from direct sunlight—faeries don't like it too hot—and some protection from the weather, like rain. Create a round fire pit where you will set the pot and position the pot with the drain hole (now the chimney hole) over the pit. When you see smoke rising from the chimney hole, you will know that your faery home has become inhabited.

Don't forget to occasionally leave fresh bread, juice, sparkling wine, or cider for your faery inhabitants, remembering the words of Walter De la Mare:

Lob-Lie-By-The-Fire

Keep me a crust
Or starve I must;
Hoard me a bone
Or I am gone;
A handful of coals
Leave red for me;
Or the smoldering log
Of a wild-wood tree;

Even a kettle
To sing on the hob
Will comfort the heart
Of poor old Lob:
Then with his hairy
Hands he'll bless
Prosperous master,
And kind mistress.

Yule Count Down

Litha is exactly opposite on the wheel of the year to Yule and is the perfect time to start counting down to that magical up-all-night family fun. You will need a wooden tile, wire, drill, primer in your color choice, beads in Yule colors (red, gold, evergreen, dark yellows, silver, white), paints in Yule colors, chalk, ribbon in your color of choice, and blackboard spray paint. First, drill two holes to hold the wooden tile where you will later use the wire from which to hang the tile. Lightly sand the wooden tile and paint with primer paint. Let dry.

While drying, create a stencil of a Yule tree, you want both the negative and positive images. Carefully place your Yule tree where desired on the tile, covering up the tile with the Yule tree cut-out. Paint around the tree with paints decorating the tile with images of holly leaves, presents, and a Yule log. Allow to dry completely. If you want a high gloss finish or a matte finish, keeping the Yule tree cutout in place, spray the tile with a finishing spray. Allow to dry completely.

Use painters tape to tape the area that will be the Yule tree ensuring the rest of the tile is covered. Now use the blackboard paint to fill in the Yule tree. It may require more than one coat of paint for complete coverage. Follow the instructions on the blackboard paint can completely for best results. Allow to dry completely.

Remove the painters tape when *completely* dry and attach the chalk to the back of the board by gluing ribbon on it and tying it to the chalk. Use the beads and wire to create a decorative hanger for the tile. Calculate the days to Yule and track them near your family altar, in your kitchen, or at the main altar.

A Family-Friendly Midsummer Ritual

Ellen Dugan

THIS OUTDOORS FAERY MIDSUMMER ritual calls on the Faery Queen Aine (pronounced *Aw-nee*). According to tradition Aine was honored on Midsummer with torch lit processionals through the fields and with bonfires. I would suggest starting this ritual about thirty minutes before sundown.

For this ritual, a small bonfire is called for. So here is your opportunity to build a nice fire in your outdoor fire pit or chiminea. Make sure you cast your ritual circle large enough to encompass the fire pit so you can easily move to it during the ritual.

Also please note that this ritual works with sparklers at the end of it, in a modern twist to "torches" that were once used in Aine processionals. If sparklers are not available or fireworks are not allowed in your area, use glow sticks instead. Finally, be smart and safe. Long, unbound hair or draping sleeves can be a fire hazard. Be careful when you work this fire festival ritual. Also, if you decide to celebrate with small children be extremely careful with sparklers around the little ones. You can always give small children a neon colored glow stick to march around with, instead of a sparkler.

Items Needed

Work surface (altar) set up with illuminator candles in your choice of color and style

Fresh summer flowers from the garden, such as meadowsweet, yarrow, herbs, and roses, scattered across the altar

Cup of wine or grape juice. You may wish to have two separate cups if children are present

Plate of sugar cookies for the "cakes"

Basket of fresh herbs. (Tie the herbs into little bundles with red thread beforehand.) Suggested herbs: Rosemary, sage, mint, lavender, or yarrow

Fire pit or chiminea set up off to the side, and ready to light with kindling

Matches or a lighter

Basket full of unlit sparklers for adults and glow sticks for the children

Bucket of water for safety and to put the hot sparkler sticks in when they are finished burning

Calling the Quarters

Have everyone gather in a circle and light the bonfire. While the fire starts to catch, allow everyone a few moments to ground and center. Then start by calling the quarters. Begin in the East:

Eastern Quarter Caller: *Element of Air, we welcome you into the circle tonight. Bless us with your inspiration, motivation and the winds of positive change. Hail and welcome!* [Now have everyone turn to face the South.]

Southern Quarter Caller: *Element of Fire, we welcome you into the circle tonight. Grant us the gifts of transformation and may passion and energy burn brightly within us. Hail and welcome!* [Have everyone turn to face the West.]

Western Quarter Caller: *Element of Water, we welcome you into the circle tonight. Bless us with your gifts of intuition and cleansing.*

Wash over us with your healing energy. Hail and welcome! [Finally, everyone turns finally to face the North.]

Northern Quarter Caller: *Element of Earth, we welcome you into the circle tonight. Bless us with the powers of stability and strength. Help us to be grounded and secure as we work our magick. Hail and welcome!*

Have the group all turn toward the center, join hands, and say together.

All: *As above, now so below. The elemental powers spin and our magick holds.* [Let everyone release hands.]

Main Ritual

Priest/ess: *Now is the time of the Summer Solstice, the greatest light. The day devoted to the Faerie Queen Aine. Astronomically, this is the time of the longest daylight hours and the day of the shortest nighttime hours. For now the Sun is at its peak in the heavens, and all of nature around us is beautiful, green, and luxurious. It is a time of great joy and fertility. Yet we remember that starting tomorrow, the light begins to wane, and the dark half of the year begins.*

Speaker #1: *Now receive a gift from the good green Earth.* [Speaker picks up the basket from the altar, with the herb bundles in it and hands it to the oldest child or youngest adult present.]

Oldest Child or Youngest Adult: [Takes the basket of herbs and beginning in the east moves clockwise around the circle allowing everyone to take a single bundle of herbs. Saying as each person takes one bundle of herbs:

Blessed be, or *Happy Midsummer.*

When everyone has their herb bundle, the basket bearer returns to Speaker #1 and takes an herb for themselves and then returns the basket. Have the basket bearer return to their place in the circle.)

Priest/ess: *Now we will each take turns casting our herbs into the flames. While we do, each of us will make a silent wish. As we cast away that which no longer serves our greatest good, we do make room for something new and wonderful to blossom and flourish within our lives.*

Priest/ess leads the processional to the fire. As they cast their herbs into the flames they say:

All: *Hail the magick of Midsummer! I embrace the light within me!*

Have adults help children with this part. Everyone should file out in a line and one at a time, toss the herbs into the flames. Afterward, file back into place in the circle. Make a continuous line of filing to the fire, stopping to toss in the herbs, and then moving back to stand in place in the circle. Once everyone is back in place, all join hands and raise energy as you move clockwise around the circle.

Everyone repeats the following chant:

Everyone: *Seed, sprout, stem, leaf, bud, blossom.*

When you feel you have reached the peak of energy, stop and throw your hands to the sky. Then ground and center.

Cakes and Ale

The Priest/ess takes the wine/ juice and the plate of cookies to bless them. Then says:

I consecrate this wine and cakes in honor of the Midsummer Faerie Queen Aine. May the elemental kingdom bless us all with happiness and abundance. May Aine bring fertility to the land. May our flowers bloom lavishly and our magickal herbs become imbued with power.

All: [Take a sip, take a cookie and pass around.] *May you never hunger,* or *May you never thirst.*

Close the Quarters

Start in the North and then continue widdershins around the circle.

Northern Quarter Caller: *Element of Earth, we thank you for joining us this day. Continue to bless us with your strength as we move beyond this circle. Hail and farewell.* [Now everyone turns to face the West.]

Western Quarter Caller: *Element of Water, we thank you for joining us this day. Continue to bless us with intuition as we move beyond this circle. Hail and farewell.* [Now everyone turns to face the South.]

Southern Quarter Caller: *Element of Fire, we thank you for joining us this day. Continue to bless us with your passion as we move beyond this circle. Hail and farewell.* [Now everyone turns finally to face the East.]

Eastern Quarter Caller: *Element of Air, we thank you for joining us this day. Continue to bless us with wisdom as we move beyond this circle. Hail and farewell.*

Ritual Closing

Now have everyone turn and face the center of the circle. The Priest/ess moves to the center.

Priest/ess: *As the Sun sets on this day of the Summer Solstice, we close our ritual. And so the wheel of the year turns toward the dark half. Tonight the Earth is beautifully green and fertile. It is Midsummer's night and the nature spirits are all around us. We give thanks to Aine, of the Faeries and the nature spirits and elementals who have gathered here with us.*

All: *The Circle is open but unbroken, Merry meet, merry part, and merry meet again!*

Speaker #2 : *Let the light grow within us all.*

Speaker # 2 [Goes around the Circle with the basket and hands each person an unlit sparkler, or glow stick.] *Now as our ritual is complete, as in days of old when the people used to carry torches* *through the Midsummer fields, receive this sparkler/glow stick. May its color and light bring you enchantment, wonder and a touch of faery magick to you.*

All: *Blessed be.*

Now light up the sparklers or activate the glow sticks for the kids and have some fun.

When finished, tidy up, put the finished sparklers in a bucket of water for safety and let the Midsummer's feasting begin!

Notes on Outdoor Ritual: This family-friendly, group ritual can be easily adapted to a solitary ritual—simply change *we* to *I* and *us* to *me*. Instead of dividing up the speaking parts, say all the lines yourself.

Options for Indoor Rituals: If you are limited to working indoors, or if inclement weather does not allow, then do as suggested earlier and group several large candles together inside of a cauldron for your bonfire. This would be a practical alternative to a bonfire. Instead of tossing the herb bundles in the flames, arrange them around the outside base of the cauldron with a wish. At the end of the ritual switch out the sparklers for small candles or use the glow sticks. Happy Midsummer!

Bibliography

Conway, DJ. *Moon Magick*. Llewellyn Publications, St. Paul, MN. 1995.

Franklin, Anna. Midsummer: *Magickal Celebration of the Summer Solstice*. Llewellyn Publications, St. Paul, MN. 2002.

Hopman, Ellen Evert. *A Druid's Herbal: For the Sacred Earth Year*. Destiny Books, Rochester, VT. 1995.

Notes

Lammas

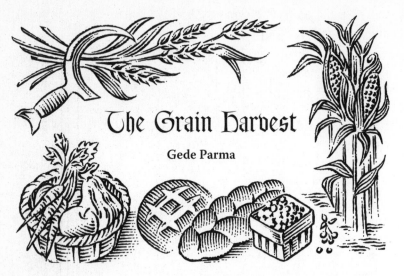

The Grain Harvest

Gede Parma

LUGHNASADH (LOO-NUS-AH), THE CELTIC fire festival of first fruits, is an ancient holy day that is now celebrated by the vast majority of Neopagans as one of the eight sabbats of the wheel of the year. Another popular name for the festival is Lammas, from the Anglo-Saxon "loaf mass," a festival of bread-baking. It is also called First Fruits, August Eve, and the Harvest Festival. Wiccans consider Lughnasadh to be the first of the three harvest festivals, the other two being Mabon (the Autumnal Equinox), and Samhain, respectively. Lughnasadh is also grouped as one of the Greater Sabbats (the Celtic-derived fire festivals), and is a crossquarter holy day. Traditionally, according to Celtic-British folklore, it is celebrated in the Northern Hemisphere on July 31 or August 1. In the Southern Hemisphere, the day is marked on January 31 or February 1.

Lughnasadh marks the time in the year when the force of summer begins to recede. The light is waning, and although the heady, scorching days still linger, there is the scent of change in the air. The Summer Solstice has been and gone and the Sun's power is now in decline. The Earth Mother gives of her bounty in the first fruits of Nature. Lughnasadh is the true beginning of the autumn season, therefore the colors that symbolize the holiday are gold, ochre-red, and deep, forest greens.

In celebrating the sabbats, attuning oneself to the cycles of nature, and honoring the tide and flow of both terrestrial and celestial currents, one discovers a rich symbolism that is called the mythos. The traditional mythos that applies to Lughnasadh is that of the sacrificed Grain God who is cut down and whose spirit enriches the food derived thereof. This is done in the name of the Mother Goddess (the Sovereign Queen) of the land and for her people. The Irish-Celtic myths speak of Lugh (loo) of the Long Arm and Taillte (tell-tay), his foster-mother, as being the patrons of this festival.

Lugh, grandson of Balor, the leader of the Fomorian tribes, son to Cian of the Tuatha Dé Danann and Ethniu, daughter of Balor, is the many-skilled "shining" solar deity of the Irish Celts. He has often been identified with Apollo of the Hellenic pantheon. In myth, Lugh's foster-mother is Taillte, a mother goddess of fertility, marriage, and competition, whose games were held annually on a cleared plain near Tara like a Celtic version of the Olympic games—the Tailltean games. It was at Lughnasadh that couples came to wed with her blessing for trial unions (a year and a day) and to ask for the gifts of fertility.

The deeper, esoteric theme of Lughnasadh is that of royal sacrifice. The king, who is married to the land (the Goddess), must give of himself and his own life force so that the people may be sustained and the harvest flourish. The old Celtic beliefs held that the king was a reflection of the land, and vice versa. Therefore if the king was ill, the land would become barren and yield no crop. If the land was unhealthy, it was the fault of the king; in order to bring back the balance of nature, the king would be ritually sacrificed. The king's blood was spilled upon the fields, and his flesh and bones were buried in the soil, so as to infuse the land with power and potency. This was the spirit of the old Grain God, the Corn King, and thus it was in this way, in the ultimate union (marriage) between God and Goddess, that the harvest was yielded and life continued as it always had.

Lughnasadh is a time to mourn the last Sun-sweet moments of summer, and also the sacrifice of the Grain God. The mantle of the Sun that once blazed on his crown has now begun to make its descent into the underworld and as the Sun enters the seed, the Goddess (the Land) rejoices and answers with golden abundance, proudly displaying her fecundity. This is a time to share with family, and to indulge in the gifts of Mother Earth, the first harvest blessings. This is the passing of summer into the season of autumn—the reaping. Therefore many Pagans today associate the tall golden stalks of corn (meaning any grain that is harvested) that wave in the fields with Lughnasadh, as well as the red poppies, which flourish this time of year in the Northern Hemisphere. In Australia, 'Wild Fire,' 'Baby Crimson,' and 'Baby Orange' (all eucalyptus trees) flower at this time, as does the famous bottlebrush tree. In the summer season, on the eastern coast especially, Australia's bush and scrubland are ravaged by wild bushfires, and in the north and south ravenous thunderstorms and cyclones shake the shores and cities. Even in the great southern land, we experience kindred mythic themes at the times of the sabbats, just through different lenses. It's easy to see how the dangers of bushfires and the threatening storms that sweep in from the sea correspond with the idea of sacrifice for a greater good and with the catalytic forces that bring destruction and devastation, only to replace them with the beauty of new, green growth as the seeds of the burnt-out trees in the bush germinate and bring rebirth to the land.

When it comes to Australian fauna at the Lughnasadh season, brolgas and magpie geese lay their eggs, estuarine crocodiles hatch, and young platypuses emerge from their burrows. Various European traditions associate lions, mice, and salmon with this festival. Stones that correspond with the energies of Lughnasadh include sunstone, amber, bloodstone, tiger's eye (gold, red, and blue—to balance the solar energy), and petrified wood.

The Corn Dolly

One of the most well-known and widely practiced customs associated with Lughnasadh is the making, blessing, and sacrificing of the corn dolly. Depending on which tradition one is aligned with, the cornhusk figurine can represent either a male or female (a god or a goddess). It is generally the last remaining stalk of grain in the fields that is "sacrificed" (made sacred) and made into the corn dolly. Because being the one whose scythe cut the last stalk of grain in the field was considered bad luck, all the harvesters would gather together and throw their tools at the stalk simultaneously so that no one would know who had actually cut down the last stalk. The general idea, however, is that the corn dolly embodies the spirit of the harvest and thus the newly created effigy will act as a talisman, ensuring the fruitful return of the harvest the following year. In many Neopagan groups, the corn dolly is burnt (sacrificed) at the Lughnasadh ritual and its ashes are scattered to ensure a good harvest the following year. Others may choose to keep the corn dolly throughout the year (garlanded and dressed appropriately) until the spring, when its seeds are scattered throughout the fields, ensuring a good crop with the next harvest.

In this day and age, we Pagans aren't exactly the farmers and herders of past centuries; the fertility of the land isn't at the forefront of our concerns anymore (even though our staple foods still require it). The idea of fertility today can mean many things. For women, it can manifest as the ability to inspire and sustain life in the womb for nine months. For a university student, it can express itself as the creativity needed to engage with assessment. Personally I relate to fertility in many aspects—the fertility of mind (intellect and thought), body (vitality and health), heart (emotions and relationships), spirit (life force and connection), and soul (being). The corn dolly today—its creation and its sacrifice—embodies the process whereby we invoke the powers of fertility, make use of them, and then disperse them. Once dispersed, they return to the primal source of their origin and ferment, enriching themselves for a future call.

To make a simple corn dolly, all you really need to do is find a piece of ripe corn (maize) and peel down the outer layers, making sure there are four separate strands—two for the arms held out either side of the cob, and two for the legs, which will dangle down beneath. Remember to tie pieces of string around the ends so that they appear as distinct hands or feet. Then all you need to do is tie in your own accessories like ribbon, bells, and other charms. Perhaps you could make a small garland of poppies or eucalyptus leaves to crown the corn dolly. At your Lughnasadh ritual, give your corn-dolly pride of place on the altar and fill it with power before separating the corncob from the husk and burying both. Place poppy flowers on the places they were buried, to signify the blood that has been spilt so that we may be nourished—the sacrifice of the Grain God. Alternatively you could leave the dolly intact, and after the ritual you could find a place in your home or garden for it and leave it there until the spring comes. By then the corn kernels should have dried out and hardened and you can scatter them in your garden or in a field to encourage the fertility of the land.

Corn dollies are not merely ancient relics that were honored as totems by our Pagan ancestors; they are also modern-day tools of power that can create focus during Lughnasadh celebrations. Corn dollies connect us with our underlying, primal nature that requires visual stimulants to encourage the childlike spirit to participate in the everyday. Remember that it is never the physical effigy itself that is the power, but the force that it represents. The effigy is the symbol that bridges this world with the Other.

Celestial Sway

Fern Feto Spring

LAMMAS BRINGS THE EARLY harvest, when we receive the first returns on our labor and take a look at what might need to be culled in
order to ensure that the final harvest on the Fall Equinox is a bountiful one. At this time, we notice the seeds planted that did not survive the summer heat, and we also recognize those that are thriving,
blossoming, and bearing fruit. During these last days of summer,
we meditate on both our hopes and our fears for the fall season.
Lammas gives us the chance to fine-tune our goals and plans for the
future, recognizing those that are truly important, and letting go of
those that hinder, rather than help.

This Lammas season is a powerful one, with the inner planets
expressing a fiery forward movement, and many of the outer planets involved in a dynamic, yet potentially explosive, relationship
with each other. The cardinal mode signs (Aries, Cancer, Libra, and
Capricorn) make a strong showing now, with six out of ten planets
representing this action-oriented astrological mode. The Sun is in
Leo, lighting up our ability to create and express ourselves. A waning Moon in Aries supports this fire-energetic combination that encourages us to act, move, do, and create. Mars, the planet of action
and movement, has just moved into relationship-oriented Libra,

making a conjunction with Saturn, opposing the Jupiter/Uranus conjunction in Aries and squaring Pluto in Capricorn. This almost grand cross influence is only missing the influence of Cancer, highlighting the need for the soothing and healing effects of water now.

With a planetary pattern of this magnitude occurring so close to the sabbat (growing exact on August 4), we are encouraged to look carefully at the meaning of the time of Lammas in light of the power of this energy. The hope, optimism, and desire to move forward and act, symbolized by the Jupiter/Uranus conjunction, are in a standoff with the need for the balance, justice, and focused calm that Mars and Saturn demand. When we add Pluto in Capricorn to square this configuration, we know that some deep, irrevocable, and long-lasting change is at hand.

Cancer is the only cardinal sign not represented here by a planet, and as always when something is noticeably missing, it makes sense to find a way to incorporate these qualities that can complete the last piece of the puzzle. Questions that can help us focus during this chaotic time include: How can we bring in the nurturing, sensitive, and intuitive flow of Cancer to help us heal wounds from the past and move forward toward the harvest time? What do we need to release or bring balance to in our personal lives and relationships in order to reap the seeds we have planted?

Spending time meditating on these questions before this powerful configuration hits exactitude August 4 will help us to navigate this time with a measure of grace and purpose.

Lammas Season Ritual

The potent energy of Lammas can be well used in some form of physical activity. A garden or plot of land is an ideal environment to work in, but failing the availability of either, you can use a cluttered area of your home as a stand-in.

Leave an offering or light a candle for Lugh, the Sun King, who is honored on Lammas. Ask him for help in culling and letting go of what is no longer needed in your life and to light the way for your hopes and dreams for the future. Choose an area to clear, either out in your garden, or a closet or room inside. Carefully weed or cull this area, thinking of the areas of your life where you also want to clear and make new room.

You may want to try a special chant that helps you release and let go as you work. When you feel complete with your labor, either plant something new outside or place a bouquet of flowers in the room you were working in, representing your hopes and dreams for the future.

Full Moon in Pisces on August 24

The Full Moon in Pisces opposing the Sun in Virgo brings us an awareness of our ability to emotionally trust and allow spirit to guide us, and our corresponding need to stay grounded in the real world. The unique way that we integrate these two qualities will be the lesson of this Full Moon, as the light of this oppositional relationship shines on our need to serve in the world of both spirit and matter. Practical expressions of spiritual inspiration will help to express the energy of this Moon.

Look to where the Full Moon falls in the houses of your chart for a more specific interpretation of how this lunar event will affect your life. Notice which house cusp Pisces rules, and also which one Virgo rules for an understanding of the house pairs to be activated.

Full Moon in Pisces through the Houses

1st and 7th: Self-identity/The Other, partnerships

2nd and 8th: Personal skills and resources/Shared energies and resources

3rd and 9th: Communication and the immediate environment/ Meaning and expansion of consciousness

4th and 10th: Home, family, and deep-self/Public persona, career, and destiny

5th and 11th: Self-expression, creativity, and spontaneity/Community, humanity, and the future

6th and 12th: Service to others and in the world/Service to spirit and retreat

New Moon in Leo on August 9

The Leo New Moon on August 9 follows on the heels of the Lammas planetary extravaganza involving Mars, Jupiter, Saturn, Uranus, and Pluto. Leo offers the opportunity to create anew in the ashes of the old. What passion or desire calls to you now? What relationships need a touch of romance and sparks in order to begin or deepen? This Leo Moon offers its gift for childlike inspiration and play to help you breathe new life into those areas of your life that are important to you. Embrace this opportunity to spontaneously express yourself, and watch your passions unfold as the month goes on.

Venus newly in Libra enhances this focus on relationships, joining Mars and Saturn in the sign of the Other. This planetary movement enhances the need to make relationships a priority now, asking you to set intentions that will help bring a newfound sense of balance and harmony to the way you interact with others.

New Moon in Leo Ritual

On the New Moon, pick one form of creative expression that you enjoy, and gather any needed materials for this form. Light an orange candle, and set an intention that as your creative energy begins to flow through you, it will affect all the parts of your life. You may want to pick one relationship or situation that you feel needs more creative, playful, or spontaneous energy. Put some symbol of this situation on your altar and as you work and play, imagine that both the Leo New Moon and your own creative flow are filling and charging this situation with fiery sparks and new energy.

The Old Ways

Dan Furst

LUGHNASADH, CELEBRATED IN THE first week of August, is the last of the four great midseason, crossquarter festivals. Long associated with the summer vegetable and early grain harvest, this is also a time to honor the Sun and ask his blessing of vitalizing warmth for the crops that grow now toward the second harvest at Mabon. The Lughnasadh celebration comes about a week after the Sun enters Leo, the sign of his rulership, so not surprisingly, Lughnasadh celebrates the kingly figure of the mature, prolific Father in his lordly abundance, and in his mastery born of experience that makes him, and other elders of his community, treasures of wisdom for the guidance of their people. This is why Lughnsasadh so often features, along with all the sprightly music for dancing and games, ceremonies of poetry, sacred music, and spiritual teaching.

The festival's name comes from the deity Lugh, who seems to have been all things to all people. Julius Caesar identified him with Mercury because of the god's practical knack for teaching many essential arts—including shoemaking—and a cleverness in commerce that naturally aroused the interest of Greeks and Romans over the centuries when Celts prospered in trading along the Rhone, the Rhine, and the Danube. Lugh is also identified with marriage—

Lughnasad may mean "give in marriage"—and with betrothals and marriage contracts for the new couples recently formed at Claiming Moon in June. The northern deep-forest peoples, such as the Teutons, celebrated fire on July 31 in the person of Loki, whose marriage to Sigyn precedes Lughnasadh in this season when both the solar king (Lugh) and the fire trickster (Loki) are honored worldwide.

While some links and shared traits between Lugh and Loki have been established, it is also possible that Lugh had in his makeup elements of a Sun god, the Prometheus who gives fire and other gifts to men, and a beneficent trickster who combines with the Goddess, strategically if not sexually, to defeat darkness and bring new life. Irish Celts recited and enacted a ritual drama of the young hero Lugh defeating the dark lord Balar the "venom-eyed," and bringing renewed plenty to the land.

Lughnasadh is said to have been instituted by Lugh himself, to honor his mother Teiltiu (also spelled Taillte). Legend has it that this goddess was so determined to help her people farm Ireland's rich soil that she worked relentlessly to clear boulders in the fields, not even resting during the blaze of summertime, so on August 1 she died of exhaustion and heat stroke. Her name comes from Tailtiu, one of the two very ancient sites—along with Carmun—that were sacred to an Earth goddess of grain and fertility, so one likely scenario of primeval Celtic mythology is that the male solar fire mates with his mother Earth now to renew the world. Whatever the mother-son relationship of Teiltiu and Lugh entails, he named the midsummer feast Teltaine in her honor. At this time, Lugh also decreed the obvious: since Father Sun is making it much too hot to work, and Mother Earth would prefer that we just let the grain grow for a while, high summer will be a time for games and contests—of poetry and singing as well as athletic sports, and for celebrating the bounty of this early summer harvest served in all its feast of color by maize, carrots, potatoes, celery, broccoli and leafy greens, and berries in black and blue and strawberry red.

The main colors of the feast, though, are always white, brown, and gold for the center and crust of the bread and the sparkling beer. For both ancient Celts and medieval Christians—who called it Lammas, meaning "loaf mass"—Lughnasadh is the Feast of New Bread, celebrated in the baking and offering of ritual bread and cakes, and the brewing of ale and beer. This time just after the first harvest was also the moment to ask Earth's blessing. When Sir Toby Belch warns Malvolio in Shakespeare's *Twelfth Night* that his piety had better not get in the way of cakes and ale, it's feasts like Lammas, with plenty of grain in both loaf and liquid form, that the old Pan-soaked knight has in mind. The German Oktoberfest—as Oktober is the eighth month—is another relic of ancient rites that rejoice in the Sun's reason in the mysteries of what grain and fire create together.

Lugh was usually imagined dressed in fire red, and he is naturally the lord of the feast's great fire. This bonfire contains the bones of the animals that our hunters have killed and will track again at Hunter's Moon. This August fire gives thanks for both bread and meat, with prayers that Lugh, the Mother Goddess, and the Horned One bless their people with abundant food and game. The Lughnasadh fire is one of those that are born each year in total darkness. All of the people douse their home fires before they come to the fire ceremony, bringing firebrands so they can carry the New Fire home to light their hearth fires again. As they have all received their light and heat from the same communal fire, they are unified now for the teamwork they will need soon for the maize harvest and the elk hunt. This sacred summer fire, one of the year's most exalted, is called the Teinne or Tan and is especially associated with the Tan Hill festival that is celebrated in the first week of August.

As Lugh is the solar deity of the Tuatha dé Danann, the Fairy people of Ireland, his feast is considered an excellent time for communication with spirit beings and with the spirits of animals. Tales of shape-shifters, tricksters, and changelings abound now, in a season considered propitious for prophecy, and for the working of white magic by figures such as Lugh himself. The son of Dagda, the "master of perfect knowledge," and Ethniu, a giant's daughter, Lugh was said to have been skilled in both the making and the use of magic ritual tools.

Prophecy is, naturally, one of the abilities that are associated with Sun gods, so it is more accurate to see Apollo, rather than Hermes/Mercury, as Lugh's counterpart. Festivals of Apollo and other lords of the Sun are held all over the Northern Hemisphere now, from Greece to Mexico—where the Aztec Sun ceremony was held August 1—to east Asia, where Japanese in their homeland and abroad build the spectacular fires of Obon every year from late July to mid-August. And there's an extra, very loud dose of summer fire at a Japanese festival that bears an astounding resemblance to the Teltaine legend.

The Kuwana Matsuri is named for the town in Mie Prefecture that hosts Japan's noisiest traditional festival. It's also called the Ishi-dori ("stone-taking") because it commemorates the day the towns-people and their friends from nearby organized a work party to do the Teiltiu-scale job of clearing the boulders from the Kuwana River, which they pulled off with classic Japanese teamwork to the beat of drums, bells, gongs, and those bronze things the size of large fry-ing pans that people today clang with wooden mallets—they may be the loudest musical instruments in the world!

The racket is tremendous at today's festival. People wear light-weight kimonos dyed with indigo and pull colorful parade floats and wagons that are draped with many drums and metal items to bop and bang—festivalgoers are welcome to jump on and play them. Much beer and cold sake will be consumed tonight, but it's improper to put it among the offerings on the floats, so men pull beer chests in little wagons between the floats. The grain here is rice, so this isn't a bread festival. But in all the other ways, it looks like Lughnasadh as usual.

Feasts and Treats

Kristin Madden

A TIME OF PEACE, games and contests, and handfastings, Lughnasadh gatherings are celebrated with fruits from the first harvest. Set with sheaves of wheat and symbolic decorations commemorating the Sun God and Earth Mother, Lammas tables often bear the bounty of the golden fields of grain through breads, cakes, and ales.

Blueberry Boxty

Taking advantage of the first of the new potatoes, boxty is a fairly traditional Irish dish at this time of year. And the blueberries commonly picked around Lammas do liven up this meal. Why not invite all your friends and family over for a joyful blueberry potato pancake breakfast?

Prep Time: 15 minutes
Cook Time: 15 minutes
Serves: 4–6

1 cup potatoes, mashed
4 tablespoons butter
2 eggs

1 cup potatoes, grated
½ cup all-purpose flour
1 teaspoon salt
¼ teaspoon pepper
¼ cup cream
¼ cup blueberries

In a large bowl, beat the mashed potatoes and 2 tablespoons of butter on low speed. Add eggs and grated potatoes and mix well. Add flour, salt, and pepper. After that, add cream and mix well. Then fold in blueberries.

In a large frying pan, heat the rest of the butter over medium-high heat. Drop 2 to 3 tablespoons of potato mixture into the pan and flatten to form pancakes. Fry until browned, flipping once. Repeat with remaining potato mixture.

Barleycorn Bannock

Another British Celtic tradition that honors the grain harvest, bannock was originally baked over a fire made from several sacred woods. It combined all of the grains from the region. A symbol representing your spiritual path, a peace sign, or simply a heart for love was often carved into the top of the bread before baking.

Prep Time: 25 minutes
Cook Time: 1 hour
Serves: 8–10

1 cup wheat flour
1 cup barley or corn flour
½ cup rolled oats
½ cup sugar
2 teaspoons baking soda
2 teaspoons baking powder
1 teaspoon each: allspice, cinnamon, cloves, nutmeg
1 teaspoon salt
½ cup butter

1½ cups buttermilk
Optional: ½ cup raisins or berries, ⅛ cup minced almonds

Preheat oven to 350 degrees F. Sift together the flours, oats, sugar, baking soda, baking powder, spices, and salt. Cut in the butter. Add buttermilk and work into a dough.

Mix in any optional ingredients you would like. Roll the dough out on a piece of parchment paper or a well-floured surface. Knead for 1 to 2 minutes and roll into a ball, or 2 balls to form 2 smaller bannocks. Cut your symbol into the top of the ball. Bake for 1 hour on a greased or parchment paper–covered cookie sheet until a knife inserted into the center comes out clean.

Pear Spice Cake

Pears are beginning to ripen around Lughnasadh and they are one of the wonderful and valued fruits of the season. This pear spice cake honors all the gifts of the land plus it is a wonderful snack for gatherings. If you prefer, serve it as a celebratory dessert after games or ritual.

Prep Time: 25 minutes   *Cook Time:* 1 hour
Chill Time: 45 minutes   *Serves:* 10–12

2 cups oat flour
1 teaspoon baking powder
1 teaspoon baking soda
½ teaspoon salt
2 teaspoons cinnamon
½ teaspoon nutmeg
⅛ teaspoon cloves
⅛ teaspoon allspice
⅔ cup butter
½ cup baker's sugar
½ cup brown sugar
2 eggs
1 cup applesauce

½ cup pear, grated
¼ cup walnuts, chopped
1 small pear, cored and sliced

Preheat oven to 350 degrees F. In a medium bowl, combine the flour, baking powder, baking soda, salt, and spices.

In a large bowl, beat the butter and sugars on medium speed. Add the eggs to the large bowl and mix well. Toss in the applesauce and grated pear to the large bowl and mix well. Then, add the flour mixture and mix well. Finally, fold in the chopped nuts.

Pour batter into a greased springform pan. Place pear slices on top of the batter. Bake for 1 hour, until a knife inserted into the center comes out clean. Cool in the pan for 15 minutes before removing the sides of the pan. Cool for another 30 minutes and remove the bottom.

Blessed Berry Lemonade

Berries are very important at this time of year and bilberries, a close relative of the North American blueberry, were particularly valued in ancient times. It is said that they were one of the offerings sent to the Irish High King as tribute at Lughnasadh. Today, we can honor their ancient value and enjoy the sweet tartness of a cooling berry-filled lemonade on a warm afternoon.

Prep Time: 10 minutes	*Cook Time:* 5 minutes
Chill Time: 2 hours	*Serves:* 8

½ cup honey
1 cup lemon juice
3 lemon chamomile tea bags
2 cups blueberries
6 cups water

In a small saucepan, dissolve the honey in lemon juice over low heat. Place tea bags in a blender and pour lemon juice over them. Allow to steep for 9 minutes. Remove tea bags and puree with blueberries and water. Refrigerate for at least 2 hours. Serve over ice.

Crafty Crafts

Silver RavenWolf

Deva of the Season: Fruition
Scents/Aromas: Sage, Lavender, Mint
Energy: Abundance
Visualization: Fill a bowl with dried lavender (stress relief), fern (prosperity), basil (melding energies), sage (cleansing), mint (mental clarity), and flower petals (the association depends on what flowers you use). Add a bit of scented herbal aromatherapy oil to heighten your visualization experience. Each evening, focus on the center of the bowl. Visualize your desires (one at a time) as you look into the bowl. Imagine each thing you desire floating up from the bowl and into your hands (or close enough to touch). Practice this visualization every day for twenty-one days beginning on the eve of Lammas. Envision yourself happily sending out and receiving the things you desire. Always end your visualization with a smile. Note: You can use fresh herbs and flowers; however, you will need to change them every few days (no longer than three, as wilting plants are thought to carry negative chi).

 Affirmation: I am grateful for the abundance of the universe and welcome this positive energy into my life.

When following Wiccan holidays, I teach my students to keep their eye on their local growing season. For example, at Lammas in South Central Pennsylvania we are at the height of garden production (not Midsummer as it may be elsewhere). Here, at Lammas, vegetables, flowers, and herbs are in full swing, filling our lives with amazing abundance. The power of this holiday can be simply stunning if you take the time to tap into it. The deva of Abundance has always been more than willing to share—we simply have to agree to accept her energy. With such high energy pulsing throughout the landscape, this is a marvelous time to make yourself, a friend, or family member a Lucky Deva Abundance Charm.

Lucky Deva Abundance Charm

There are two variations of this charm, both using two, 1 × 3-inch glass slides (like those you put under a microscope). The first uses a hinged memory frame to hold the two slides together. The second employs specialty metal craft tape and wire. Either way, you will need:

Four glass slides (I say four because the slides can easily break if you apply pressure the wrong way, or if you have made your charm too thick—a simple bounce can shatter the glass. Having extras will lower your frustration level.) You can find a distributor in your area or purchase online. **Cost:** $3.75 for package of 72 (estimated)

Dried herbs of your choosing (make sure your choices are not thick—bits of leaves work well or very thin flower petals).

Craft glue (for affixing herbs to paper) If your glass sandwich is tight enough, you may not need the glue.

Designer paper or a focus/background design drawn on paper. (Best to choose designer paper that has printing on both sides—or draw on both sides of the paper. I also used rubber stamp art on photo paper with indelible ink for one of my charms.)

Scissors

Ribbon to attach to bail, or cord or chain if you plan to use your charm as a necklace or hang it over your work desk or your altar.

Variation One Supplies:

Memory Frame made by Ranger, www.rangerink.com. These frames have a convenient soldered bail affixed to the top to easily turn your charm into a necklace. **Cost:** About $5.00

Variation Two Supplies:

Metal tape (several varieties are available). Any self-adhesive tape that creates a protective accent around the glass slide. The ¼-inch thick by 9-foot long variety, which is available through Sunday International www.sundayint.com (among other places) is enough to do several charms. Decorative craft wire and beads. Wire is wrapped around slide in a decorative way to include a bail (hanger) at the top. Glass "E" beads to string on the wire. You will need a pair of jewelry pliers for easier wire wrapping. **Cost:** $3.50 for 9 feet of tape; $3.00 for craft copper wire (or you can visit a hardware store and choose the weight of wire that you will feel comfortable working with).

Instructions: As you are making your charm, you might want to use the affirmation given for Lammas as a mantra. Trace the slide shape onto decorative paper. Cut shape out precisely. If your paper is too large, the frame will not close properly or the tape will look crumpled and bulky on edges. Best to cut a bit short on all sides— just enough to be covered by edge of frame or width of tape. Also, some designer papers may be too thick for this particular project. Note: You can even design your charm using computer art. You can reduce pics, positive words and symbols to fit in your 1×3-inch space. Think of your working area as a mini-canvas and concentrate on the overall theme you wish to promote. Sandwich your picture between the two pieces of glass, checking to make sure the image does not extend over the edges. Lift the top glass and add herb bits, glitter, or a flower petal or two. Replace glass. Align edges. Slip into memory frame or secure edges with metallic tape.

For Variation Two, string beads randomly onto wire. Wrap wire in decorative pattern around sandwiched slide. You really only need enough to secure the bail you create at the top to finish, but if you like, you can certainly get wild and crazy with your wire art! To complete the project, string bail with ribbon or a chain. Note: If you desire to make a mini-collage, Variation Two may work better as Variation One does not leave much leeway on paper thickness. Although Variation Two takes a bit more time due to the tape, the charm may not crack as easily and may be preferable if you are turning your piece into jewelry art.

Bless your Lucky Deva Abundance Charm on Lammas Eve. Use the affirmation, if you like, as part of your blessing ceremony. You can also find blessing ideas and herbal correspondences in my book *HedgeWitch*!

Cost of this project: $3.50 (estimated) per charm. You may wish to make several as gifts, for resale, or as a group project. Because the glass breaks easily during construction, this project is not recommended for children under thirteen.

Time to complete: To assemble: 10 minutes. To design: Entirely up to you.

Fostering Family

Lydia M. Crabtree

IN YOUR LIFE, AS you have prepared, planted, and muddled through, have you ever reached the point where you can see the beginning of the completion? Where you can look forward through the mists of the future and begin to know that you will harvest what you planned? Have you wondered when the harvest really begins—will it be enough? Then you have experienced one of the spiritual lessons Lughnasadh brings for family covens.

Summer is winding down and the faint smell of fall is drifting into the air. Berries are out everywhere—blackberries, blueberries, raspberries, cranberries—and a tree here and there is beginning to lighten its green and shed any flowers that might have hung on through the heat of July. These sweet tastes are the first of the harvests family covens are about to experience.

Further, for family coven, Lughnasadh marks the most important harvest—the harvest of grain, wheat, and barley. This essential harvest forms the base diet most ancient Pagans would use to sustain themselves through the long winter. Corn would feed the cattle, cattle would feed the clan. This raises the second lesson of Lughnasadh—what is the most important harvest for a family coven? Each family coven must answer this question for themselves, and

Lughnasadh is the time to question if there is enough to sustain the group through the darkest and scarcest of winters.

Lugh is honored and revered with his adoptive mother Taillte, which makes the relationships between family coveners another spiritual lesson of Lughnasadh. Lugh wanted to honor his adoptive mother for her sacrifices and lessons, so he organized a gathering in which skills were tested—the first "county fair"—in honor of a mother who was not required by birth to tend to and love Lugh, yet did anyway.

The time of Lughnasadh represents the time for children of ages between nine and tween, a time when they first begin to reap and test the lessons of childhood in a world increasing with pressure and requirement. The word "harvest" may mean little to these children until the time of Lughnasadh is upon them, then they learn that harvest can be translated as "reward from work."

For partner(s), Lughnasadh marks the time in their lives when they first see benefit from years of struggle and learning. Many in the Lughnasadh of their lives no longer feel like they might be an adult someday. Suddenly, they are an adult today, a startling harvest in itself.

Lughnasadh for the family coven is the cautious entry into abundance. The wheat, corn, barley, and grain have come to fruition; however, other things need to be harvested to ensure a full belly, spiritually and physically, during the coming death that is winter.

Family covens then use Lughnasadh to celebrate what they have in the current harvest—to live in the moment. Do not put too much hope or stock in the future harvests to come and do not look back to the joy and carefree days of Litha and Beltane. Practice the art of presence. As a common ritual saying goes, "Be here now!"

Activities

Make Bread

What better way to celebrate the harvest of grain than to make bread? Once the dough is made, roll it out and use cookie cutters to identify the things that are finally coming to harvest in your life. This is an excellent time for family covens to take a lesson in symbols, their general meanings, and the meanings that have been developed by each family covener.

Family Game-Off

Starting on Lughnasadh, begin a Family Game-Off in honor of Taillte. If you have enough family coveners, divide into two teams and select a series of games to play over a period of two to four weeks. Keep score of what team wins the most games. Vary the games in skill level so that all family coveners have an opportunity to win. If you don't have enough family coveners to divide into teams, play individually. The person who wins should be given a reward—either a cash reward, the temporary relief from assigned chores, or some other special gift, like a pentacle necklace bought specifically as a prize.

Find Outdoor Projects to Complete

Lughnasadh sits opposite on the wheel to Imbolc, which was all about cleansing and clearing inside the covenstead. Take this time to cleanse, clear, and beautify the outside of your covenstead. Weed the garden beds, mend fences, paint shingles, fix leaky roofs, and complete any other odd outdoor job that has been ignored long enough.

Play, Sing – Bard

All skills were part of the scope of Lugh's celebrations, including play-acting, music, and storytelling—skills that the Druids would find in their Bards. Find a myth of your family's favorite pantheon, then create a play around that myth. You can do this in your family room without an audience or invite other family covens to celebrate Lughnasadh and view the play that you have created.

If acting isn't your family's cup of tea, then now is the perfect time to pick up and learn to play an instrument or sing. Pretty soon you could be the next traveling Pagan family band.

Celebrate Lughnasadh

Gede Parma

THIS RITUAL IS APPROPRIATE for both solitaries and groups and can be tailored to suit most European-derived Pagan traditions. Ideally the ritual should be held in a farmer's field or at the least outdoors, with the Sun shining brightly down upon the gathering.

You will need the following items for the ritual:

On the altar—one white taper candle and candleholder, frankincense incense (stick-variety), a dish of rock salt, a chalice filled with spring water, and a basket filled with ready-baked bread covered with grain stalks covered with poppy flowers (or bottlebrush flowers if in Australia).

To Ground and Center

Before embarking on any magickal or ritualistic work, it is important to clear the mind of extraneous thoughts and to find one's center. This allows for the steady flow of universal life force (that thing I like to call "Magick") through the body. In doing this, one safeguards against energy-depletion during or after the work/rite and ensures that the entirety of his/her focus is on the moment of present being. It is also a good idea to connect energetically with the energies of the dark, moist Earth and the limitless, overarching sky.

This is the act of grounding and aligning and brings one's awareness to the All that is Nature and the Cosmos.

The following guided meditation can be read aloud for a group Lughnasadh ritual. If you are solitary, either memorize the words so that you can follow the imagery as you go along, or record it onto an audio device and play it back to yourself. All participants should be standing for this meditation, and if working in a group, it is a good idea to hold hands to emphasize the connection of all things.

Take a deep breath in, and as you do, see and feel white light come down from the heavens. It enters your crown, traveling down and enlivening every cell in your body. Your muscles and joints relax. When you exhale, allow all stress, fear, and anxiety to leave your body. Let it go. Release it. Remember to always breathe deeply, allowing your abdomen to expand and your chest to rise and fall naturally. Feel the white light as it cleanses you and brings you to wholeness. Focus only on your breath and the light and come to your center.

Now bring your focus to your feet and see and feel ancient roots stretch long and deep into the Mother. Feel as they pass through layers of soil and compacted dirt; through veins of minerals and gold and through pockets of chthonic water. Your roots reach the molten core of the Mother and there they stop. They draw up the fire from the beating heart of the Earth and it travels through your roots into your body, which is the trunk of an ancient tree. You feel as the serpentine force settles within your being and then you bring your awareness to your crown. You feel and see strong branches emerge from your crown, and you feel the sensation of growing taller. Your consciousness is placed high in the sky-realms, and higher it climbs, through the stars and into black, limitless space. There your branches receive the white light of this realm and it travels like quicksilver down into your body, which is the trunk of an ancient tree. There the white light meets with the fire of the Earth and they dance and become one in spirit and ecstasy. You are now grounded and centered and ready for magick. Blessed be.

To Affirm the Space

In many Neopagan traditions, a circle is cast to delineate this earthly realm from the ethereal realms of the gods. A cast and consecrated circle is a place between the worlds and in all the worlds. It is also a psychic container for the power that is raised within it, until it is to be released for its intended purpose. However, many Pagans today do not find the practice of circle-casting to be for them or are otherwise engaging with spiritual traditions that are not Wiccan-based or influenced. Therefore, this rite to "Affirm the Space" is a "Pagan-ecumenical" method of doing just that.

Light the altar candle and the frankincense incense from the flame and walk in a sunwise direction (clockwise in the Northern Hemisphere, counterclockwise in the Southern Hemisphere) once around the altar, fanning the smoke and saying:

Here I walk by Air and Fire and thus do I call upon their blessings. May the serenity and swiftness of Air imbue our (my) mind(s) with clarity and may the warmth and radiance of Fire kindle the heart-flame of Life. Blessings by the Air and the Fire!

Now, back at the altar, sprinkle the rock salt into the chalice of spring water and stir three times sunwise with the forefinger of your power hand, charging it with cleansing light. Walk once around the altar, asperging with the water and salt, saying:

Here I walk by Water and Earth and thus do I call upon their blessings. May the fluidity and depth of Water open the floodgates of love and may the solidarity and resilience of earth keep and guard us (me). Blessings by the Water and the Earth!

It is now time to acknowledge the shamanic Pagan cosmology of "the Middleworld, the Upperworld, and the Underworld" or as the Celts call it—the Land, the Sky, and the Sea. This practice helps align you with the "center" of the universe.

Beginning with the Land/Middleworld, crouch down and place both hands (groups may assign three people to acknowledge the three realms) on the ground, saying:

By the Land . . .

Next, stand and with both hands and head raised to the sky, say:

By the Sky . . .

And now to acknowledge the Sea/Underworld, cup your hands before you as if cupping water and say:

By the Sea . . .

To seal the invocation, say:

By the ancient trinity, Blessed be.

The space is now affirmed and the invocation/acknowledgement of the Divine may begin.

To Acknowledge the Divine

Now is the time for you to call upon and acknowledge the presence of the Divine as it is related to the sabbat of Lughnasadh in whichever way it expresses itself to you or your group.

The following invocation should be spoken aloud (in both solitary and group rites) and addresses the forces of the Grain God/Corn King and the Sovereign Queen/Mother Goddess of the Land.

We (I) call to you, O great Grain God, that you may bless our/my Lughnasadh rite. You are the spirit of the harvest and you have fallen only to rise again in the bread of this season that we (I) are/am nourished by. You are the golden hue of the afternoon Sun as it moves farther into the West. Blessings to thee O dying God who gives us/me life.

We/I call to you, O Sovereign Queen, that you may bless our (my) Lughnasadh rite. You are the spirit of the land and you are eternal in your grace and presence. It is your earthly labor that brings the harvest and it is you that we are (I am) nourished by. You are the golden fields as they wave in the afternoon breeze. Blessings to thee Great Mother of the Land who keeps us (me).

Gesture to the altar and to the offerings of harvest you have collected in the names of the gods.

To State the Purpose

Now is the time to state the purpose, to define the intent of the ritual and to direct one's awareness to the celebration at hand. The following words can be used to state the purpose.

> *Lughnasadh, your light grows dim*
> *Across the fields of golden grain,*
> *Lughnasadh, we (I) call you here*
> *To see the year-king rise again.*
> *For harvest's come,*
> *The year has turned,*
> *And we (I) thresh grain upon the floor;*
> *The Mother's Earth is rich and brown,*
> *The first fruits of her labor show.*

To Enact the Mythos

In celebrating any sabbat, it is important to engage with the mythos or mythic themes/cycles of the festival and what they represent. This can be done quite effectively through mummery (dramatic enactment via characters and costume) or drawing down (ritual "possession" by the gods). In this ritual the ancient practice of mummery will be invoked.

If you are a solitary then you may visualize the following mythic drama; in a group setting, different people may personify each of the forces/deities that are involved. Each person should wear an appropriate costume to aid in the mummery. For example the Grain God could wear a robe of deep brown and gold and wear a garland of poppy flowers and wheat on his head.

The Sovereign Queen, standing in front of the altar and holding a basket of bread covered in poppy flowers and stalks of grain, speaks:

I am the Great Mother of the Land. You call me Goddess. I am she who is life and nourishment; however, I am also the barren, withholding crone of the wintertime. I walk among you all wearing the rags of the gnarled woman begging and asking for alms. Those whose compassion turns their hearts to me, so does my heart turn to them; and as good always answers good thus my gifts are offered up from my rich, brown womb. Take of the Earth's bounty and be blessed my children. This is my charge. Be kind to one another and to your Mother, the Earth, who is Sovereign.

The Grain God kneels before the Sovereign Queen and rises to take the basket from her, removing the poppy flowers (letting them fall to the ground). He turns to the gathering and speaks:

I am the Grain God. You call me Corn King and Dying Lord of the Sun. I am he who is the sacrifice that brings in the harvest. I am the Lord of the Dance of Life who rises and falls in rhythm with the cycles of the Earth. Though I die, I live on in those who remember me and nurture that memory until once more I am reborn with the Sun. These are the gifts the Great Mother has given me to give to you. Cut me down and take of her bounty. Be blessed children of the Old Ones, and be good to one another, and to our Mother, the Earth, who is Sovereign.

The harvester walks forth to kneel before the Grain God and rises, with scythe in hand, to cut him down and take up the basket of first fruits, removing the stalks of grain and letting them fall to the ground. The harvester speaks:

I am he who brings the scythe of pale death to the Grain God, the spirit of the harvest in the golden fields. It is my duty to my people and to the Great Mother to aid in bringing forth the bounty of the Earth to the mouths of those who yearn to be nourished. I pass on the messages of the Old Ones who say, "take of these gifts and be blessed."

Hold dear to your heart the memory of the Year King who ever returns and the Great Mother who, though her face changes, is constant and all-loving. Be good to one another, and to our Mother, the Earth, who is Sovereign.

The harvester then walks around the circle of those gathered and each person takes a piece of the bread to eat, remembering to leave some to sprinkle as an offering to the Goddess.

To Raise and Release the Power

Now it is time to raise power to aid the harvest and send blessings to the fields and the farmers for their good and necessary work.

If you are solitary, stand in the center of your space and take a power stance—feet spread evenly apart, with shoulders in line with your hips, standing straight and tall. Return to and affirm your center and then begin to clap a beat steadily with both hands as you focus on the harvest of the land that nourishes and sustains you, your friends, and your family. Feel the sovereignty and power of the land beneath you; it is your foundation, without it you would not, could not, be. As you clap, remember to always breathe, and with each breath in, the power surges. Gradually as you quicken the pace, the energy level will climb until you feel the urge to throw your arms up and release the power to bless the fields and the farmers who work in them. After releasing the power, you should crouch down and place your head to the Earth to ground the excess energy and to return your awareness to the mundane.

In a group setting, the same idea can be utilized, however the participants should join hands and raise the power by moving in a sunwise direction and walking the grapevine. To do this, the first foot to move (the right for those in the Southern Hemisphere and the left foot for those in the North) will step to the side and then the second foot will step over the placement of the first foot. The first foot will then step to the side again and the second foot will proceed to step behind the placement of the first foot, and so on. Gradually quicken the pace until the time is intuited to release the power.

The following chant can be used to aid the power:

Deep below we (I) call ye up
Power of Earth, raise the Power,
Twist and turn and fuel our (my) spell
In this time and in this hour.

When celebrating in a group it is good to ground by hugging! The positive power of embracing cannot be beaten and the emphasis of physical connection is a beautiful thing.

To Seal the Ritual

A closing statement should be read aloud so that the intent is sealed and the rite is properly closed. The following is ideal:

We (I) have come to the end of our (my) celebrations, though Life in its myriad forms and expressions is constant in its revelry. The sabbat/festival of Lughnasadh is here and as the wheel turns, so does the Earth reflect the inner changes of the Mythos that occur on a deeper level in the primordial unconscious. Blessed be the Sovereign Queen who is the holy Mother of Life. Blessed be the Grain God, who has fallen to bring forth the harvest. Blessed be the harvester, he who wields the scythe, for he teaches us that what we sow we reap. Blessings to the season of Lughnasadh!

To Disperse the Space

The three worlds are blessed either silently or aloud, as are the elements who helped in the affirming of the space. The altar candle is snuffed out and the space is then declared open. Now the feasting and merriment may begin.

If the ritual was a group celebration, perhaps some competitive sports could be organized to commemorate the Tailltean games held in honor of Lugh's foster-mother near Tara in ancient Eire. Alternatively, a game of tug-of-war would work wonders! Prizes could also be arranged for winning teams or participants.

Blessed Lughnasadh!

Notes

Mabon

Summer's End

Oberon Zell-Ravenheart

Autumn Equinox is the point of the year opposite the Vernal or Spring Equinox, when the path of the Sun in the sky crosses the plane of the ecliptic. Just as on Ostara, the day and night are of equal length, and light and dark are in balance. This is the day of the year when the Lord of Light is defeated by his twin and alter ego, the Dark Lord. The Autumn Equinox is considered the only day of the whole year when light is vulnerable and it is possible to defeat him. Because of leap year, the exact date of the Autumnal Equinox fluctuates each calendar year between September 20 and 23, but most traditions celebrate it on September 21.

Also known as Harvest Home, Kirn Feast, Mell Day, Ingathering, and Harvest's Height, this is the second of the three Celtic harvest festivals, between Lughnasadh and Samhain. In medieval Europe, the Autumn Equinox marked the middle of the harvest season, when farming communities began the intensive preparations against the looming barren months of winter. This season was known as the Harvesting or Reaping Tide, a time of inward turning as well as celebration and gratitude for a bountiful harvest

In England, the traditional name for this feast of thanksgiving is Harvest Home, a feast given by farmers for their workers. But the Plymouth Pilgrims had a late harvest, so America's Thanksgiving is celebrated much later. In Ireland, Michaelmas (around September 29) was the time of the goose harvest and apple picking for making cider. In Latvia, one of the last European holdouts of the old Paganism, this harvest festival is called *Vela Laiks*, the "Time of the Dead."

The last stand of grain in the field marked the end of the harvest, and the cutting of it was attended with some ceremony; the way the last sheaf was cut was held by many to affect the destiny of its cutter. Small ornamental twists or knots of plaited straw, called "harvest knots," were made and worn as a sign that the harvest was complete. The most universal tradition throughout Europe was the corn dolly made from the final sheaf. Called in Ireland the *Cailleach* or "hag," this was prominently displayed in the house, replacing the one from the previous year.

Sometimes the vegetation spirit was represented by a large, man-like wickerwork figure. It was believed that the spirit of the grain resided in this effigy, and it was dressed in good clothes, addressed by name, and carried from the field, where it was usually burned as a mock sacrifice, amidst much rejoicing, similar to the modern "Burning Man" festival held each year at this time in the Nevada desert.

Mabon is the Welsh God of the Harvest, *Mabon ap Modron*, meaning "divine son of the divine mother." As told in the *Mabinogion*, Mabon was stolen from his mother three nights after his birth, and dwelt in Annwfn (the Welsh underworld) until he was rescued by Culhwch. Because of his time in the underworld, Mabon stayed a young man forever, and he was equated with the Roman Apollo. He is the Green Man whose blood is an intoxicating beverage. Other examples of this archetype are Dionysos (wine), Osiris (beer), and John Barleycorn (whiskey). Indeed, the traditional song, "John Barleycorn," epitomizes the spirit of the season.

The name of Mabon was given to the Autumn Equinox sabbat by Aidan Kelly around 1970, and it has become widely adopted throughout the Pagan community. However, this name does not appear to have been historically attributed to any festival.

This festival commemorates the ritual sacrifice of the God and his descent into the underworld, and the brewers' art that produces the sacrament of this season. In the California Wine Country, where I live, this is the festival of the grape harvest, often dedicated to Bacchus. Whiskey and brandy, as the spirit of the barley, is also readily consumed during this festival! The bay tree is sacred to Mabon, as its magical action is preservation, a time-honored harvest-tide occupation.

It is important to note that the Full Moon closest to the Autumn Equinox is the traditional time of the ancient Greek Eleusinian Mysteries, in which Persephone, the Flower Maid, is abducted by Hades, lord of the underworld, to reign as his queen for the next six months, until she returns to the surface at the Vernal Equinox. Versions of these mysteries have been re-created and conducted annually for decades by a number of modern Pagan traditions—including the Church of All Worlds.

Celebrating Mabon

Most of us enjoy this time of year for the beauty of the fall colors and the energy felt in the cool air, which seems to put an added spring in our steps. It can be great fun hunting for just the right harvest symbols. Mabon is a good time to cut new wands and staves of willow. Make a little corn dolly for your garden altar from an ear of corn by twisting and binding the shucks into a body, legs, and arms (you can make the head by breaking off part of the cob, leaving a short piece attached to the rest). Bring it inside after Mabon and hang it up in your kitchen for the rest of the year.

Your altar is a great place for fruits such as squash and apples set in an old wooden bowl. You will also want to add pomegranates, in honor of Persephone, who is bound to the underworld half of the year for eating three pomegranate seeds. Decorate your altar with orange, brown, and yellow altar cloths and candles. A cornucopia (horn of plenty) is the perfect item to serve as a centerpiece on table and altar. Arrange colorful autumn leaves and small gourds, nuts, apples, dried corn, seeds, acorns, pine cones, etc. You might want to add a shallow bowl of water, because autumn is associated with water, emotions, and relationships. If the inside is black, this same bowl of water can later be used for scrying at Samhain.

You might throw a "going away party" for the Green Man, and charge seeds for next year's crop. If you use those little packets of seeds from a garden store, everyone can then take them home to plant in the spring. Prepare a thanksgiving harvest feast for your loved ones—or at least make some special food to share. The vegetables and fruits should be in season in your area, such as corn, squashes, beans, and berries. Give thanks at this time for all that you have harvested in the past year. Remember, "An attitude of gratitude is the guidance of the Gaia-dance!"

A favorite ritual in our circle has been to write on a piece of paper the things you have planted in your life this year that you are now harvesting—or wish to. Read your list aloud, saying, "For all these things, I give thanks." Then burn the paper in a cauldron. I first performed this little rite in our nest at Mabon of 1973, and the next day I met my eternal soul mate, Morning Glory!

We did many variations of this simple Mabon Thanksgiving over a couple of decades, but in 1990, our community began an entirely new seasonal cycle that subsumed both Mabon and Ostara into the cycle of the Greek Eleusinian Mysteries. Morning Glory and I conceived and created these rituals, and over the past eighteen years, our Eleusinian Cycle has expanded from an initial weekend Mystery rite at each equinox into an eighteen-month series of special events, dinners, enactments, and performances—all based on what was done in ancient Greece, but updated and modernized as if the entire cycle had continued to evolve uninterrupted since 395 AD, when Alaric the Goth demolished Demeter's temple at Eleusis, and these annual rites came to an end after 1,600 years of continuous celebration.

When we set out to re-create the Mysteries of Eleusis, we began with the Homeric Hymn to Demeter, which provides the text for the exoterica, or outer mysteries that everyone knew. The hymn (which we enact as an elaborate series of costumed performances from late afternoon all through the Full Moon night at various appropriate sites along the trails, reservoir, and caves of Pinnacles National Monument near Gilroy, California) tells how the Flower-Maiden Koré, daughter of the Grain-Mother Demeter, is abducted into the underworld by Hadés, grim Lord of Erebos, land of the dead.

In her grief, Demeter is inconsolable, and roams the world searching for her missing child. During all this time, she abandons her life-giving duties. Crops die, animals cease to bear young, and the land grows ever colder and darker. The other gods, headed by Sky Father Zeus, fear that humanity will die out, and with them, the sacrifices and belief that sustain the gods. They appeal to Hadés to relinquish Koré, but he refuses. Finally, Demeter comes as an old woman to the city of Eleusis, where she is taken in by its queen, Metaniera, to serve as a nurse to her new baby. She reveals herself to the kind woman and her daughters and commands that her temple be built below the town. There, the goddess installs herself, but continues to withhold her bounty until her daughter (whom she now knows has been stolen by her brother Hadés) is returned to her.

And this is where the esoterica, or inner mysteries, begin. The gods have failed to convince Hadés to give up the maid he has taken, and in desperation, the task falls to the mortal pilgrims, who must descend one at a time down the long, dark, winding stair to confront the Lord of Death, and try to persuade him to release Koré.

But things turn out not to be as they seemed, and deep within the boulder caves at the heart of the San Andreas Fault, the pilgrims learn things they never could have imagined. . . . They emerge as Mystae—Initiates of the Mysteries.

And every Autumn Equinox since 1990, a dozen prior Mystae have been conducting another twenty or so pilgrims through these ancient mysteries.

About the HOME Tradition

If celebrating Mabon as part of an elaborate eighteen-month cycle sounds a bit more involved than most covens, it's because our group is not a typical coven. We are a community. I'd like to take this opportunity to explain how we evolved.

In 1962, Lance Christie and I co-founded a Neopagan religion called the Church of All Worlds, which was formally incorporated in Missouri in March 1968. Two years later, I was introduced to modern Witchcraft and ceremonial magick, receiving initiation in April 1971.

My publication of *Green Egg* magazine, and early articles on what later became known at "The Gaia Thesis," brought me into national attention, and I started getting invitations to travel and lecture. I was presenting such talks at Llewellyn's Third Gnostic Aquarian Festival in Minneapolis, Minnesota, over Autumn Equinox 1973, when I met my lifemate, Morning Glory. Our wedding at Llewellyn's Spring Witchmoot the following Easter was officiated by CAW High Priestess Carolyn Clark and ADF ArchDruid Isaac Bonewits. As one of the first Pagan handfastings published (in *Green Egg*), it became widely adopted as a model throughout the Pagan community.

Morning Glory and I headed to the West Coast. In the autumn of 1976 we arrived in Eugene, Oregon, where we met fellow Witch Anna Korn. The three of us organized all our respective training into a coherent amalgam, and formed the Coven of Ithil Duath to practice it. Our first Mabon sabbat featured a ritual based on a pantomime of "John Barleycorn" to the music and lyrics of Steeleye Span.

In July of 1977, Morning Glory and I moved to Coeden Brith, a 220-acre parcel owned by Alison Harlow on the 5,600-acre Hippie homesteading community called Greenfield Ranch near Ukiah, NorCalifia. Coeden Brith ("speckled forest" in Welsh) was adjacent to the 55-acre parcel recently acquired by Gwydion, which he called Annwfn (the Welsh underworld). The Holy Order of Mother Earth (HOME) was conceived there, as a magickal monastic order of stewardship and ritual, and was chartered as a subsidiary organization of the Church of All Worlds on September 21 (Mabon), 1978.

Other Pagan residents of Greenfield Ranch when Morning Glory and I moved in included Anodea Judith, Sequoia, and Molly. Shortly thereafter, Eldri Littlewolf came up from Berkeley. When my old friend Orion decided to leave St. Louis and join us, and Anna Korn moved in with Gwydion, we had a foundation for a solid working magickal group composed of people from several distinctly different traditions—including Faerie Triad, Dianic, Strega, Ozark "Druidic" Witchcraft, and CAW.

Due to Gwydion's influence, HOME developed as a "Bardic" tradition—with ritual elements composed as poetry and song more than prose. Also, because of the incredible creativity among such a diverse group, we never did the same ritual twice—especially for sabbats. Each year, someone else would step up and offer their own original ritual creation, and our Book of Lights and Shadows became an entire file cabinet! Indeed, creating an original ritual for a major sabbat became a "final exam" for our clergy training.

As other members of the Greenfield Ranch community came to join our HOME circles, we grew beyond any coven and became a community. We planted trees and gardens; raised goats, deer, and Unicorns; sang our songs; and told our stories around the campfire. Babies were born on the land, blessed in ritual, and raised up in Circle, assimilating our customs and traditions into each new generation. In our growing magickal community, we actually lived the semi-mythical lives of our ancient Pagan tribal forebears.

Although Morning Glory and I moved from Coeden Brith in 1985, our HOME tradition retained the unifying designation for the rites and rituals we had developed during those years on the land, and which we have continued to practice, refine, and expand upon to the present day.

Note: The author acknowledges Ruth Barrett, She' D'Montford, Janet & Stewart Farrar, Marian Green, and Shekhinah Mountainwater, whose works were consulted in compiling this introductory section.

Celestial Sway

Fern Feto Spring

THE HARVEST SEASON BEGINS with the Sun's entry into Libra on September 22. At this moment of perfect balance, light and dark are equal in length, and we rest in this breath of transition, appreciating the calm and harmony of nature before the balance tilts once again. The Fall Equinox offers us the chance to recognize and show gratitude for the fruits and harvests of our lives—a moment of appreciation and pleasure, when we can immerse ourselves in the beauty and peace that surrounds us.

We also may be moved to share the bounty of our labor with others, creating a communal feast for all to share, as we come together in celebration, before the cold and dark of winter grows.

A Full Moon follows this equinox with the Sun in Libra and the Moon in Aries. This lunar cycle continues to activate the ongoing Saturn/Pluto square, with the Sun conjunct Saturn and square Pluto, and the Moon opposing Saturn and also in square to Pluto. Changes we might have instigated during Lammas' stormy planetary weather may arise once more, giving us a chance to revise and fine-tune our approach to areas in our lives where we would like to improve.

The Full Moon serves to amplify and highlight whatever sign it is in. With the Moon in Aries, we may feel an emotional need for honesty, courage, and frankness. Impulsive reactions to others and our own needs for space and independence can create tense relationships now and a need to renegotiate agreements and commitments. Pluto in Capricorn squaring the Moon, and Saturn in Libra opposing the Moon brings resistance to this need for change and a desire to maintain the ongoing patterns of relationships, while at the same time calling for a restructuring of the underlying foundations and traditions that the relationship rests upon.

We are learning about integrating complex and opposing energies now, and as individuals we may need to radically alter and revolutionize our approach to life, as we stretch to accommodate the stormy planetary weather that shapes this time.

Mercury, newly direct in the sign of Virgo, and trine Pluto, helps us process and organize the enormous amount of information and ideas that are flowing toward us now. Providing a grounded, practical approach to communication, Mercury in Virgo helps us to create systems and an order to our days and routines. List making, strategizing, and planning systems for growth will help us create some sense of calm in the midst of chaos. As Mercury moves through its shadow phase from September 12 to 27, we can slowly begin to pick up speed in our efforts to plan and organize the information and communications in our lives.

Mabon/Fall Equinox Harvest Ritual

Spend some time contemplating what you have harvested during this equinox season. What are some apparent fruits of your labors throughout the year? Are there projects, relationships, tasks, or creative works that you feel proud of and/or grateful for? Note the people who were involved with these experiences, meditating on all the ways big or small that you benefited from their involvement.

Take a moment to write a short (or long) note to as many people as you like, expressing your appreciation for their help, presence or support in your life. Charge up the notes with energy by chanting over them or using any other mode of charging or raising energy that inspires you. When you are ready, deliver these notes to everyone living that you wrote them to; if anyone involved is no longer living, you could bury, burn, or float (in a bottle or boat) the note away. If you have the time and energy, you may also want to host a Mabon feast and invite all the people who you wrote notes to, giving them your gratitude messages as party favors.

Full Moon in Aries

Bringing even more power to this equinox season is the added influence of two Full Moons in Aries. One is at the beginning of a run of Sun in Libra and Moon in Aries, and the other is at the very end. The first takes place the day after the Fall Equinox, September 23, and the second, just before Samhain season on October 22. This rare occurrence emphasizes the lessons of these two signs, asking us to pay careful attention to the archetypes and energies they represent and serve.

Libra is associated with balance, justice, harmony, and relationships, and helps us negotiate and facilitate interactions with those around us. Aries, the sign opposite Libra, emphasizes the self, bravery, courage, risk-taking, and action, and brings zest and flavor to life, encouraging us to be true to our own essence and capabilities.

Look to where the Full Moon falls in the houses of your chart for a more specific interpretation of how this lunar event will affect your life. Notice which house cusp Aries rules, and also which one Libra rules for an understanding of the house pairs to be activated.

Full Moon in Aries through the Houses

1st and 7th: Self-Identity/The Other, partnerships

2nd and 8th: Personal skills and resources/Shared energies and resources

3rd and 9th: Communication and the immediate environment/ Meaning and expansion of consciousness

4th and 10th: Home, family, and deep-self/Public persona, career, and destiny

5th and 11th: Self-expression, creativity, and spontaneity/Community, humanity, and the future

6th and 12th: Service to others and in the world/Service to spirit and retreat

Venus Retrograde

Venus goes retrograde in Scorpio on October 8, asking us to reassess, review, and rethink our relationships and patterns of relating. Old lovers and partners from the past may return to our lives now, or we may find ourselves in relationships that rekindle long-forgotten patterns and habits. The Scorpio influence encourages us to courageously face our fears of loss or abandonment in love and cultivate the ability to love unconditionally—letting go of any need to control or manipulate to gain love or affection. If our current relationship shows signs of stress, we would do well to embrace change and deeply examine our own contributions to conflicts or problems. When Venus turns direct in November, we may gain new clarity and a feeling of choice or possibility in how we relate to others.

Venus Retrograde Ritual

On the day of the Venus retrograde, take a bath with Epsom salts and essential oils (rose, sandalwood, and ylang-ylang are a few Venus-friendly oils). Light a pink candle to honor Venus, and as you bathe, imagine that all the patterns and habits that have caused you pain in relationships are being gently cleansed away. Set the intention that by the time Venus turns direct, you will feel inspired about new ways to connect and build intimacy with others. When you feel complete, open the drain and allow the water, charged with your old patterns and habits, to release down in the direction of the Earth, letting her absorb and transform your old energy to something new. On the next New Moon after Venus goes direct (November 6) you may want to do another ritual, setting new intentions around what you want to create in a new or already existing relationship.

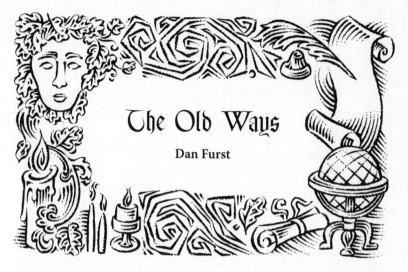

The Old Ways

Dan Furst

MABON IS THE LAST of the eight sabbats. And like the last child in a birth order of eight, it might have to struggle for recognition with older, more brilliant siblings. Like Litha, Mabon was one of the two great festivals that was apparently not even big or popular enough to have its own traditional Celtic name, so it had to be named by Aidan Kelly in the 1970s. Some British Wiccans have even dismissed Mabon as a fabrication or exaggeration by Americans who want to make a small "festival" sound more important and more authentically Celtic than it really is.

One wonders if such critics have ever actually managed a feast, or put much love into the food if they have, or whether the Celts living in the colder crags of the British isles in the middle ages would have had any interest in such things, especially if the question came up at the Harvest Home Week of September 20–26. A Celtic householder who had such a foolish quibble dropped on his table in harvest week would likely have said: "We dinna have time for this now. We have crops to get in and thrash. Animals to slaughter and dress. There's not a moment to lose. Are our cousins here yet? Here, put these on. They're for wurrk."

Why the hurry? Because in cultures all over the Northern Hemisphere, the Autumn Equinox is the time when the grain harvest must be done, and done fast before rain or cold can kill much of the wheat. While the September harvest is not the only one in the year, this is the one that gets urgent because it saves the grain that makes our bread in winter. For many thousands of years, before modern farming technologies and markets began to disconnect people from the skills and experience of growing and reaping food, September always brought the biggest, most demanding communal project of the year. Especially for people like Celts living in raw weather.

Cutting, threshing, weighing, and storing a big grain crop is a huge operation even when the fields are flat and free of stones. But for Celts in the British Isles and Gaul, who had to get the sheaves out of the rain and wind and into barns, it must have been a wet, numbing business best done by many hands. This is why the Mabon season is better known as Harvest Home or Homecoming, when students and travelers come home to help their families bring in the crops, then celebrate Earth's bounty with a feast. The basic plan is to get the crop in before September 21, when we do the ritual of weighing the grain, vegetables, and fruits. Then comes the Night of the Hunter. Livestock who will not improve with age in the winter, and may not survive it, are killed and prepared for the next day's feast and for the cold months. At night, the hunters run a wild, singing chase in the woods, not to catch game, but to wish a happy, fruitful time to the deer who are in mating season now. On September 25, everyone sits down to a feast of mutton and goose, bread and cakes, beer and ale, cider and wine, yams and squash, and maize and apples.

The symbolism and practice of this season are consistent through cultures everywhere. Families gather—as at Sukkot, the Feast of Ingathering that follows the Jewish high holy days—to share Earth's bounty and affirm that all are included and welcome. Accounts are to be settled now too. The theme of balancing and equity is unavoidable, as this is an equinox. The month is even represented by Libra's scales of justice as well as measure, and this is why medieval Christians paid rents and settled contracts at Easter and Michaelmas (September 30), and other ancient peoples likely settled such matters in the same half-year rhythm in March/April and September.

The word Mabon is said to have come from a hero by that name, also called *Maponos*, meaning "Divine Son" or "Divine Boy." Some Celts say he is the son of Dagda and Modron—that is, Matrona, "Divine Mother"—and he is thus the half-brother of the solar god Lugh. The Irish say that Mabon's mother is Boann, the sacred river. He is said to have been born on December 25, as the sacred figure that Welsh legend, in the *Mabinogion*, calls the Bringer of the Light. He mysteriously disappears just after birth, carried away from his mother when he is three nights old. He can be found again only with the help of animals who tell the seekers to look for him on a blest island in the otherworld, from which Mabon will come to be born again at Yule. He appears, then, to be another of the many lover-trickster figures who die every spring to be born again at Yule.

Here again, it seems, the available surface folklore tells the story of a god, while the true people's practice, as usual, honors the Goddess. One of the best clues to this is in the enormous variety of local folk customs at the cutting of the last sheaf of grain at the end of the harvest. Some communities, it is said, managed the harvest as a speed competition among families, and ridiculed, even penalized, the slow, lazy, or unlucky farmer who was the last one to get his crop in. Some people thought the last sheaf of wheat was unlucky, and would cut it only while blindfolded, or by throwing the sickle at it. Whether the last sheaf was considered baleful, and it would be ritually burned or grains from it would be fed to the next goose to be slaughtered; or it was thought lucky and treated well, one way or another, the reaper who would cut it was carefully chosen, and farmers would come from neighbor fields to witness the moment of completion.

Thankfully, not all clans liked to punish the last handful of barley or wheat. Some would save it to use for festive hair ornaments, or to strew into the field at the next Planting Moon to promote the growth of the new year's crop. Others would weave the last grain stalks, charms, and other luck attractors into a corn dolly that would be placed over the mantel or dining table to ensure plenty until the time of the next harvest. A rite like this, of course, almost shouts Demeter, Uma, Ceres, the Native American Corn Maiden, and every other grain goddess who pours the people's health from her horn of plenty.

She is in ripeness now as the Matron, who thrives and is fulfilled at this turn of the year when the Sun enters Libra, ruled by Venus the Mother. The sabbat that many Wiccans now call Mabon might better have been called Modron, the Divine Mother, for she is the one who has come to fruition now from having birthed her own children and from having won the authority of the Lady of the House. Now, at the peak of her power, she manages all matters pertaining to the home and family, and, on a larger scale in relation to other matrons, the town as a whole. Why is Modron not the central figure at this festival?

Perhaps she was, but the Celts, close-mouthed as always about their rituals and choosing to keep mum in more ways than one, chose not to say anything more than was absolutely needed about why the Matron is too busy right now to be a festival star. She is out in the woods and the stream, gathering herbs for winter food, health, and magic. She is, as usual, running the show on the ground while the feast honors her son. And as she will soon begin to turn into the Wise Woman, she tends to seek solitude when the feast is done.

Feasts and Treats

Kristin Madden

THE SEASON OF DEEPENING light and luxurious color blesses our tables with apples, grapes, and rich, warming meals. As darkness and light are held in balance, we work toward harmony in our selves and our lives. Tradition is coupled with new ideas as the foods of the season balance colors, tastes, and textures in a grand feast to honor the coming dark half of the year.

Salmon Dinner with Leek Cream

In the Welsh tale of Culhwch and Olwen, a search was undertaken to find Mabon, the child stolen from the Earth Mother days after his birth. It is said that light had disappeared from the Earth with the grief of the Earth Mother. The salmon, oldest and wisest of the animals, took Culhwch and his companions to where the child had been hidden. We give thanks for the myriad blessings of salmon with this dish.

Prep Time: 10 minutes
Cook Time: 45 minutes
Serves: 2–4

3 tablespoons olive oil
2 salmon filets
½ onion, chopped
½ cup broccoli florets
¼ cup mushrooms, chopped
1 teaspoon rosemary
2 medium leeks
2 garlic cloves, chopped
2 tablespoons butter
¼ cup dry white wine
½ cup sour cream

Preheat oven to 400 degrees F. Oil the bottom of a baking pan and add the salmon and vegetables. Sprinkle with rosemary and cover with aluminum foil. Bake for 30 minutes.

Rinse leeks and finely chop the white part and up to 2 inches of the green part. In a small saucepan, cook the leeks and garlic in butter over medium heat until tender. Reduce heat to low and add the wine. Simmer for 5 minutes. Add sour cream and stir until dissolved. Serve cream sauce on top of salmon and vegetables.

Apple Butter Nut Bread

Autumn apples are the source of enough different foods that some areas hold apple festivals to showcase the many wonderful tastes of this versatile fruit. Among all those delicacies, apple butter is one of the smoothest and sweetest. This bread is mouth-wateringly good as a side to a meal or as a dessert offering.

Prep Time: 15 minutes
Cook Time: 90 minutes
Serves: 8–10

2 cups all-purpose flour
1 teaspoon baking powder
¼ teaspoon baking soda
1 teaspoon cinnamon

1 teaspoon nutmeg
1 cup olive oil
3 eggs
½ cup brown sugar
¾ cup apple butter
½ cup raisins
½ cup pecans or walnuts, chopped

Preheat the oven to 375 degrees F. In a large bowl, mix together the flour, baking powder, baking soda, and spices.

In another large bowl, mix the oil, eggs, and sugar on medium speed. Add apple butter, raisins, and nuts to the egg mixture and mix well. Add the flour mixture and mix well. Bake for 90 minutes in a greased and floured cake pan.

Cranberry-Apple Cobbler

Apple cobbler is a big favorite at most apple festivals and it goes quickly because it is so good. Taking the best advantage of many of the foods of the season, this dish is truly delightful. Best served warm with vanilla ice cream, this combination of sweet apples, tart cranberries, and crunchy pecans is a fantastic finish to any Mabon meal.

Prep Time: 25 minutes
Cook Time: 60 minutes
Serves: 8–10

4 apples, peeled, cored, and cubed
1 cup frozen cranberries, thawed
¼ cup sugar
1 teaspoon cinnamon
½ teaspoon nutmeg
½ teaspoon cloves
½ teaspoon allspice
1 cup oat flour
1 cup brown sugar
1 teaspoon baking powder

1 egg
½ cup evaporated milk
⅓ cup butter, melted
¼ cup pecans, chopped

Preheat oven to 350 degrees F. In a large bowl, mix together the apples, cranberries, sugar, and the spices. Cover the bottom of a greased baking dish with this mixture.

In a large bowl, combine the flour, brown sugar, and baking powder. In another large bowl, combine the egg, evaporated milk, and butter. Whisk together well. Add egg mixture to flour mixture and mix well. Pour over apples and top with pecans. Bake for 60 minutes.

Autumn Nog

This tasty twist on eggnog will take the edge off those chilly autumn nights. It combines many of the flavors of the season in one deliciously creamy drink that can be served warm or cold. For a non-alcoholic nog, use cider in place of the brandy and keep it in the refrigerator instead of the freezer.

Prep Time: 10 minutes
Optional Chill Time: 2 hours
Serves: 6–8

⅔ cup honey
1½ cups brandy
2 tablespoons vanilla extract
½ gallon cream
3 teaspoons nutmeg
6–8 cinnamon sticks

Warm the honey, brandy, and vanilla in a large saucepan over medium-low heat until the honey dissolves. Add cream and 1 teaspoon nutmeg and stir again. Pour into a large pitcher and serve warm, sprinkled with nutmeg and with a cinnamon stick garnish. To serve cold, place pitcher in the freezer for at least 2 hours. Then serve, sprinkled with the remaining nutmeg and with a cinnamon-stick garnish.

Crafty Crafts

Silver RavenWolf

Deva of the Season: Generosity
Scents/Aromas: Apple, Cedar
Energy: Magnetism
Visualization: Fill a bowl with red apples. For at least a few minutes each day, visualize the apples filled with love. Practice this visualization every day for twenty-one days beginning on the eve of Fall Equinox. Change the apples every week, sharing them with family and friends. Envision yourself happily sending out love as you give each apple away. Always end your visualization with a smile.

Affirmation: I attract to myself all that I want and need, and in turn, I experience and act upon the divine nature of generosity.

The month of September has always been a natural time of closure, a period when people, items, experiences, and energies extricate themselves from our lives. If we allow these things to naturally leave us, the separation will be smooth and painless. If we hold onto those unhealthy energies, the extrication may be emotionally painful. Generosity, and the love behind it, as in the visualization above, helps us to move forward as the harvest energies cycle to a close at

Samhain. This month allows us to happily let go of those people, things, and experiences that no longer serve us well.

Just as Spring Equinox is a natural time of cleansing after a dark and cold winter, so Fall Equinox provides cleansing energy after a vibrant and exciting summer. Nature always gives us opportunities to touch the balance of life and harmonize the spirit. As the Fall Equinox approaches, it is time once again to banish negative energy from our homes or apartments. In keeping with the balance of the season, we should remove the clutter that has grown over the spring and summer months. Remember to clean carpets, curtains, and bare floors. Throw out broken items and paper trash. Sell or give away objects in good repair that are no longer useful to you. Enjoy the spirit of generosity! This is also the time to clean garden tools that you will no longer use and thank them for their hard work over the growing season.

Working in your garden and preparing it for winter can be a wonderful, anti-stress activity. As you clean up the beds, feel free to visualize what you would like to grow next year. Use the affirmation given as a mantra while you work. I guarantee you'll feel refreshed and at peace when you finish for the day!

If you are having trouble disengaging yourself from a particular person or experience, use a black-ribbon ceremony to cut the ties and distance yourself in a peaceful way.

Black-Ribbon Ceremony

The black-ribbon ceremony is exceptionally easy to perform. All you need are two black candles, a 19-inch piece of thin, black ribbon, a pair of scissors, two 3 × 5-inch cards, and the resolve to release negativity from your life. On one card write your name. On the other, write what or whom you want removed from your life. Put both candles in appropriately sized candleholders. In sacred space, place the card with your name under one candle. Place the card with what you wish to banish under the other. Next, connect the candles by tying the base of the candleholders together with the ribbon. Stretch the candles out so the ribbon is taut. In a magick circle, light both candles. Allow them to burn for at least five minutes. Then, clearly state what you wish to banish from your life. Cut the ribbon and say, "It is done!" (and mean it). Release the magick circle. Each hour as the candles burn, move them farther and farther apart. This reinforces to the mind that the separation is wanted and needed. When the candles completely burn out, throw the candle end of what you wish to banish in flowing water or at a crossroads. Bury your candle end on your property. Burn both 3 × 5-inch cards and the ribbon.

The black-ribbon ceremony can be used for almost any situation in which you need to find release. Psychologically, doing this ceremony in a sacred, magick circle allows you to let go of limiting beliefs and make an active decision to free yourself from negativity.

Cleansing and release naturally leaves room for drawing positive energies toward you. Once you have completed the black-ribbon ceremony, design a Collage Spell Board to draw new energies and exciting experiences to you in the coming months.

Collage Spell Board

Supplies

8 × 12-inch piece of chipboard
Pictures of items, places, and energies you wish to draw toward you
Craft glue

Instructions: From magazines, photos, or drawings, cut out what energies you wish to bring into your life over the coming holiday season. Paste the pictures onto the chipboard until the board is completely covered. Add inspirational words from newspapers, magazines, or computer art. The board should embody your hopes, dreams, desires, and visions for the coming months. Be sure to add a picture of an apple to symbolize love and generosity. You may wish to use the affirmation given as a mantra while you work on your spell board. When you are finished, hang the spell board where you will see it first thing in the morning when you wake up. This helps to reinforce your pathway to success. You can also seal your board with Liquitex Matte Gel (or another sealer) to protect the surface. Allow to completely dry. Now you have a ready-made spell mat or a mini-altar! Empower your spell board in a magick circle on the Eve of Fall Equinox. Dot with cedar or apple magick oil to seal your work.

Cost of this project: About $3.00 to $5.00 (with sealer).

Time to complete: Give yourself plenty of time in the creative, collage process.

Fall Equinox Collage Board Spell

On the day of the equinox, place your board flat in a special place. In the center, put a bowl heaping with dried beans and dried coconut (both are symbols of money, good fortune, and abundance in the home). Cast your magick circle. Light a brown candle dressed with brown sugar (this is a hoodoo practice for creating miracles and drawing abundance). As the candle burns, repeat the affirmation given nine times, then surround the candle with apple slices (another symbol of abundance and good fortune). Release your magick circle. Allow the candle to burn completely in a safe candleholder that will not drip on your board. When the candle has finished burning, bottle the beans and coconut and use as a decorative focus piece for the next thirty days. Throw out the candle end. Give the apple slices back to Mother Nature.

Fostering Family

Lydia M. Crabtree

THE ANTICIPATION THAT WAS Lughnasadh ends when Mabon descends. Equality of the work and toil and the harvest and gain has been reached by the family coven. You aren't anticipating many other crops, and you are sure the ones you have harvested will sustain you and yours. This time period for partner(s) of family covens can last for years. There is a sense of satisfaction with life that is reached. Their individual and spiritual needs are met daily during the Mabon of their life and for partner(s) whose lives have been long-lived, staying in the balance of Mabon becomes a goal that is strived for daily: a balance of work and family; a balance of spirituality, individuality, and of the family; a balance of the individual dreams and goals within the group goals of family coven.

Children have a way of challenging this balance, because during the Mabon of their lives, they have come of age and are completing a rapid harvest of many things. Finally, the promise of Lughnasadh is bared for them and worlds of emotions, feelings, and physical sensations come flooding in. They long to stretch their new wings and test the boundaries and balances the family coven has gained. They eagerly dive into the work of harvesting, often bringing home more emotions than the family coven can handle.

However, this is exactly why Mabon is a celebration. Instead of looking at these teen years with dread, the family coven has an opportunity to view the bounty as a thing to be celebrated, examined, and encouraged. What better place to do this than around the table of the harvest? After all, if even a teenager has nowhere to place the fruits of their labors where they can be appreciated, then the harvest is as barren as a table full of food surrounded by empty chairs.

Activities

Cornucopia of Thanks

On September 1, set out an empty cornucopia basket, a bowl full of clear glass ornament balls (the type that can be opened and filled), paper in the colors of autumn, and pens. Tell the family coven that before the Feast of Mabon, the cornucopia basket should be overflowing with balls filled with things the coveners are thankful for. You could even make this a daily event leading up to Mabon. Before bed, have everyone fill a ball and place it in the basket.

At the Mabon feast, have family coveners randomly draw and read the thanks on the papers. This promises to be a moving activity for any family coven.

Harvest the Apples

Apples are one of the symbols of Mabon. To get your family coven outdoors, have them harvest apples together at a local apple farm, then use the apples for pies and other craft activities.

Make Candied Apples

Make candied apples then give them as gifts to people in your life for whom you are thankful: teachers, high priests or high priestesses, elders in the community who don't get a lot of attention, friends, neighbors, the mail carrier, etc.

Apple Faces

Have each member of the family coven carve a face in an apple, then allow the apple to dry out over several days. Later, at Samhain, these apples can be hung outside as extra wards against the spirits of the dead and as an offering to the living creatures who are looking for life-sustaining food before the onset of winter.

Apple Warding

Cut the apples in the center and wrap a bay leaf over the exposed star. Place them under the bed of children who may be having sleeping problems or nightmares. You can also place the apples in the four corners of your land lot (away from the house), as a symbolic warding and gift to the Earth in thanks for the bounty.

Make Fire Starters

To prepare a harvest for the darkness to come while pine cones are in abundance, make fire starters to give to people for whom you are thankful. You will need wax, tongs, a double-boiler or candle-wax melting pot, wax-coated string, and some crushed leaves, twigs, and cinnamon sticks in a wax paper–coated pan. Melt the wax in a double-boiler or candle-waxing pot. Using tongs, dip the pine cones in the wax for a good coating, carefully placing the waxed string somewhere into the pine cone. Dip the pine cone again, ensuring a good coating, then roll the pine cones in the pan with the leaves, twigs, and crushed cinnamon sticks.

Make Pine-Scented Wards

You will need glue; cinnamon powder, clove powder, allspice powder, salt, and any other autumn-type herb you can think of; big sealable plastic bags; a large bowl big enough to completely submerge your pine cones; wax paper; and string. Submerge the pine cones completely in the glue. Lift them out, letting the excess glue drip off the pine cones. Fill a plastic bag with the different powders and salts. Place the gluey pine cone in the plastic bag, seal it, and shake until the cone is completely covered. Remove the pine cone and let dry on the wax paper. Attach string and give as gifts to those for whom you are thankful or hang as extra wards to the coming of Samhain.

A Mabon Mystery: John Barleycorn

Oberon Zell-Ravenheart

THE VERSION OF THE SONG JOHN BARLEYCORN used in this ritual appeared in the *Journal of the Folk-Song Society* 1:3 (1901) pp. 81–82. First printed in that form during the reign of James I, the original song is said to be much older. An early version of the ballad is included in the Bannatyne Manuscript of 1568, and broadside versions were common in seventeeth century England. Variations from Sussex, Hampshire, Surrey, Somerset, and Wiltshire were published in subsequent issues of the *Journal of the Folk Song Society*. Robert Burns published his own version in 1782, and modern versions abound. The most famous of these is by Traffic, on their album *John Barleycorn Must Die*. The song has also been recorded by Steeleye Span, Jethro Tull, Fairport Convention, Heather Alexander, and many others.

The ballad relates the life and death of the Corn King, the Green Man of the barleycorn—an ancient crop that was the chief bread grain in Europe as late as the sixteenth century. According to *The Golden Bough* by James Frazier, the Corn King was selected from the men of the village and treated as king for a year. Then at harvest time, he danced the corn maze and was killed. His body was dragged through the fields so his blood would fertilize the next barley crop, and afterward, according to Frazier, he himself may have been eaten.

Then the harvested barley was made into brandy and cakes, which were stored for the winter, according to folk musician John Renfro Davis. His interpretation continues that at Winter Solstice, the cakes were given to children to imbue them with the spirit of the Corn King. They were called "soal cakes" (soul cakes), and in England today, children still go "a-soalin'" for cookies at Yuletide.

For the following ritual, the traditional lyrics were slightly adapted by Oberon Zell.

Production Notes

First performed in 1976, and created by Morning Glory and Oberon, who wrote all portions unless otherwise noted, this Mabon Mystery ritual is not meant for solitaries, but it can work for a fairly small group such as a coven. As is common in the HOME Tradition and the Church of All Worlds, this ritual is very "Bardic"-oriented, all in poetry and song. Ideally, there should be a Bard or at least a strong singer to carry the song, "John Barleycorn," which is central to the rite. However, if no one can sing it, the recorded version by Traffic will suffice—as long as someone is there to pause the recording after each verse for pacing. The Mystery Play, which comprises the main part of the ritual, is designed to be performed in the round, within the open arena of space inside the circle. As individuals may play several parts, the entire play can be performed with as few as four actors, or as many as ten.

Altar Setup

An altar is set into the western side of the circle. On it are a sheaf of barley or wheat, a large brandy snifter filled with brandy, a plate with an uncut loaf of good bread, and a large chalice of water. Other altar items might include appropriate images of the Goddess and the Green Man, as well as candles, seasonal fruits, nuts, and fall leaves. Also on hand (under the altar) are a bottle of brandy and a bottle of water for refills.

Cast, Costumes, and Props

High Priestess: Beautiful robe; crescent Moon crown.

High Priest: Beautiful robe; horned crown.

Norns or Fates (3): Three black hooded robes; a large brown blanket.

John Barleycorn: Straw-colored tunic and pants; a bright green clock that ties at the neck; a long, fake blond beard with a string tied behind the neck.

Hired men 1 (2): Tunic and pants; a plastic scythe for a Grim Reaper costume; a 10-foot length of brown rope.

Hired men 2 (2): Tunic and pants; two plastic pitchforks.

Hired men 3 (2): Tunic and pants; four rough sticks, each about a foot long.

Circle Casting

To be done by High Priestess using a sheaf of barley or wheat.

I cast the Circle round and round—
Shadow of Moon upon the ground.
I cast the Circle round about—
A world within; a world without.
Between the worlds a sacred field—
What lies within, now stands revealed.
By magick deep and Mystery—
The Circle is cast; so mote it be!
All respond: *So mote it be!*

Invoking the Guardians of the Four Directions

To be done ideally by four different people, with final verse by High Priest or Priestess. These invocations should be made by "cross-calling." Each Quarter-caller stands on the opposite side of the circle from their direction, facing inward so all can hear.

O Guardians of the Airy East,
Attend and sanctify our feast!
At dawn of day, your winds blow free,

Hail and welcome; blessed be!
All respond: *Hail and welcome; blessed be!*

O Guardians of the Fiery South,
Plant your hot kisses on our mouth!
By flames and lightning, burning tree,
Hail and welcome; blessed be!
All respond: *Hail and welcome; blessed be!*

O Guardians of the Wat'ry West,
Your sacrament defines our Nest!
By rain and river, lake and sea,
Hail and welcome; blessed be!
All respond: *Hail and welcome; blessed be!*

O Guardians of the Earthen North,
We summon, stir, and call ye forth!
By bud and branch, by root and tree,
Hail and welcome; blessed be!
All respond: *Hail and welcome; blessed be!*

O Guardians of the Quarters all,
Hearken ye unto our call!
Protect our Circle through the night,
And lend your pow'r unto our rite!
    So mote it be!
All respond: *So mote it be!*

Invoking the Goddess and the God
May be sung by the Bard, the High Priestess, and High Priest.

The Lady's Bransle (to the tune of "Nonsuch")
For She will bring the buds in spring
And laugh among the flowers
In Summer's heat, Her kisses are sweet
She sings in leafy bowers
She cuts the cane and gathers the grain

When fruits of fall surround Her
Her bones grow old in wint'ry cold
She wraps Her cloak around Her!
   —Hope Athern

The Lord's Bransle

O, He will call the leaves in the fall
To fly their colors brightly
When warmth is lost, He paints with frost
His silver touches lightly
He greets the day in the dance of the May
With ribbons wound about Him
We eat His corn and drink from His horn
We would not be without Him!
   —Artemisia Barden

The Mystery Play

Enter three women with great solemnity from behind the western altar (the Norns or Fates). All wear long hooded black robes in which their faces are shrouded. They surround and shepherd a bowed male figure hidden under a large brown blanket. The Bard begins to sing the song, "John Barleycorn" (or it may be played from a recording). As the first verse is sung, the players pantomime the action: In the center of the Circle the three women lay the blanketed figure down on the ground flat on his back, and arrange the blanket to cover him completely. Then they stand up in a ring around him, clasp their right hands together in the center over the body, and then raise their clasped hands high as if making a vow. Afterward, they retreat back into the Circle, leaving the covered body lying there.

There were three women came out of the West,
Their fortunes for to scry,
And these three women made a solemn vow,
John Barleycorn should die.

They ploughed, they sowed, they harrowed him in,
Threw clods upon his head,
And these three women made a solemn vow,
John Barleycorn was dead.

The song stops for a moment. A large bell or gong is struck: "Bong!" Then the song resumes with the next verse to be pantomimed. The male figure ("John Barleycorn") pokes his head out from under the blanket, then stands up strong. He wears a bright green cloak over a straw-colored tunic and pants.

They let him lie for a very long time
Til the rains from heaven did fall,
Then little Sir John sprung up his head,
And soon amazed them all.

Pause the song for a moment, as John arises and stretches his arms. As the next verse is sung, he bows his head and unfastens his green cloak, while simultaneously pulling a long blond fake beard up over his ears and adjusting it to his chin. As he lowers his arms and raises his head, the green cloak falls to the ground, revealing him standing in straw-colored raiment.

They let him stand til Midsummer's day
Til he looked both pale and wan.
And little Sir John grew a long, long beard
And so became a man.

The song stops for a moment. A large bell or gong is struck: "Bong!" Two people enter the circle and stand to either side of John. One brandishes a scythe, like the Grim Reaper; the other holds a 10-foot length of rope. Then the song resumes with the next verse to be pantomimed. The reaper swings his scythe across in front of John's legs; John drops to his knees. The other man quickly ties him around the waist, leaving a few feet of rope dangling for a lead. Then both men retreat back to the circle.

> *They hired men with the scythes so sharp*
> *To cut him off at the knee.*
> *They rolled him and tied him by the waist,*
> *Serving him most barbarously.*

Pause the song as two more people (or even the same ones, if there aren't enough players) carrying fake pitchforks enter the circle to stand at the front and back of John. Then the song resumes with the next verse to be pantomimed. The pitchfork wielders dramatically "stab" John in the back and chest, then drop their weapons and roughly raise John to his feet. The one in front takes up the end of the rope around his waist. The other places his hands on John's back.

> *They hired men with the sharp pitchforks*
> *Who pricked him to the heart.*
> *And the loader he served him worse than that,*
> *For he bound him to the cart.*

The song stops for a moment. A large bell or gong is struck: "Bong!" Then the song resumes with the next verse to be pantomimed. The two players roughly push and pull John one turn around the inside of the circle, going deosil (clockwise). Then they bring him back to the center, where they release him, exaggeratedly shake hands with each other, retrieve their pitchforks, and retreat back into the circle.

> *They wheeled him around and around the field*
> *Til they came unto a barn.*
> *And there they made a solemn vow*
> *On poor John Barleycorn.*

Pause the song for a moment, as two other players enter, each carrying a foot-long stick in each hand. As the song resumes, they encircle John, beating at him all over with the sticks. After one round, they drop the sticks and embrace John in a double bear hug.

They hired men with the crab-tree sticks
To cut him skin from bone.
And the miller he served him worse than that,
For he ground him between two stones.

The song stops for a moment. A large bell or gong is struck: "Bong!" The players drag John over to the western altar, and fade into the circle. John turns around bearing a large glass snifter full of brandy. Then the song resumes as he carries this around the inside of the circle deosil, offering everyone a drink.

Here's little Sir John in a nut-brown bowl,
And he's brandy in a glass;
And little Sir John in the nut-brown bowl
Proved the stronger man at last.
For the huntsman, he can't hunt the fox,
Nor so loudly blow his horn,
And the tinker, he can't mend kettles or pots
Without a little Barleycorn.

The Mystery Play is complete. If John is still going around with the brandy, this verse can be sung again by everyone until all have drunk. When the song ends, a large bell or gong is struck: "Bong!"

Communion of Bread & Water

High Priest takes up the plate of bread from the altar, and turns to face the circle.

The seed of life is roused to grow
By the passionate heat of the Sun's desire.
Thus we're nourished; this we know
By Earth and Sun; Rain, Wind, and Fire.
    May you never hunger!

He passes it to the person on his left, who tears off a piece, eats it, and passes it on, repeating, "May you never hunger."

High Priestess takes up the chalice of water from the altar, and turns to face the circle.

From the Sea we all were born,
Within the womb our souls ensnared.
Unto the Well we shall return,
Our lives, through Water, ever shared.
*   May you never thirst!*

She passes it to the person on her left, who drinks and passes it on, repeating, "May you never thirst."

Thanks and Dismissal of the Deities
To be sung by the High Priestess and High Priest in unison.

Give Thanks to the Mother Goddess
Give thanks to the Father Sun!
Give thanks to the children in the garden where
The Mother and the Father are one!
(repeat three times; on the last, sing:)
. . . The Mother and the Father have fun!
*   Hail and farewell!*
All respond: *Hail and farewell!*

Dismissal of the Guardians
To be done by the same people who invoked them at the beginning of the rite—"cross-calling" as before from the opposite sides of the circle.

O Guardians of the Watchtower of the frozen North,
(watery West; fiery South; windy East),
We thank you for attending our rites.
Go if you must; stay if you will.
And ere you depart to your fair and lovely realms,
We bid you hail and farewell!
All respond: *Hail and farewell!*

Opening the Circle

To be done by High Priestess.

All from air, into air
Let the misty curtains part.
All is ended, all is done,
What has been must now be gone!
What is done by ancient Art
Must merry meet and merry part—
And merry meet again!
—Gwydion Pendderwen

Notes

Notes